IMAGE COMICS, INC.
Robert Kirkman – Chief Operating Officer
Erik Larsen – Chief Financial Officer
Todd McFarlane – President
Marc Silvestri – Chief Executive Officer
Jim Valentino – Vice-President

Eric Stephenson – Publisher
Ron Richards – Director of Business Development
Jennifer de Guzman – Director of Trade Book Sales
Kat Salazar – Director of PR & Marketing
Corey Murphy – Director of Retail Sales
Jeremy Sullivan – Director of Digital Sales
Emilio Bautista – Sales Assistant
Branwyn Bigglestone – Senior Accounts Manager
Emily Miller – Accounts Manager
Jessica Ambriz – Administrative Assistant
Tyler Shainline – Events Coordinator
David Brothers – Content Manager
Jonathan Chan – Production Manager
Drew Gill – Art Director
Meredith Wallace – Print Manager
Monica Garcia – Senior Production Artist
Jenna Savage – Production Artist
Addison Duke – Production Artist
Tricia Ramos – Production Assistant
IMAGECOMICS.COM

EAST OF WEST

JONATHAN HICKMAN
WRITER

NICK DRAGOTTA
ARTIST

FRANK MARTIN
COLORS

RUS WOOTON
LETTERS

EAS

W

T OF

EST

PEACE IS BUT A **PRELUDE** TO **WAR.**

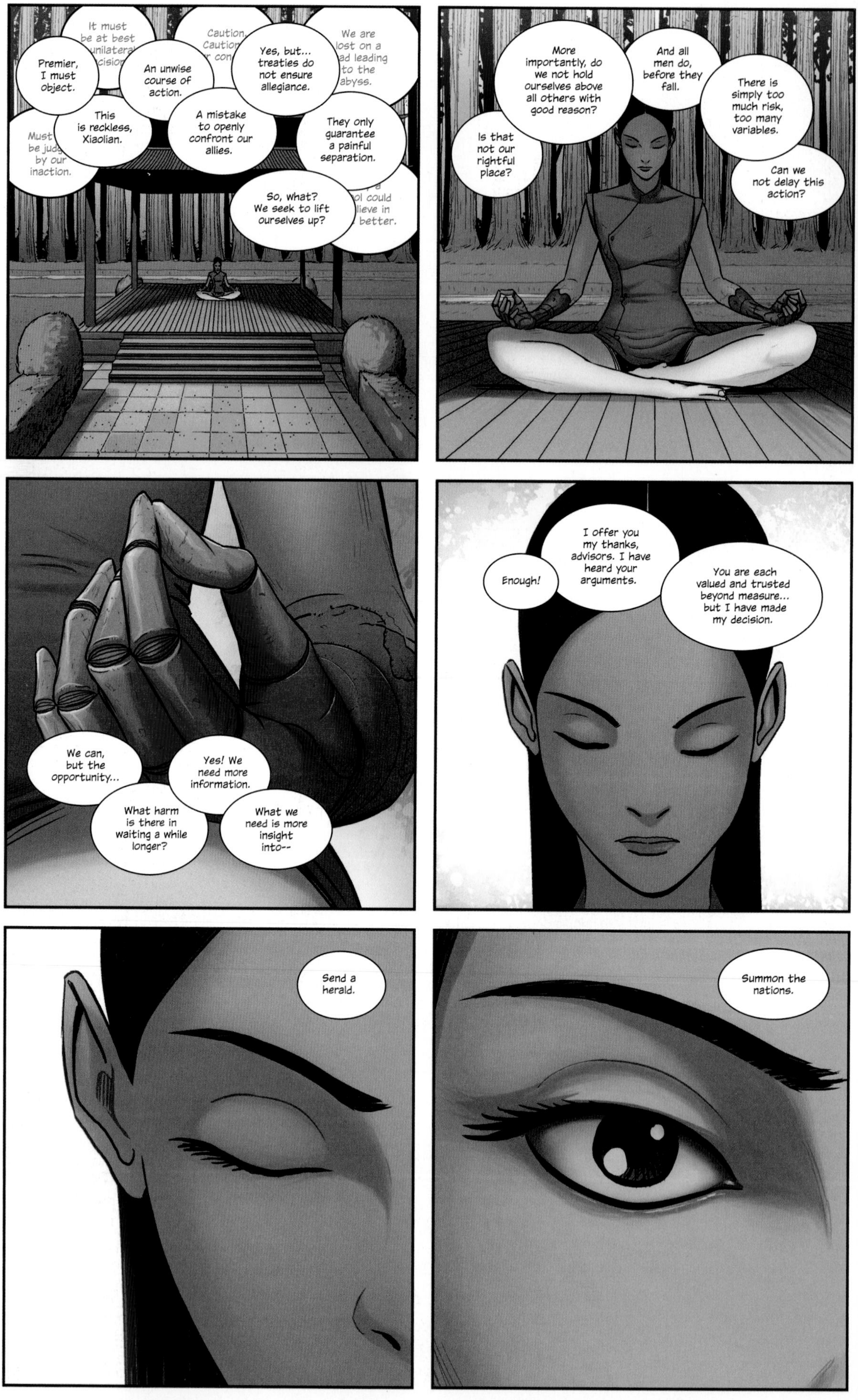
Premier, I must object.
An unwise course of action.
Yes, but... treaties do not ensure allegiance.
This is reckless, Xiaolian.
A mistake to openly confront our allies.
They only guarantee a painful separation.
So, what? We seek to lift ourselves up?
More importantly, do we not hold ourselves above all others with good reason?
And all men do, before they fall.
There is simply too much risk, too many variables.
Is that not our rightful place?
Can we not delay this action?
We can, but the opportunity...
Yes! We need more information.
What harm is there in waiting a while longer?
What we need is more insight into--
Enough!
I offer you my thanks, advisors. I have heard your arguments.
You are each valued and trusted beyond measure... but I have made my decision.
Send a herald.
Summon the nations.

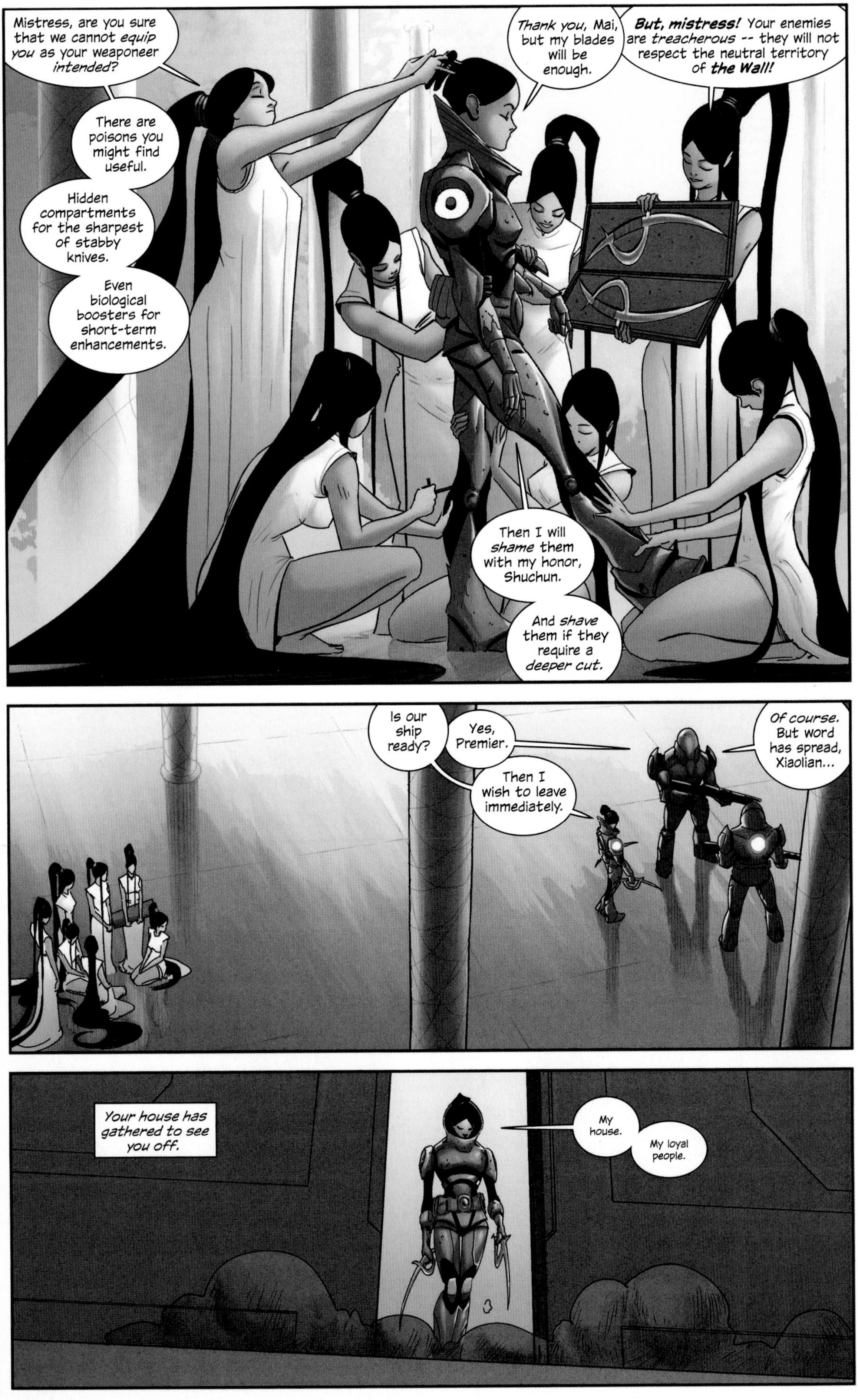
Mistress, are you sure that we cannot *equip you* as your weaponeer *intended?*
There are poisons you might find useful.
Hidden compartments for the sharpest of stabby knives.
Even biological boosters for short-term enhancements.
Thank you, Mai, but my blades will be enough.
But, mistress! Your enemies are *treacherous* -- they will not respect the neutral territory of ***the Wall!***
Then I will *shame* them with my honor, Shuchun.
And *shave* them if they require a *deeper cut.*
Is our ship ready?
Yes, Premier.
Then I wish to leave immediately.
Of course. But word has spread, Xiaolian...
Your house has gathered to see you off.
My house.
My loyal people.

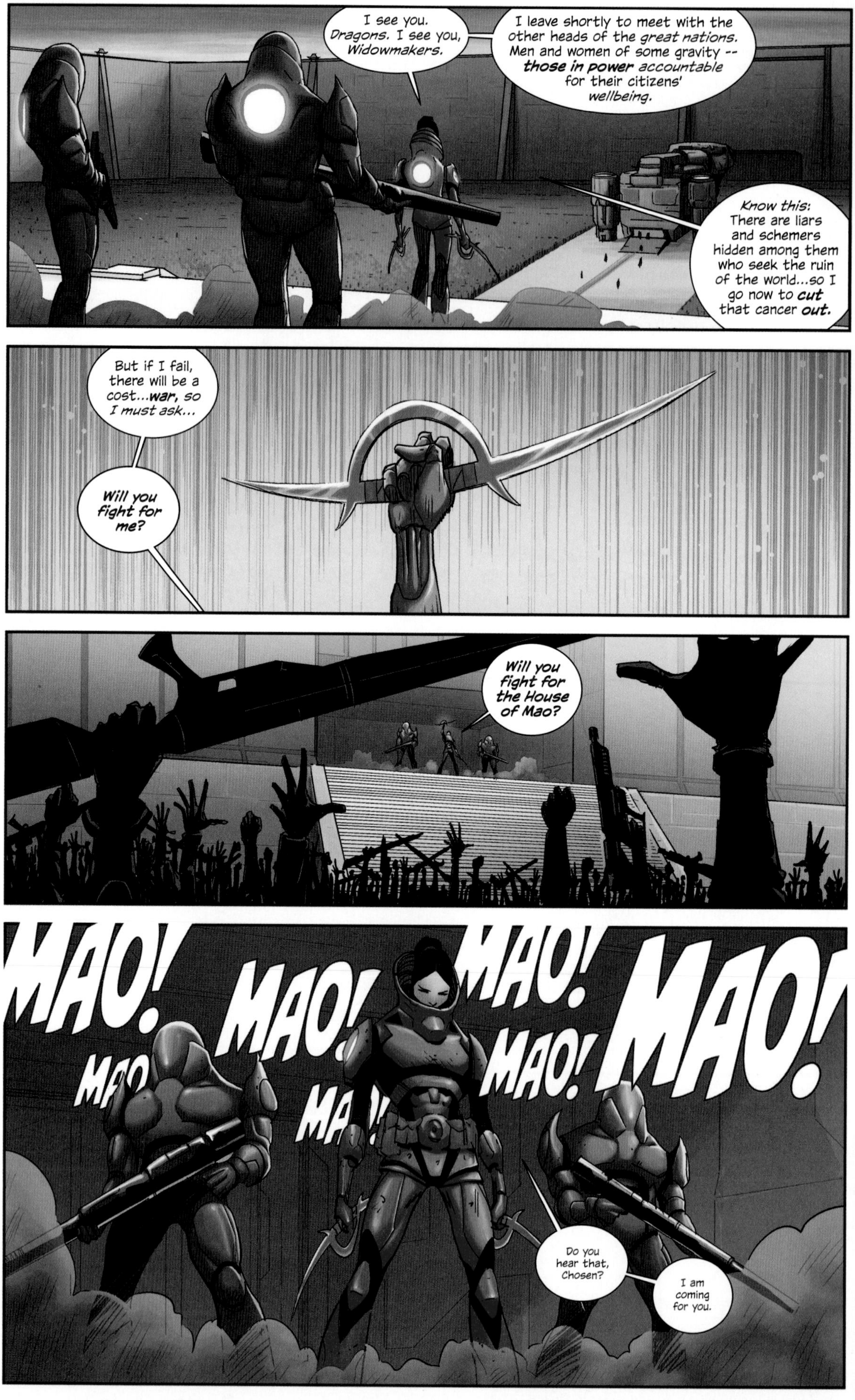

I see you. Dragons. I see you, Widowmakers.
I leave shortly to meet with the other heads of the great nations. Men and women of some gravity -- those in power accountable for their citizens' wellbeing.
Know this: There are liars and schemers hidden among them who seek the ruin of the world...so I go now to cut that cancer out.
But if I fail, there will be a cost...war, so I must ask...
Will you fight for me?
Will you fight for the House of Mao?
MAO!
MAO!
MAO!
MAO!
MAO!
Do you hear that, Chosen?
I am coming for you.

THERE IS NO US.

THERE NEVER WAS.

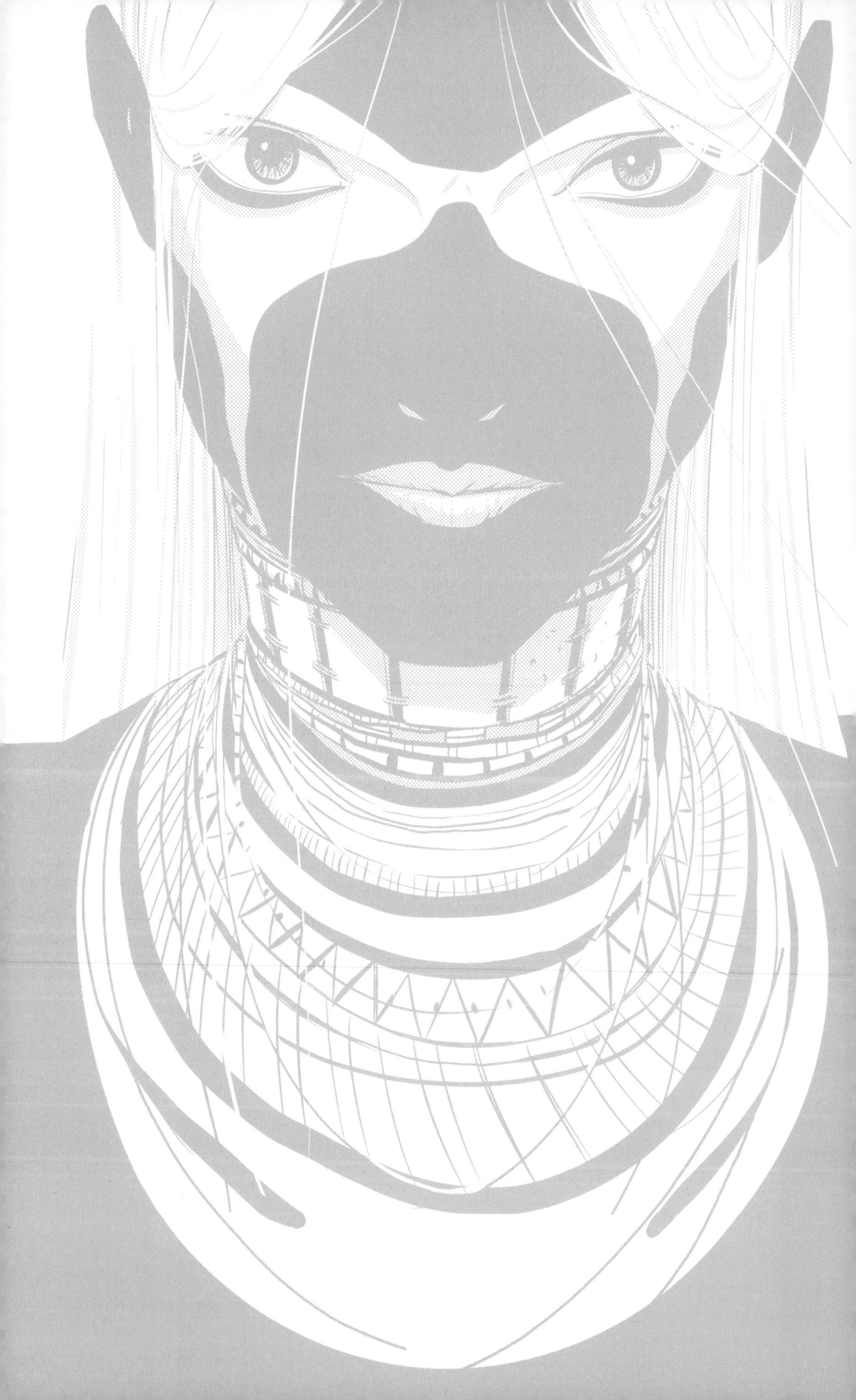

 ELEVEN: THE
WALL BECKONS

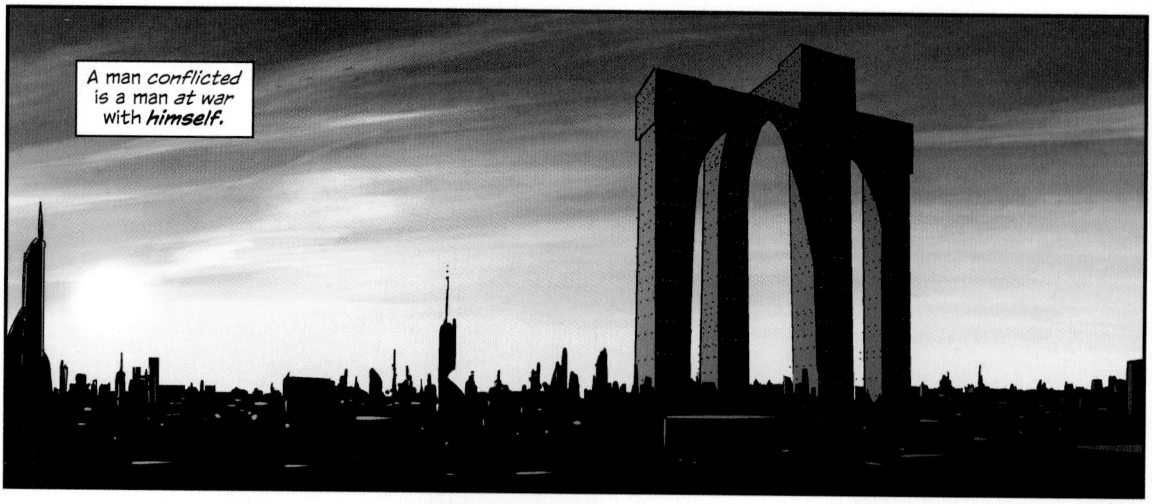
A man *conflicted* is a man *at war* with ***himself.***

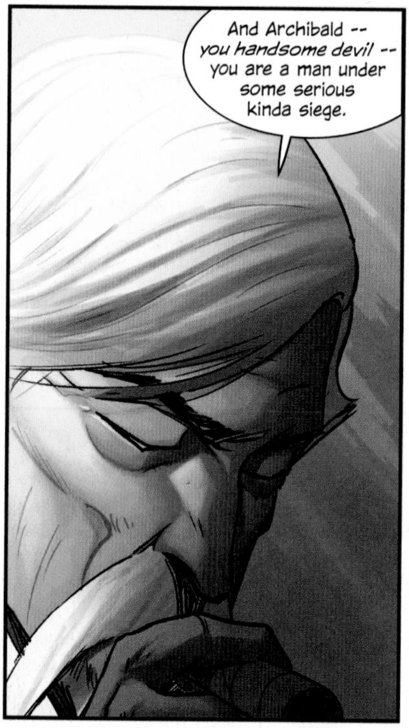
And Archibald -- *you handsome devil* -- you are a man under some serious kinda siege.

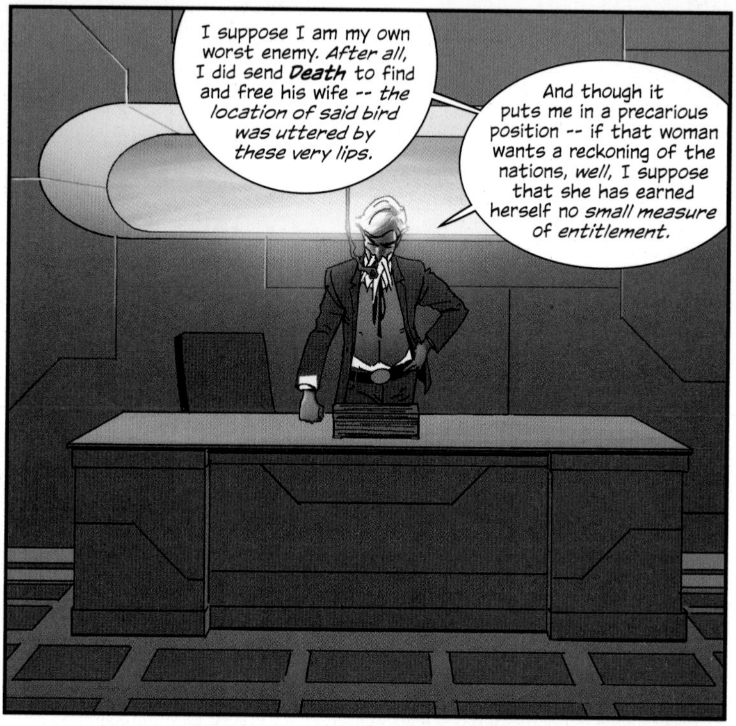
I suppose I am my own worst enemy. *After all,* I did send ***Death*** to find and free his wife -- *the location of said bird was uttered by these very lips.*
And though it puts me in a precarious position -- if that woman wants a reckoning of the nations, *well,* I suppose that she has earned herself no *small measure* of *entitlement.*

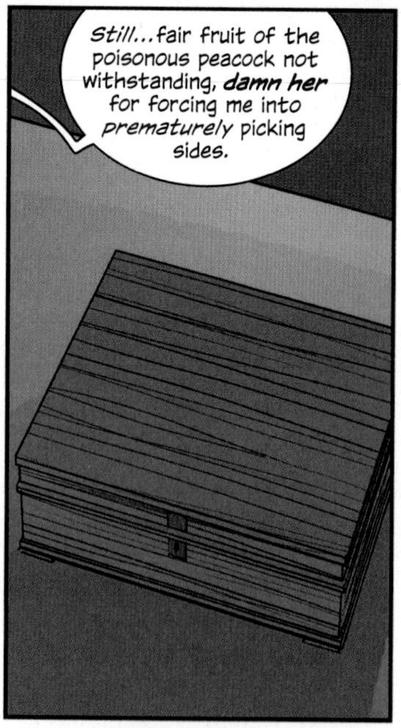
*Still...*fair fruit of the poisonous peacock not withstanding, ***damn her*** for forcing me into *prematurely* picking sides.

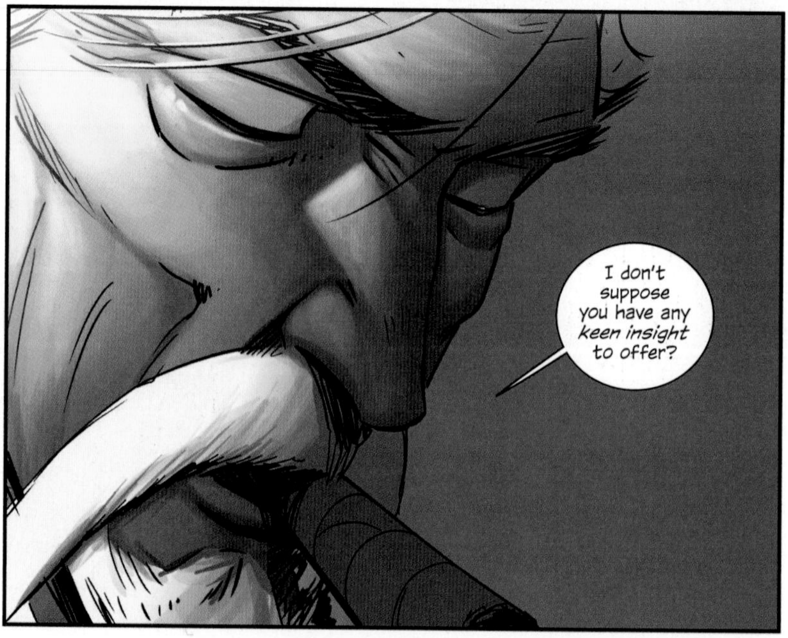
I don't suppose you have any *keen insight* to offer?

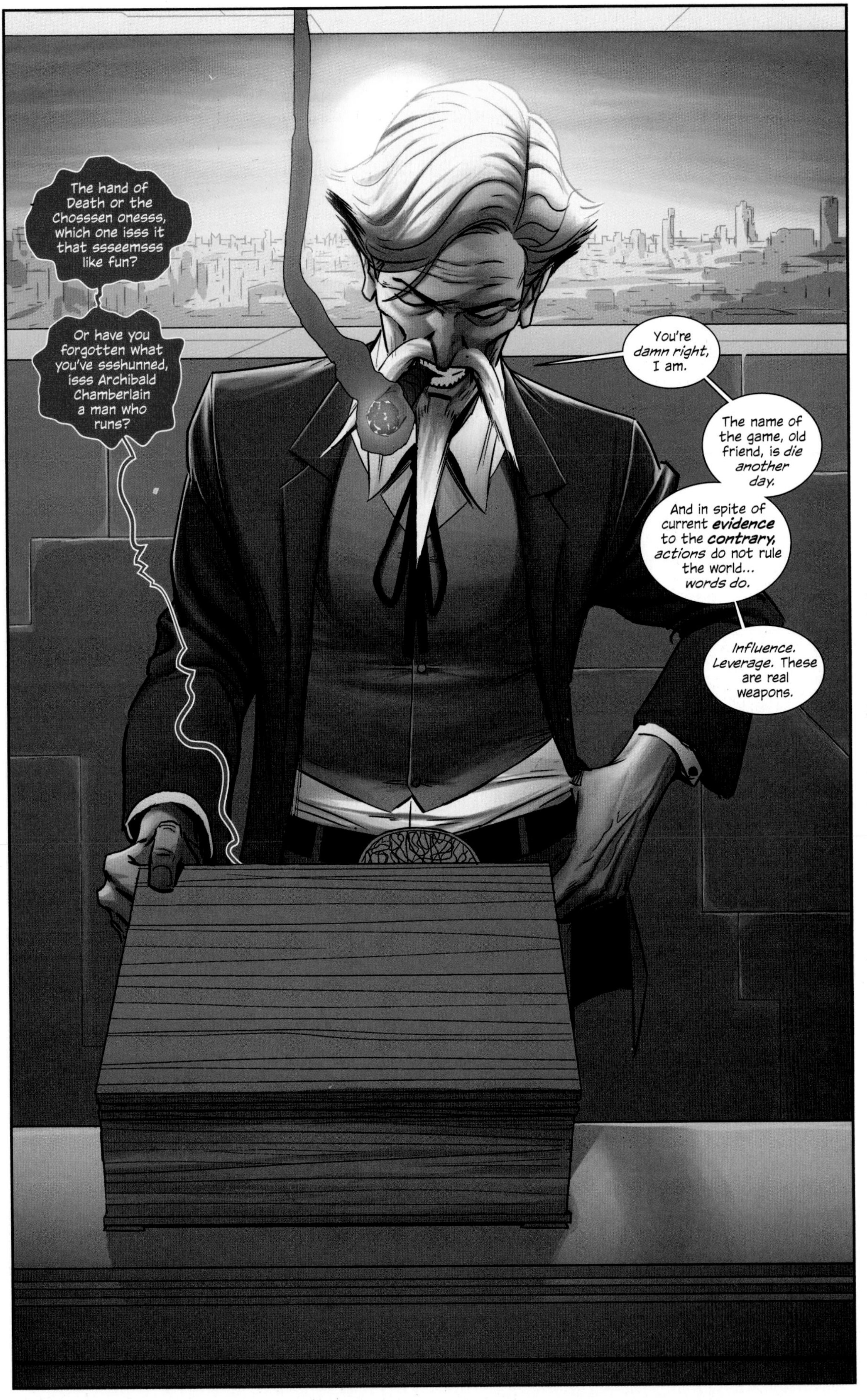
The hand of Death or the Chossen onesss, which one isss it that ssseemsss like fun?
Or have you forgotten what you've ssshunned, isss Archibald Chamberlain a man who runs?
You're *damn right*, I am.
The name of the game, old friend, is *die another day*.
And in spite of current ***evidence*** to the ***contrary***, *actions* do not rule the world... *words do*.
Influence. *Leverage*. These are real weapons.

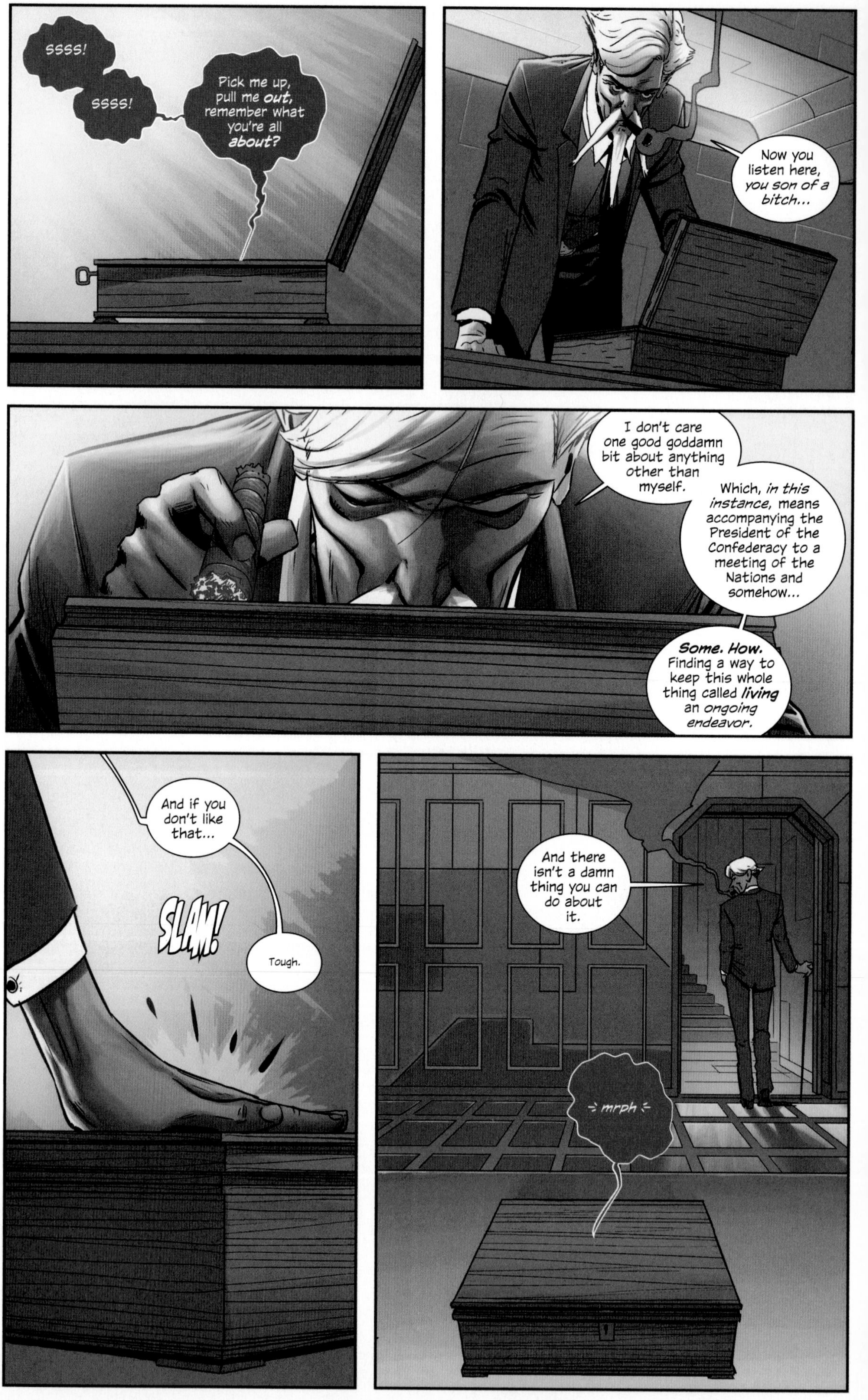
SSSS!
SSSS!
Pick me up, pull me *out,* remember what you're all *about?*
Now you listen here, *you son of a bitch...*
I don't care one good goddamn bit about anything other than myself.
Which, *in this instance,* means accompanying the President of the Confederacy to a meeting of the Nations and somehow...
Some. How. Finding a way to keep this whole thing called ***living*** an *ongoing endeavor.*
And if you don't like that...
SLAM!
Tough.
And there isn't a damn thing you can do about it.
mrph

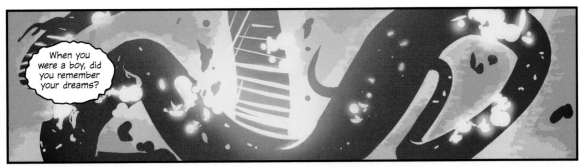

When you were a boy, did you remember your dreams?

Did you wake up and not know the difference between the dream and the world you lived in?

Do you remember those days, Bel Solomon?

Mourn that hazy divide... as all you have now is the waking world...

For your dreams...

They are mine.

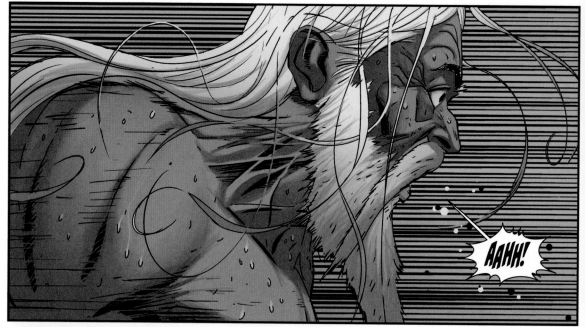

AAHH!

∹ Hack! Hack! ∺

Damn it...

Damn it!

∹ Huf! Huf! ∺

∹ Huf! ∺

Same thing every time I close my eyes...

Every damn time I fall asleep...

Oh, you think this isn't *real*, Bel?

That there's not something crawling around inside your head?

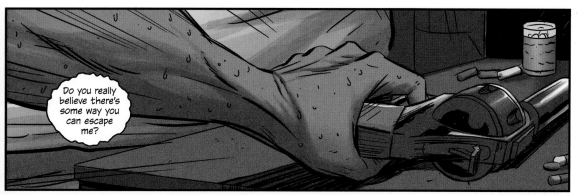

Do you really believe there's some way you can escape me?

How about this?

How about I blow my goddamn brains out -- *spare* you and me both from any more of this madness.

Sincerity begins at you pulling back the hammer, Bel...

CLICK!

Believe me now?

Yes.

Yes, I do.

So pull the trigger. Pull it before you can *betray* us any more.

For what are you if you're not *Chosen*, Bel? Just a bag of bones like any other man.

These are the end times, my friend, let's get them started earlier than all the rest..

Pull. That. Trigger!

No. Not yet...

There's still too much to be done...

And this would be... *too easy.*

Father... why complicate things? I can handle this on my own.

Son, if it **would not** undo decades of protocol, it would be I attending this meeting at the Wall...

And **you** would be serving as **my second**. So take the privilege for what it is:

An opportunity to look in the eyes of both our friends and our enemies.

So that you can divine which of our friends will soon be enemies, and which adversaries might offer some opportunity in the coming days.

Do we understand one another, son?

Yes, Father.

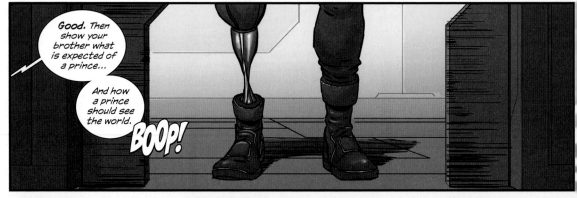

Good. Then show your brother what is expected of a prince...

And how a prince should see the world.

BOOP!

Better to blind the fool if you ask me.

Hey!

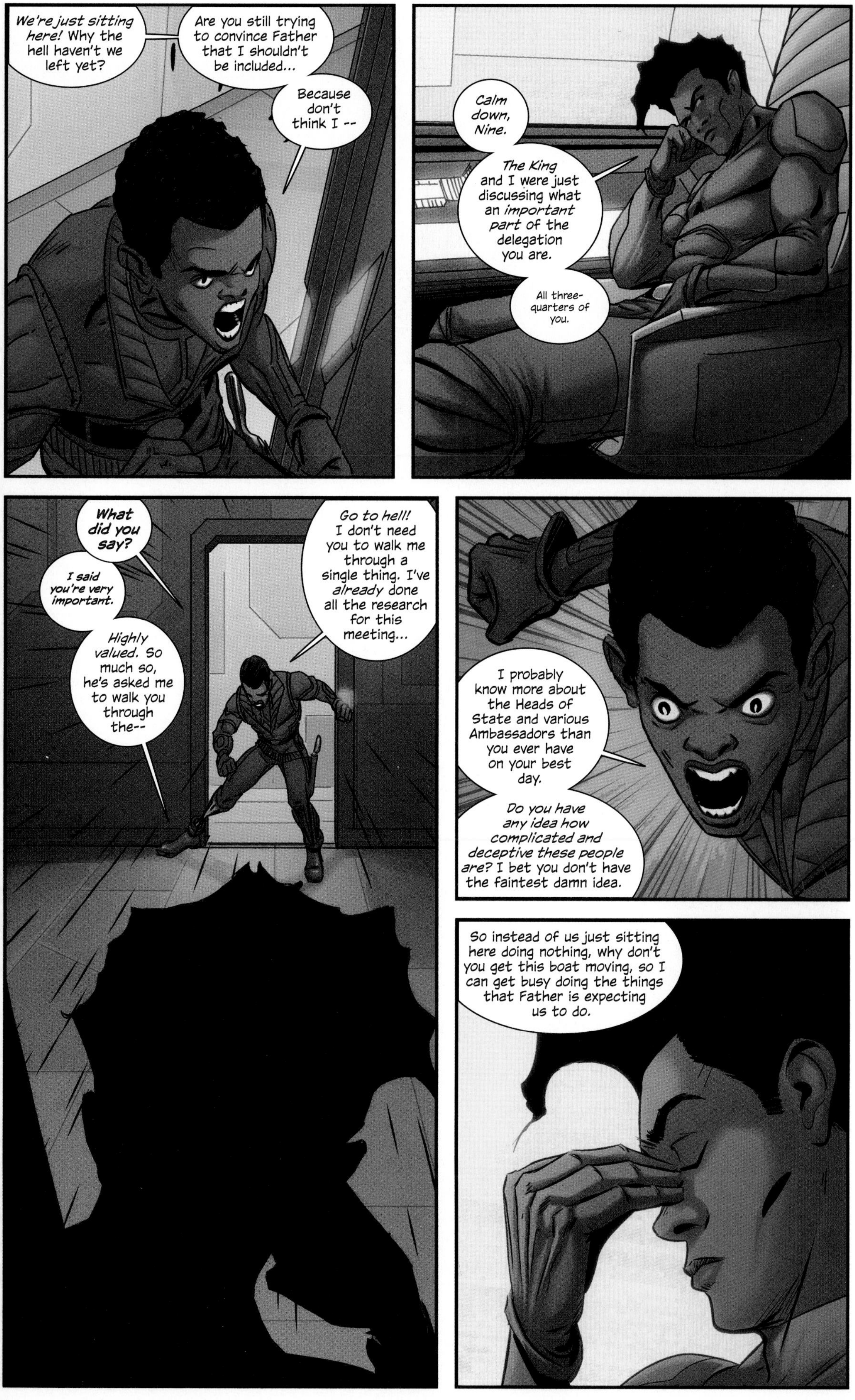

We're just sitting here! Why the hell haven't we left yet?
Are you still trying to convince Father that I shouldn't be included...
Because don't think I --
Calm down, Nine.
The King and I were just discussing what an *important part* of the delegation you are.
All three-quarters of you.
What did you say?
I said you're very important.
Highly valued. So much so, he's asked me to walk you through the--
Go to hell! I don't need you to walk me through a single thing. I've *already* done all the research for this meeting...
I probably know more about the Heads of State and various Ambassadors than you ever have on your best day.
Do you have any idea how complicated and deceptive these people are? I bet you don't have the faintest damn idea.
So instead of us just sitting here doing nothing, why don't you get this boat moving, so I can get busy doing the things that Father is expecting us to do.

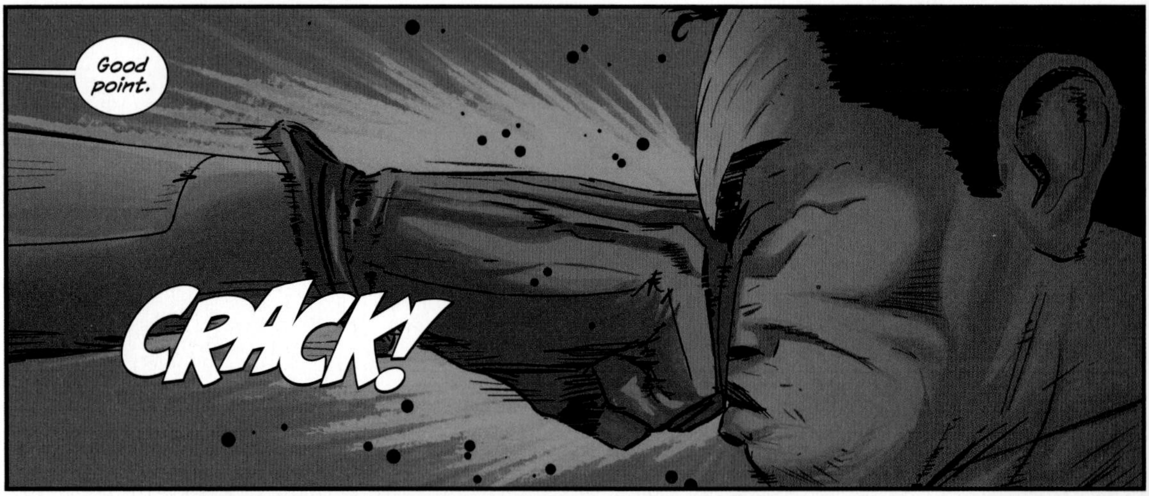
Good point.
CRACK!

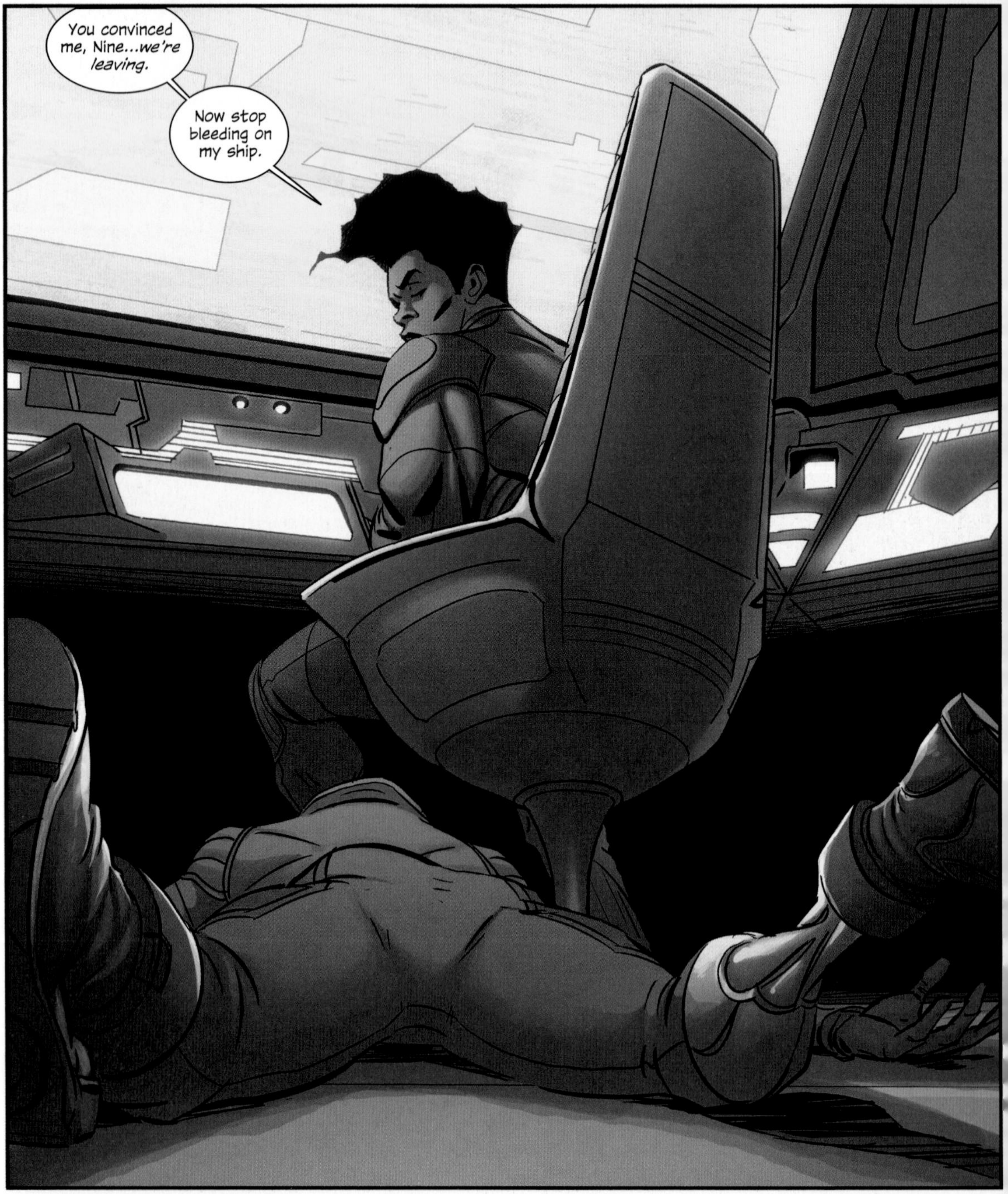
You convinced me, Nine...*we're leaving.*
Now stop bleeding on my ship.

BBZZZZZ ZZZZ ZZZZZ ZZZZ ZZZZZ

BOOM

Gods! Another one?

That's the second this week.

I'll have a *damage assessment* as soon as possible, Madame President.

Waste of time...

Child dissidents storm a local heliopad, steal a hopper, and -- because they can't handle the incredible pressures that come with living in a modern society -- crash it into the largest authoritarian *bullshit bullshit childish fecking bullshit.*

What I want, Doma Lux, is for you to quietly have their families killed.

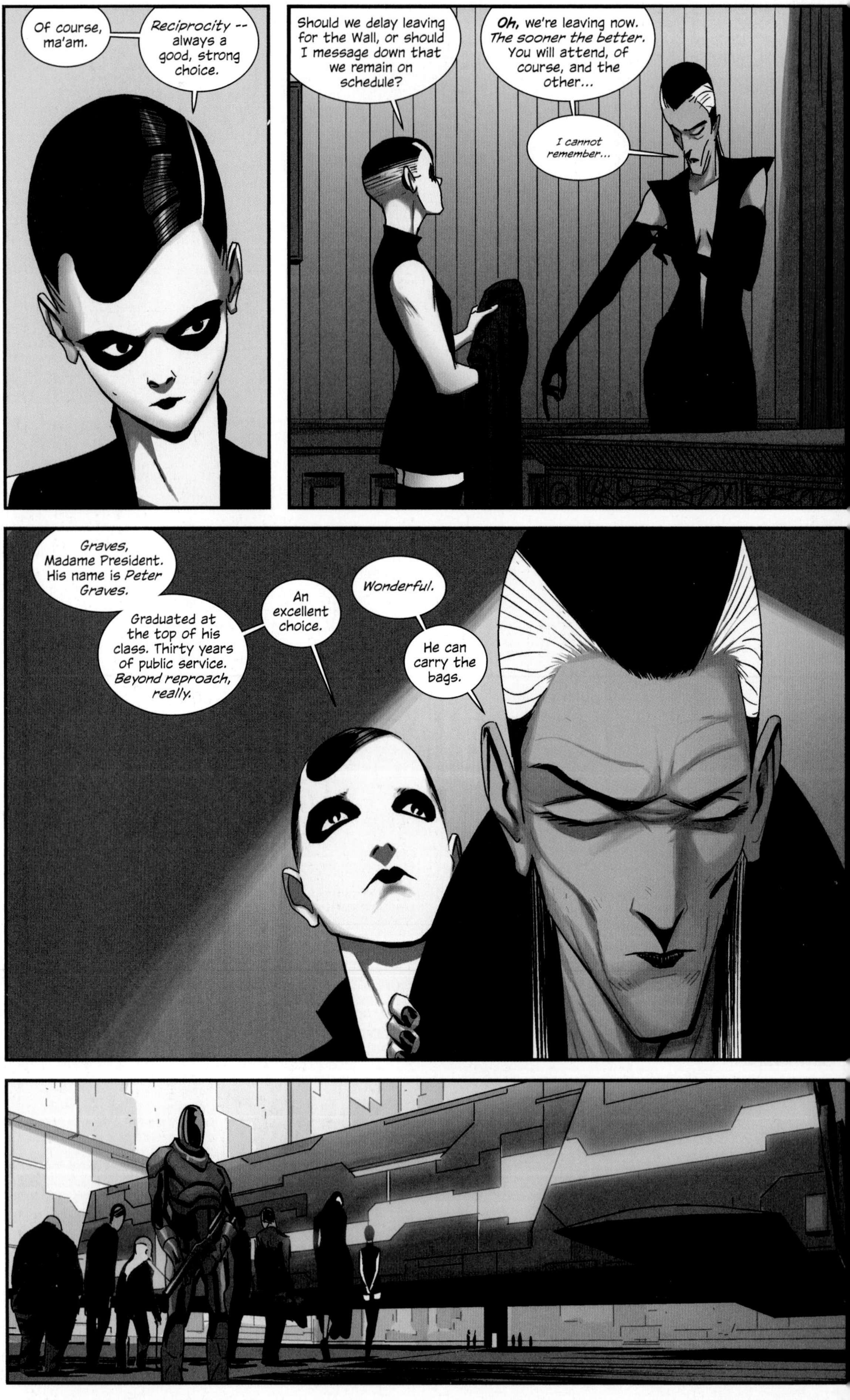
Of course, ma'am.
Reciprocity -- always a good, strong choice.
Should we delay leaving for the Wall, or should I message down that we remain on schedule?
Oh, we're leaving now. *The sooner the better.* You will attend, of course, and the other...
I cannot remember...
Graves, Madame President. His name is *Peter Graves.*
Graduated at the top of his class. Thirty years of public service. *Beyond reproach, really.*
An excellent choice.
Wonderful.
He can carry the bags.

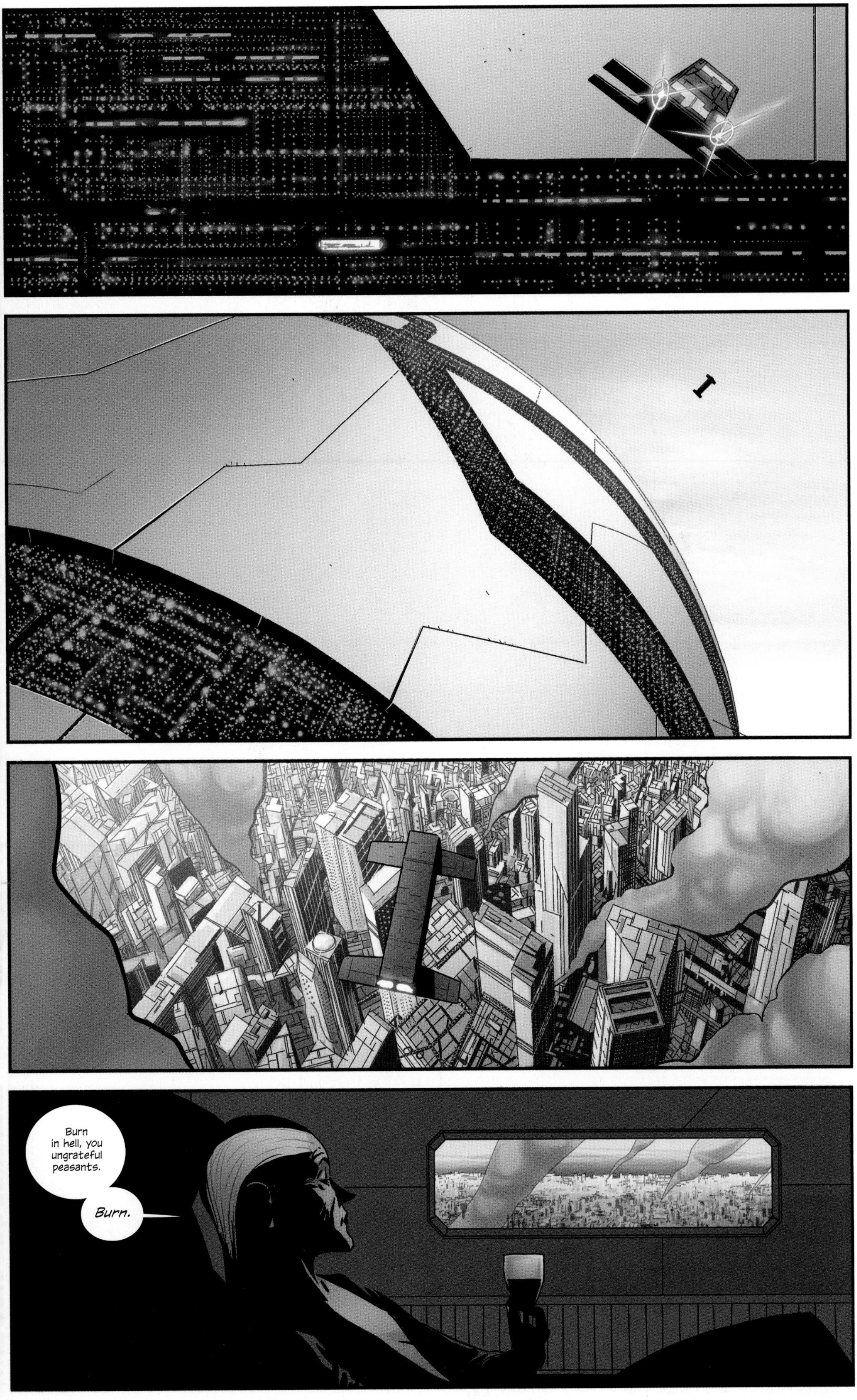
Burn in hell, you ungrateful peasants.
Burn.

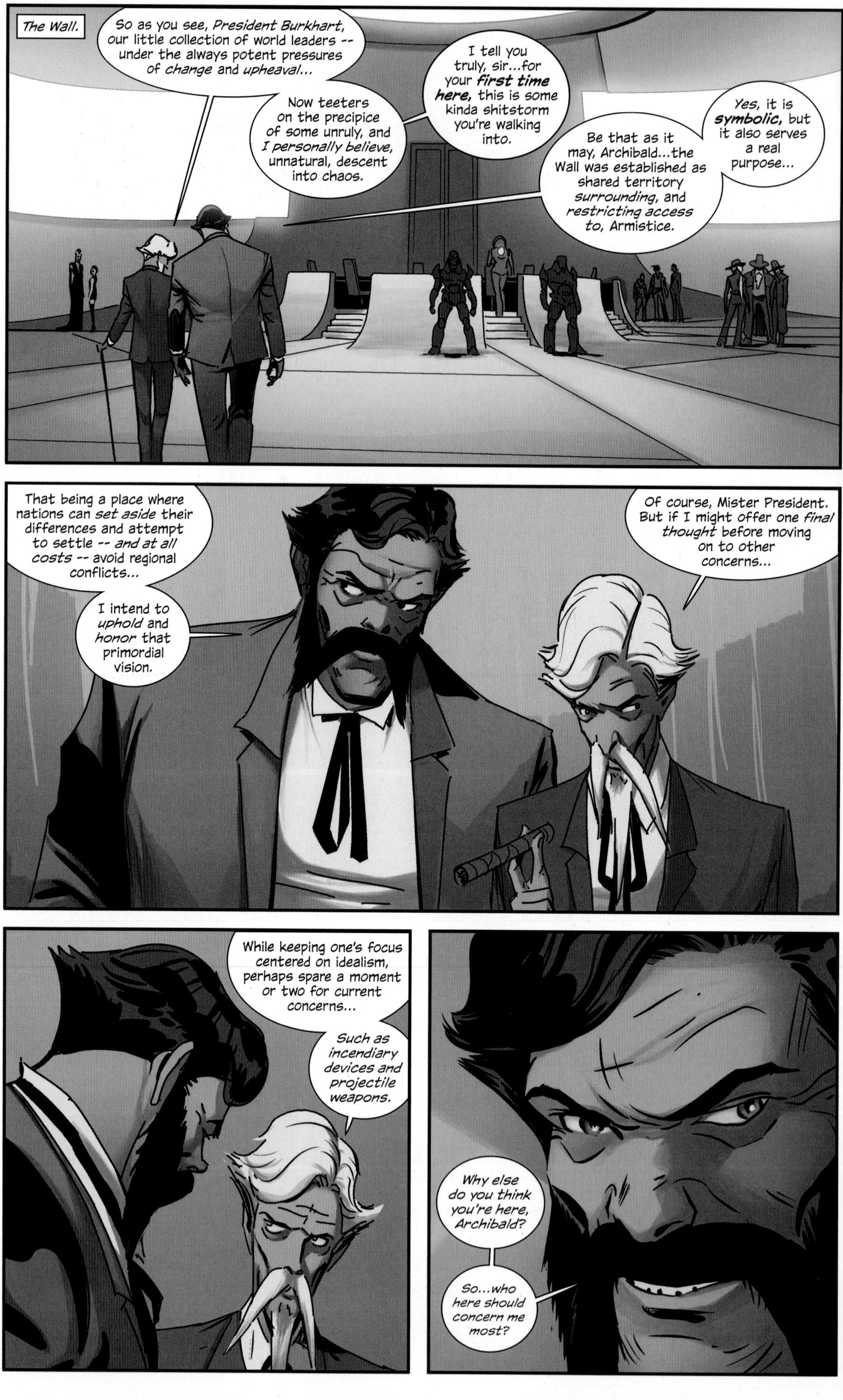

The Wall.
So as you see, *President Burkhart*, our little collection of world leaders -- under the always potent pressures of *change* and *upheaval*...
Now teeters on the precipice of some unruly, and *I personally believe*, unnatural, descent into chaos.
I tell you truly, sir...for your ***first time here***, this is some kinda shitstorm you're walking into.
Be that as it may, Archibald...the Wall was established as shared territory *surrounding*, and *restricting access to*, Armistice.
Yes, it is ***symbolic***, but it also serves a real purpose...
That being a place where nations can *set aside* their differences and attempt to settle -- *and at all costs* -- avoid regional conflicts...
I intend to *uphold* and *honor* that primordial vision.
Of course, Mister President. But if I might offer one *final thought* before moving on to other concerns...
While keeping one's focus centered on idealism, perhaps spare a moment or two for current concerns...
Such as incendiary devices and projectile weapons.
Why else do you think you're here, Archibald?
So...who here should concern me most?

With all due respect, sir. *Everyone* should concern you.

I do not need to belabor both the duplicitous and feral nature of our northern neighbors, *the Union.*

Nor should I dwell on the machinations of *the Kingdom...*

Both of these are well known to you.

And while we have enjoyed a long-term relationship with *the Texas Republic,* we should take pause at the recent ramp-up of nationalism.

I believe the border closings and their comprehensive withdrawal of all diplomats hints at a much larger problem. It's speculation, *of course,* but I believe there is a sickness growing there.

Some kind of... *inner decay.*

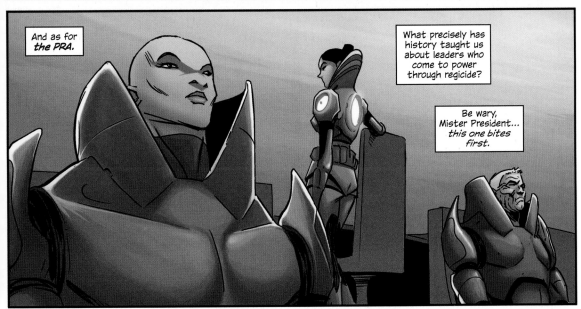

And as for *the PRA.*

What precisely has history taught us about leaders who come to power through regicide?

Be wary, Mister President... *this one bites first.*

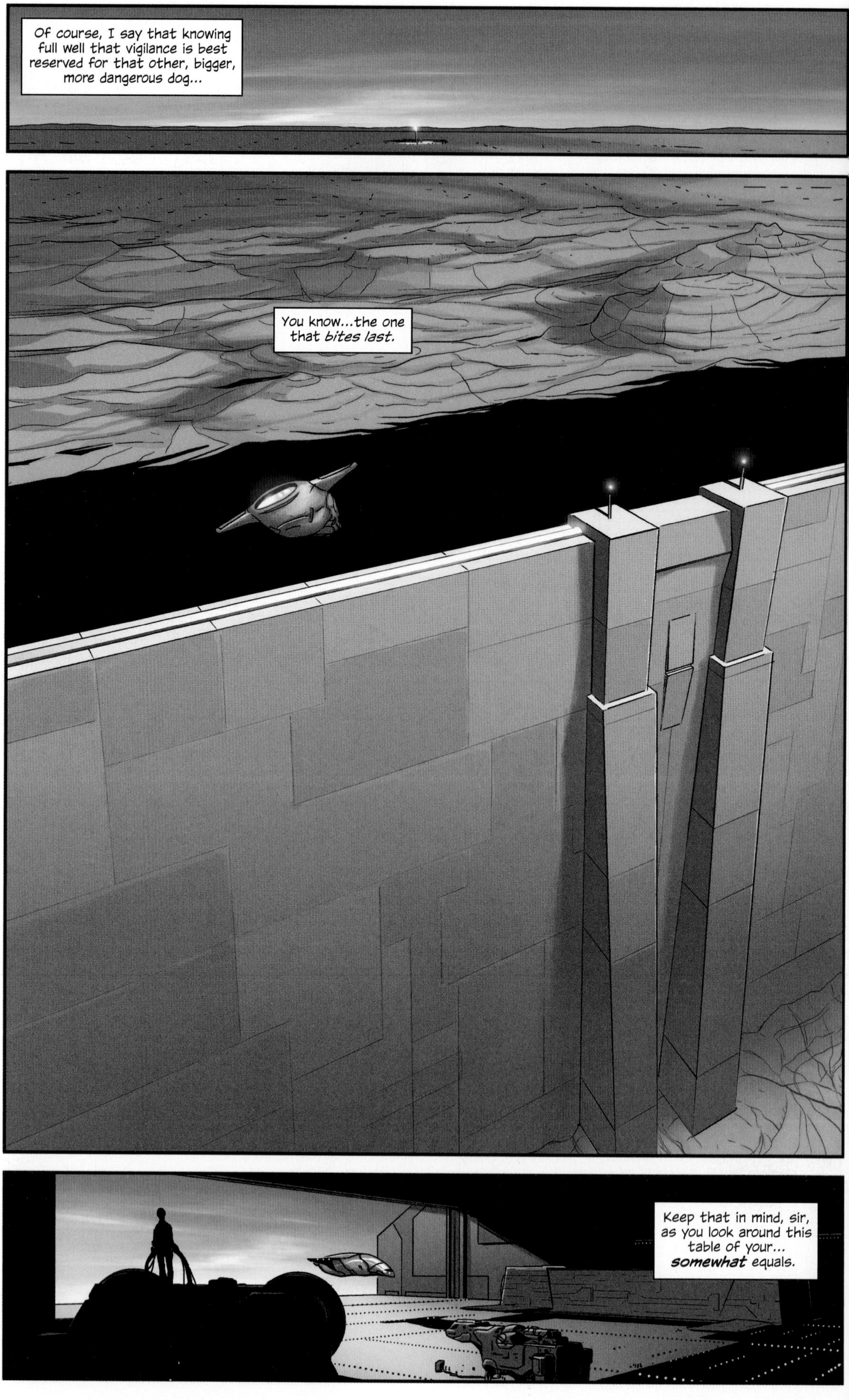
Of course, I say that knowing full well that vigilance is best reserved for that other, bigger, more dangerous dog...
You know...the one that *bites last.*
Keep that in mind, sir, as you look around this table of your... ***somewhat*** equals.

Ask yourself, what is it that separates the upper strata of aristocracy?

What makes one sovereign state better than another?

Is it having fractionally more money...or power... or influence? Yes. Of course it is.

Is it having a greater power to destroy? Or to build? Yes. *That also.*

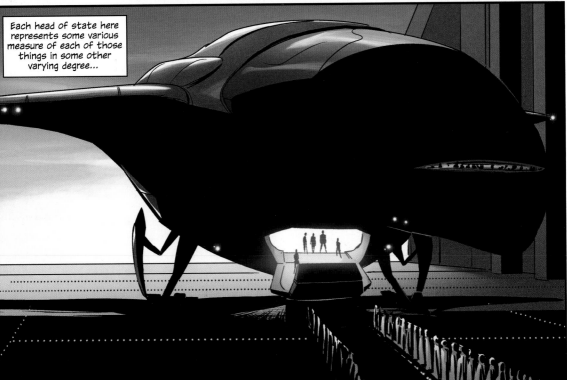

Each head of state here represents some various measure of each of those things in some other varying degree...

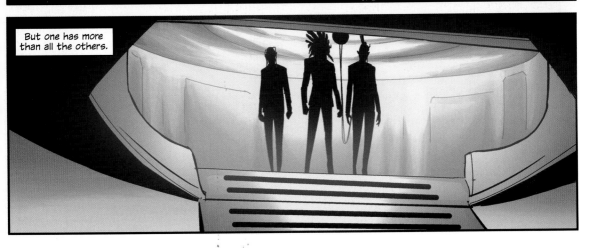

But one has more than all the others.

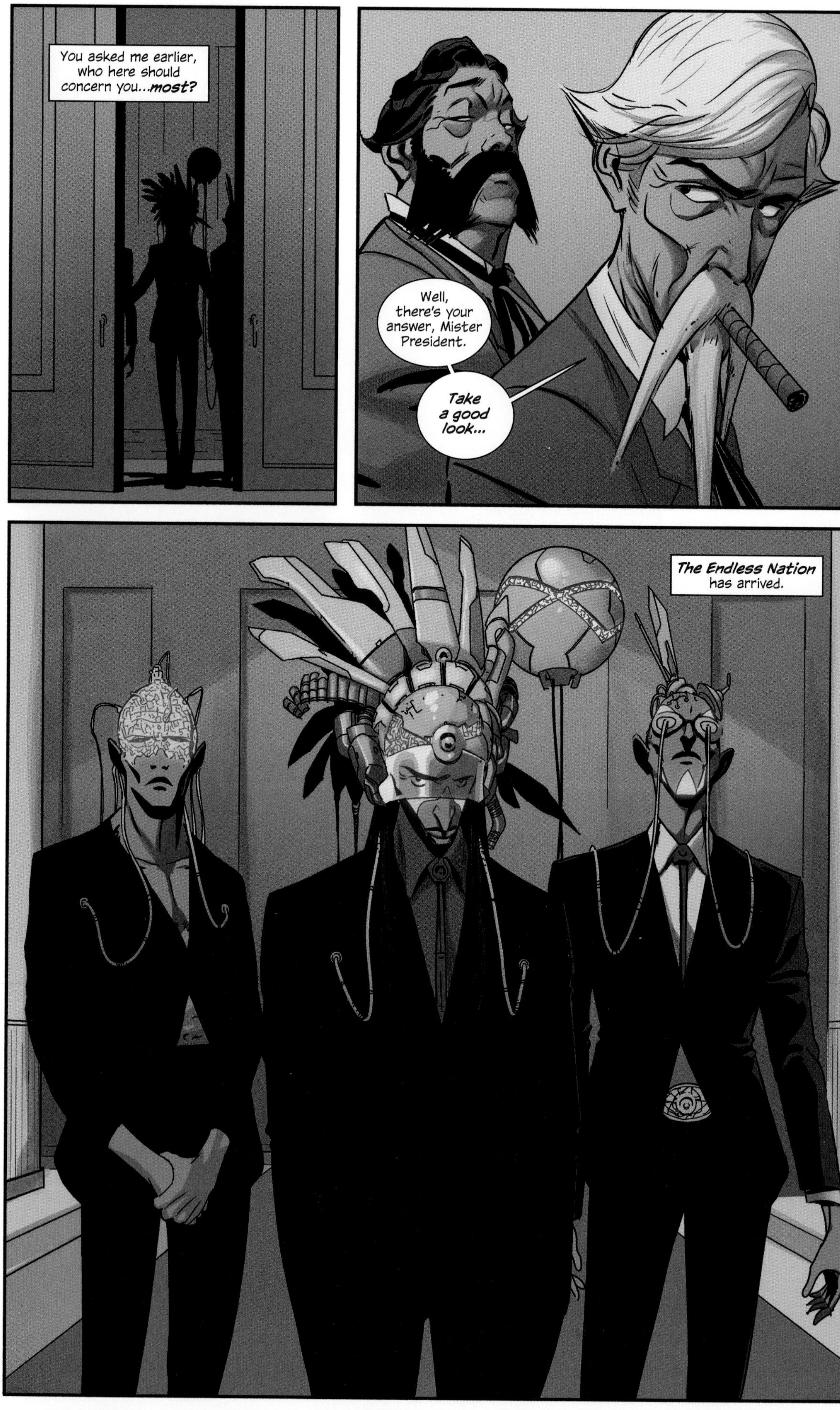
You asked me earlier, who here should concern you...*most?*
Well, there's your answer, Mister President.
Take a good look...
The Endless Nation has arrived.

REVENGE IS FOR THE **RIGHTEOUS.**

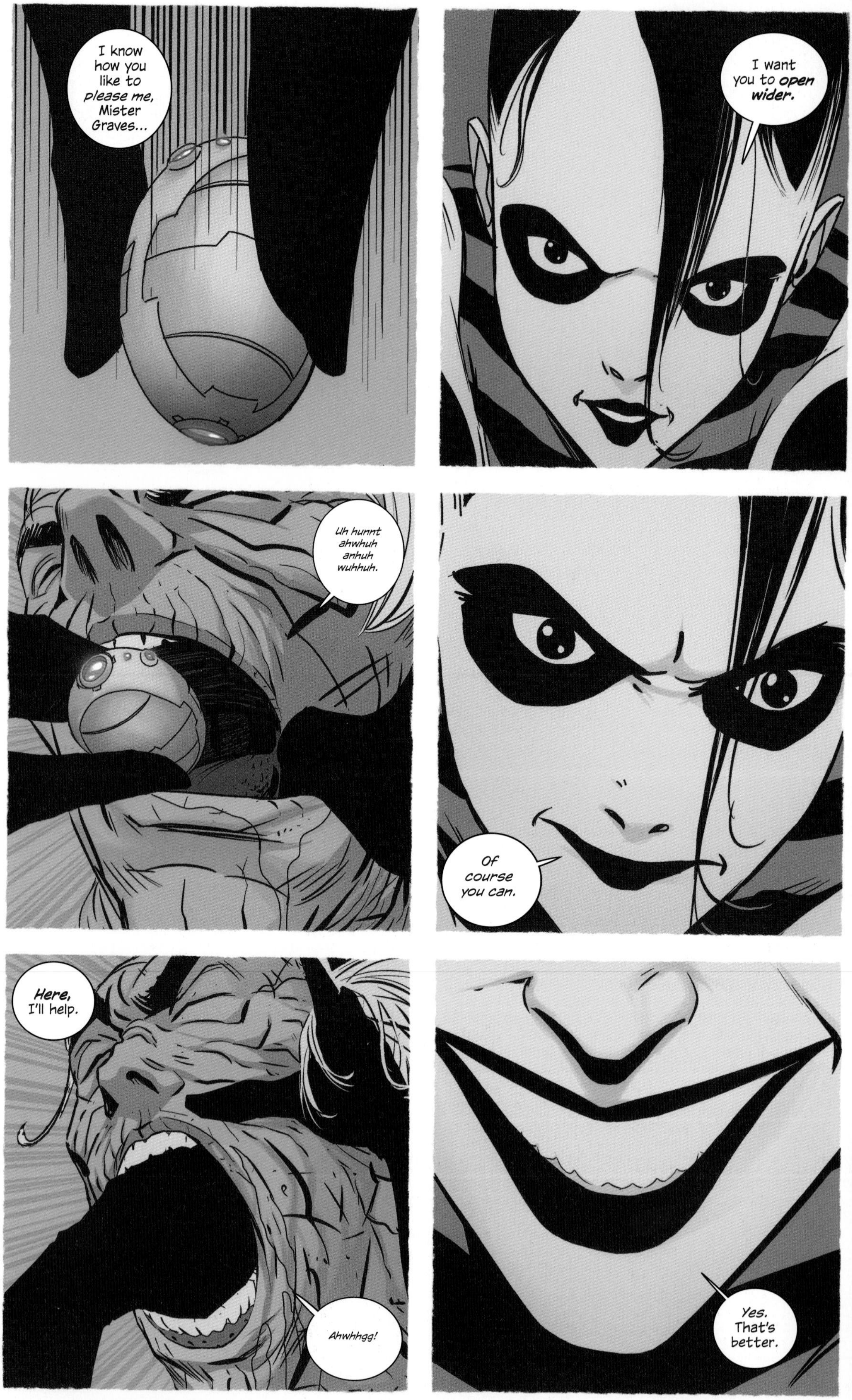
I know how you like to please me, Mister Graves...
I want you to open wider.
Uh hunnt ahwhuh anhuh wuhhuh.
Of course you can.
Here, I'll help.
Ahwhhgg!
Yes. That's better.

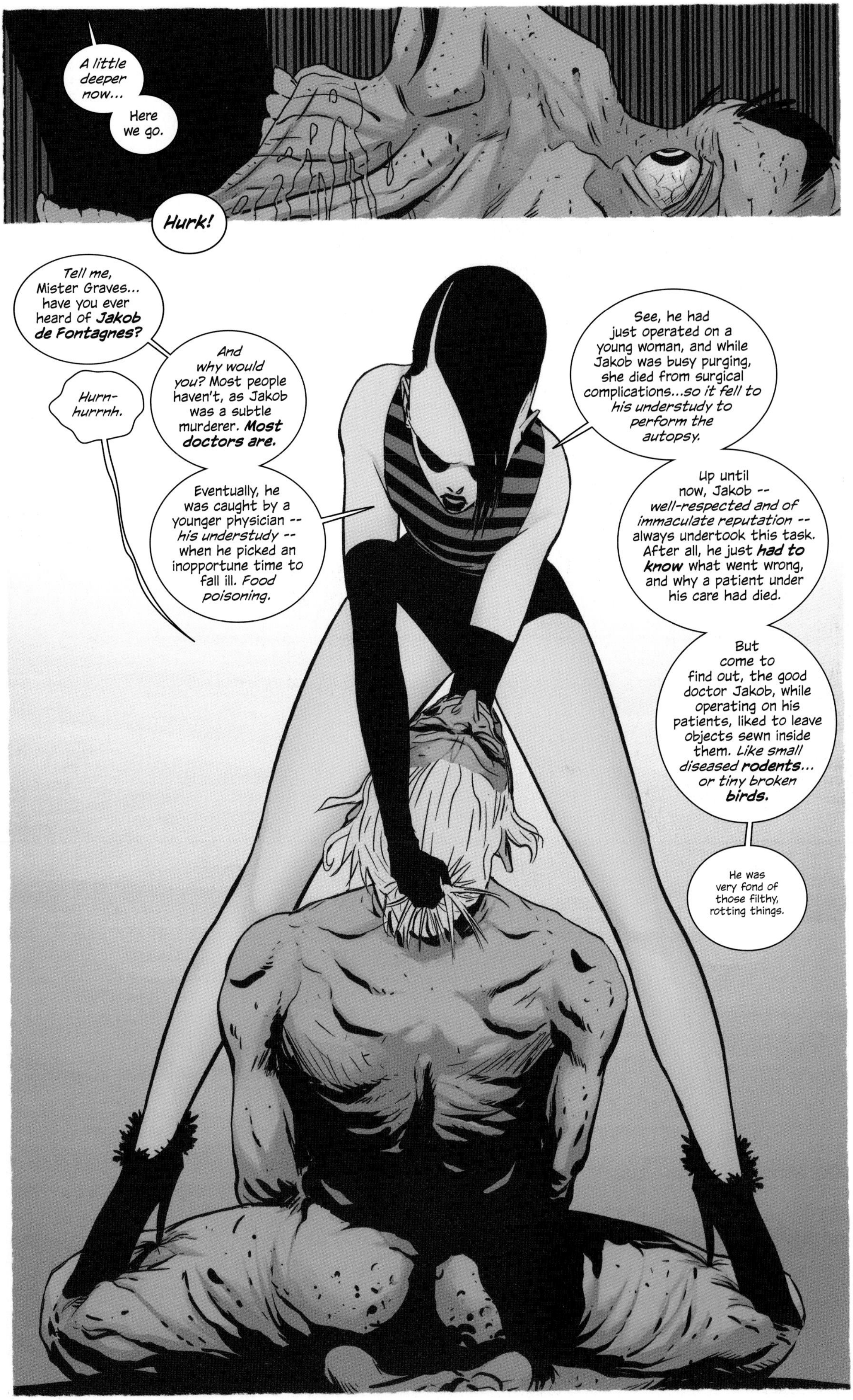
A little deeper now...
Here we go.
Hurk!
Tell me, Mister Graves... have you ever heard of Jakob de Fontagnes?
And why would you? Most people haven't, as Jakob was a subtle murderer. Most doctors are.
Hurn-hurrnh.
Eventually, he was caught by a younger physician -- his understudy -- when he picked an inopportune time to fall ill. Food poisoning.
See, he had just operated on a young woman, and while Jakob was busy purging, she died from surgical complications...so it fell to his understudy to perform the autopsy.
Up until now, Jakob -- well-respected and of immaculate reputation -- always undertook this task. After all, he just had to know what went wrong, and why a patient under his care had died.
But come to find out, the good doctor Jakob, while operating on his patients, liked to leave objects sewn inside them. Like small diseased rodents... or tiny broken birds.
He was very fond of those filthy, rotting things.

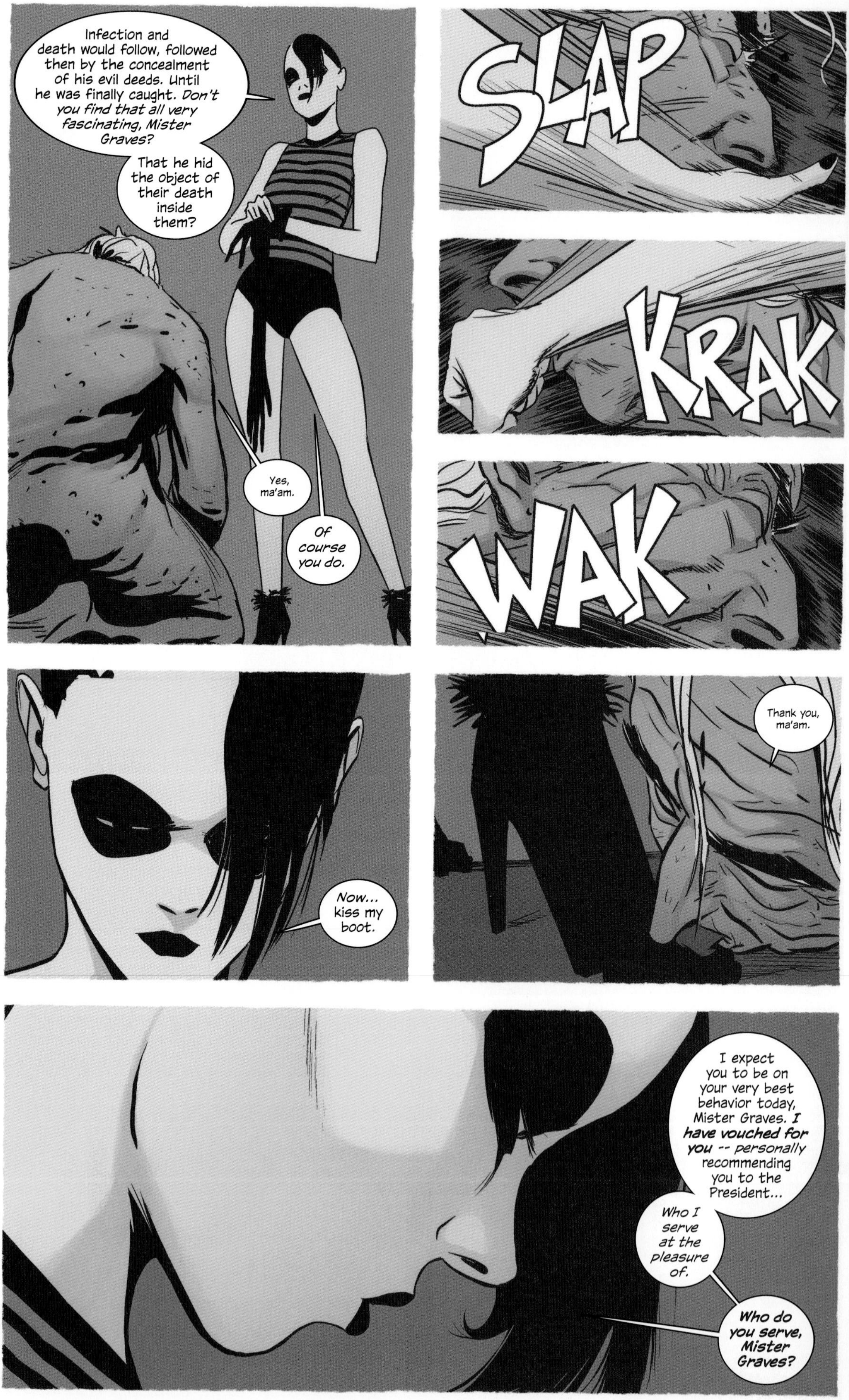
Infection and death would follow, followed then by the concealment of his evil deeds. Until he was finally caught. *Don't you find that all very fascinating, Mister Graves?*
That he hid the object of their death inside them?
Yes, ma'am.
Of course you do.
SLAP
KRAK
WAK
Now... kiss my boot.
Thank you, ma'am.
I expect you to be on your very best behavior today, Mister Graves. ***I have vouched for you*** *-- personally* recommending you to the President...
Who I serve at the pleasure of.
Who do you serve, Mister Graves?

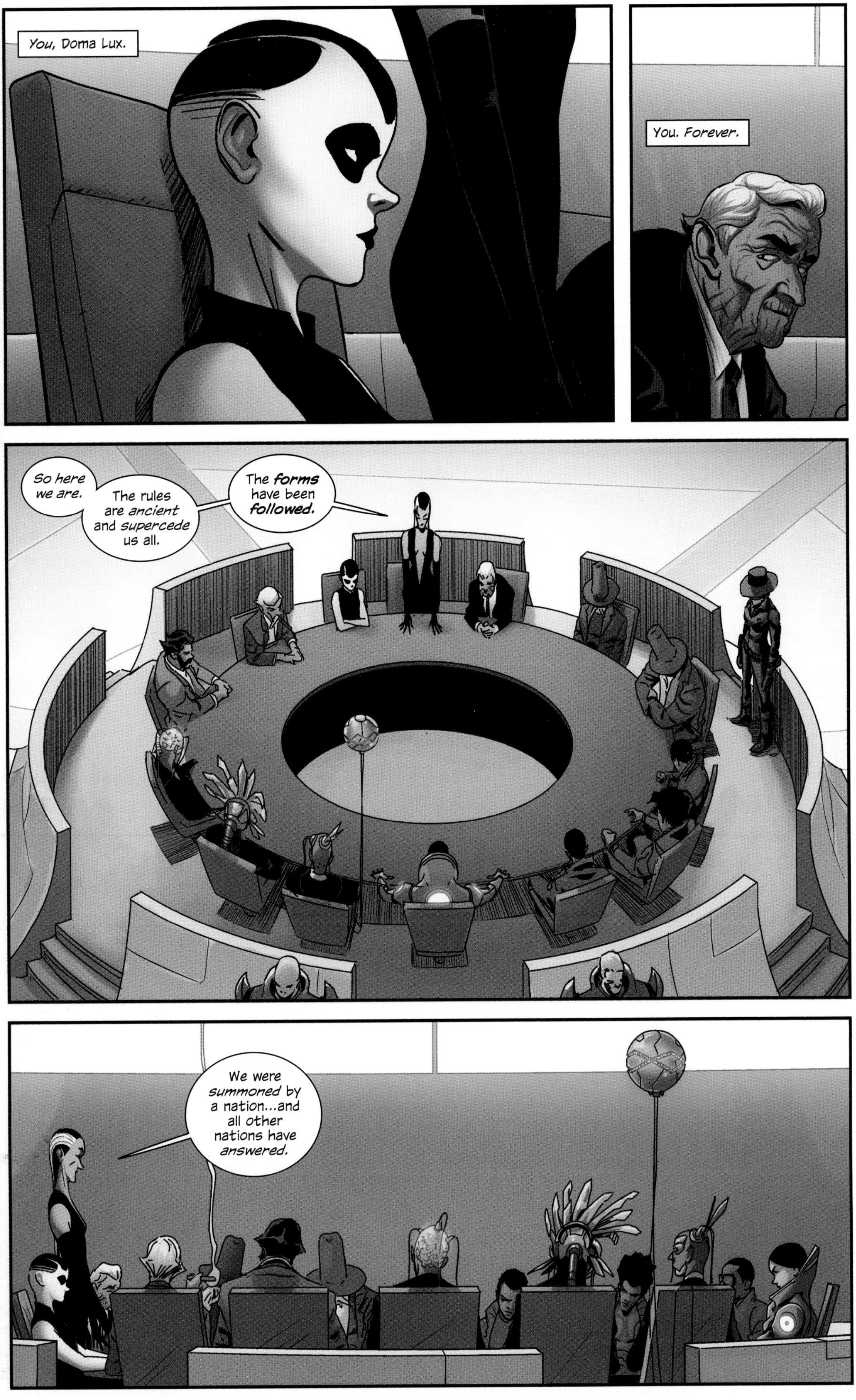

You, Doma Lux.
You. *Forever.*
So here we are.
The rules are *ancient* and *supercede* us all.
The ***forms*** have been ***followed.***
We were *summoned* by a nation...and all other nations have *answered.*

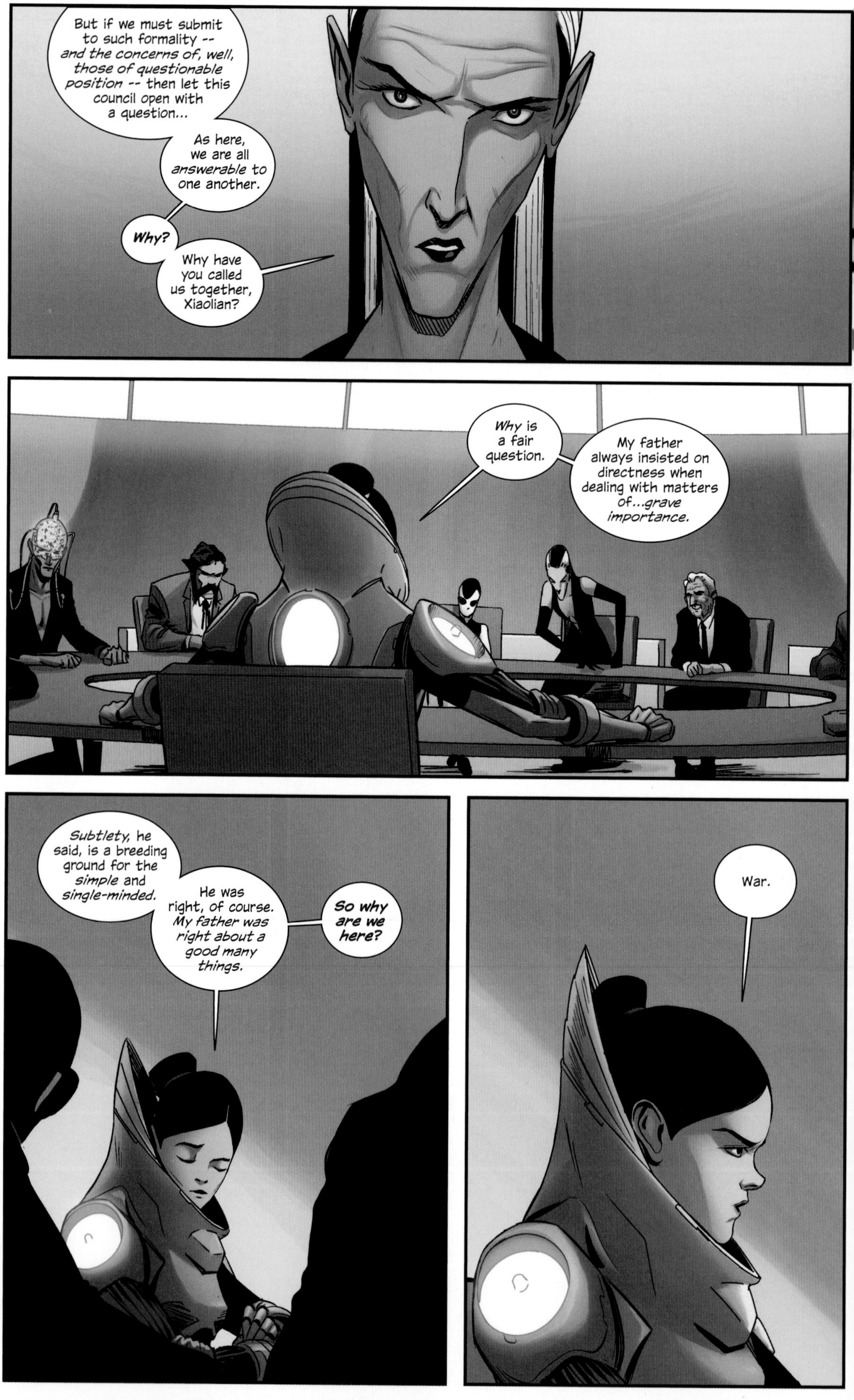
But if we must submit to such formality -- and the concerns of, well, those of questionable position -- then let this council open with a question...
As here, we are all answerable to one another.
Why?
Why have you called us together, Xiaolian?
Why is a fair question.
My father always insisted on directness when dealing with matters of...grave importance.
Subtlety, he said, is a breeding ground for the simple and single-minded.
He was right, of course. My father was right about a good many things.
So why are we here?
War.

MAN IS A MOST **COMPLEX** **SIMPLE** CREATURE.

SEE WHAT HE **WEAVES,** AND HOW **BASE** HIS REASONS FOR DOING SO.

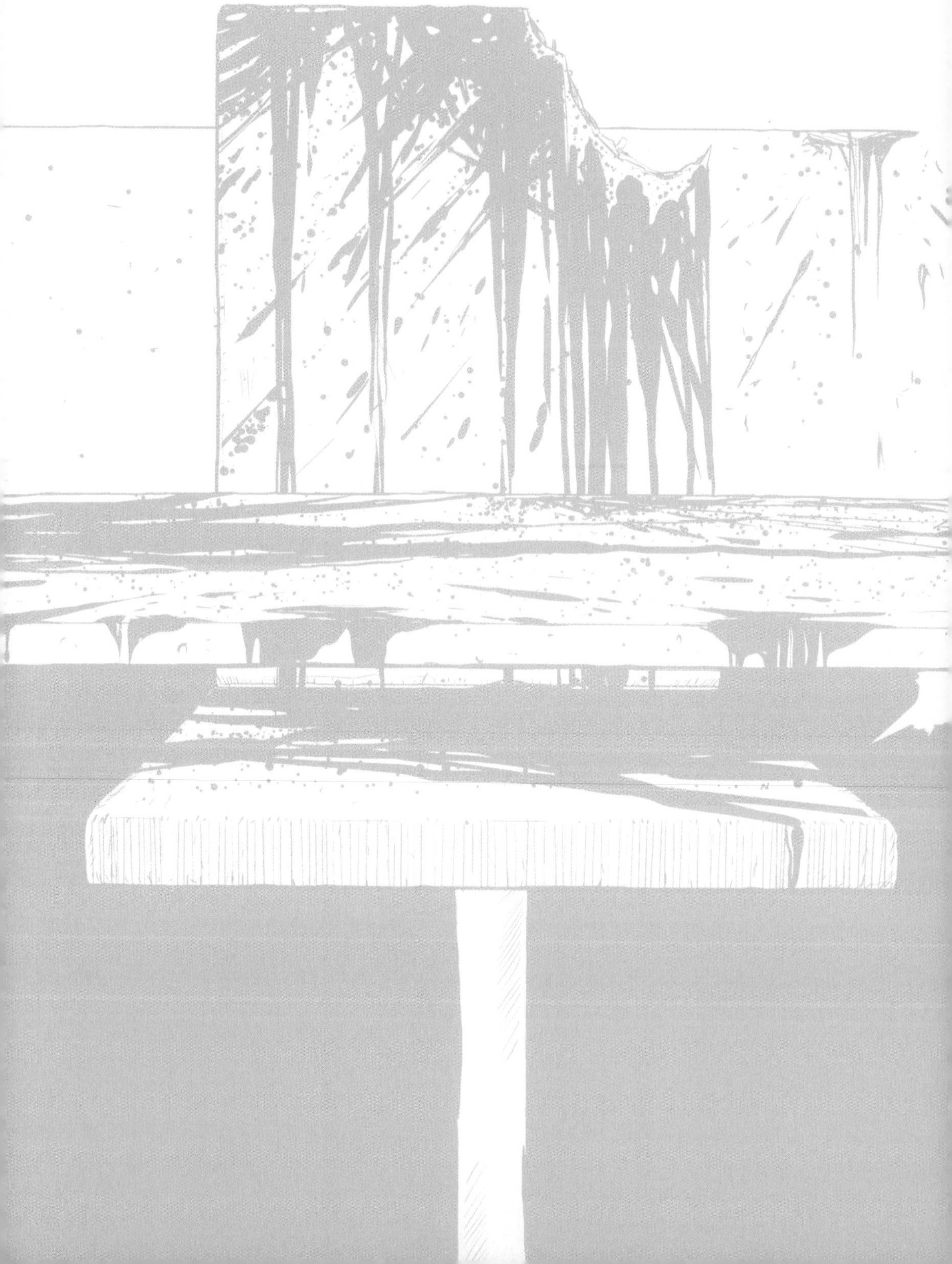

TWELVE:
WORSHIP GOD
WAR

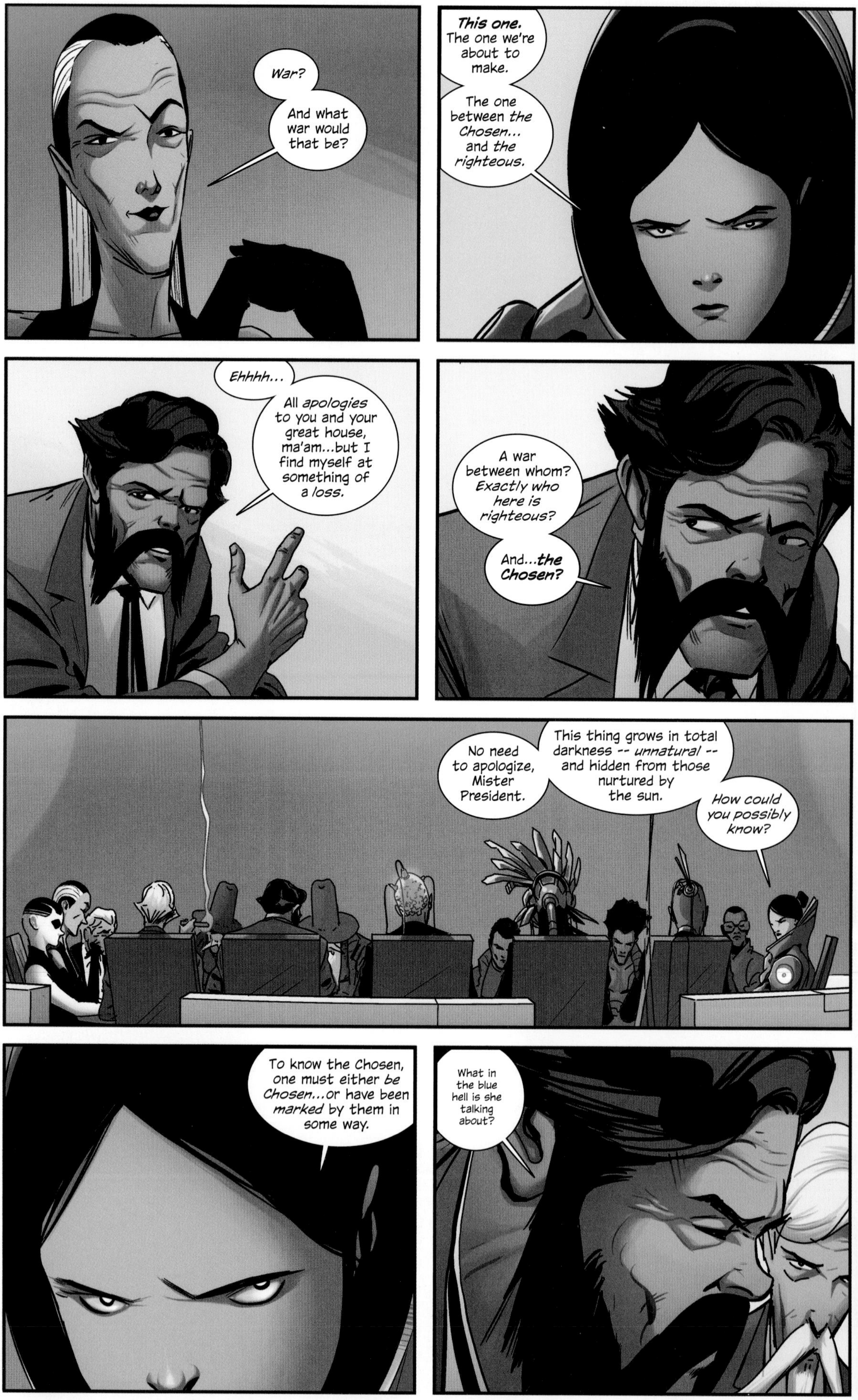
War?
And what war would that be?
This one. The one we're about to make.
The one between the Chosen... and the righteous.
Ehhhh...
All apologies to you and your great house, ma'am...but I find myself at something of a loss.
A war between whom? Exactly who here is righteous?
And...the Chosen?
No need to apologize, Mister President.
This thing grows in total darkness -- unnatural -- and hidden from those nurtured by the sun.
How could you possibly know?
To know the Chosen, one must either be Chosen...or have been marked by them in some way.
What in the blue hell is she talking about?

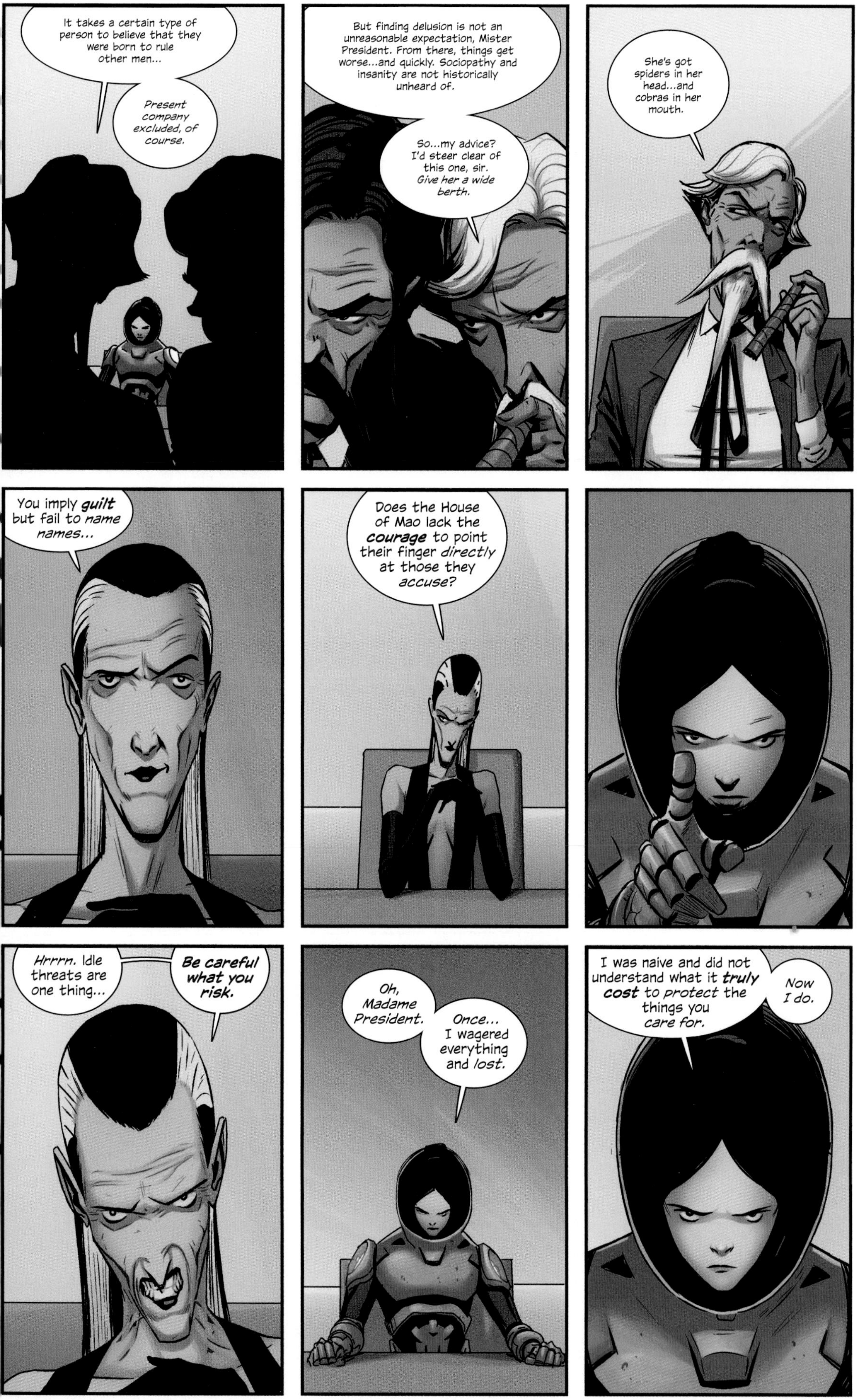
It takes a certain type of person to believe that they were born to rule other men...
Present company excluded, of course.
But finding delusion is not an unreasonable expectation, Mister President. From there, things get worse...and quickly. Sociopathy and insanity are not historically unheard of.
So...my advice? I'd steer clear of this one, sir. Give her a wide berth.
She's got spiders in her head...and cobras in her mouth.
You imply guilt but fail to name names...
Does the House of Mao lack the courage to point their finger directly at those they accuse?
Hrrrn. Idle threats are one thing...
Be careful what you risk.
Oh, Madame President.
Once... I wagered everything and lost.
I was naive and did not understand what it truly cost to protect the things you care for.
Now I do.

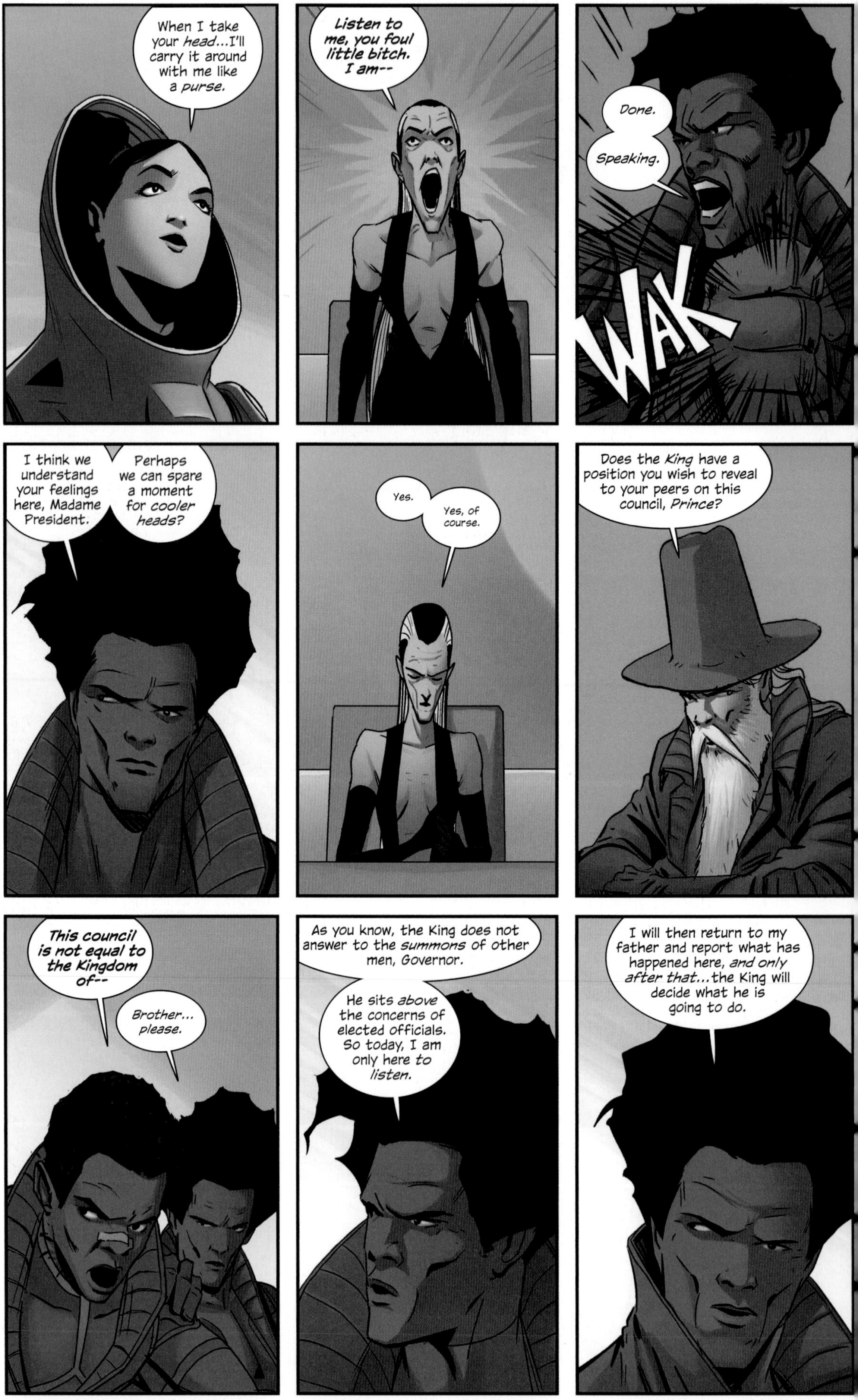
When I take your *head*...I'll carry it around with me like a *purse.*
Listen to me, you foul little bitch. I am--
Done.
Speaking.
WAK
I think we understand your feelings here, Madame President.
Perhaps we can spare a moment for *cooler heads?*
Yes.
Yes, of course.
Does the *King* have a position you wish to reveal to your peers on this council, *Prince?*
This council is not equal to the Kingdom of--
Brother... please.
As you know, the King does not answer to the *summons* of other men, Governor.
He sits *above* the concerns of elected officials. So today, I am only here *to listen.*
I will then return to my father and report what has happened here, *and only after that*...the King will decide what he is going to do.

Your father... always waiting to see what cards other men hold.

Be grateful he is the one who rules the Kingdom, Bel -- for I am not so patient, and you and I...

We have some unfinished business.

Can you feel the noose tightening around your neck, Mister Solomon?

Get out of my head.

You're surrounded... surrounded by your enemies...do you have any friends left in this world?

What are you going to do when these jackals begin to feed on each other?

I...I... see the... the Nation is here.

The rare occurrence that it is.

You want to fill us in on what you're thinking -- your take of the situation?

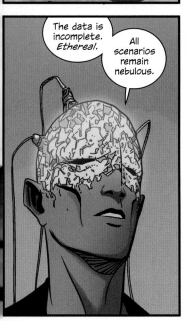

The data is incomplete. Ethereal.

All scenarios remain nebulous.

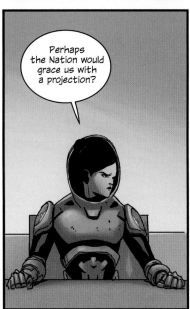

Perhaps the Nation would grace us with a projection?

For the Great House? Of course.

Shaman... a divination, please.

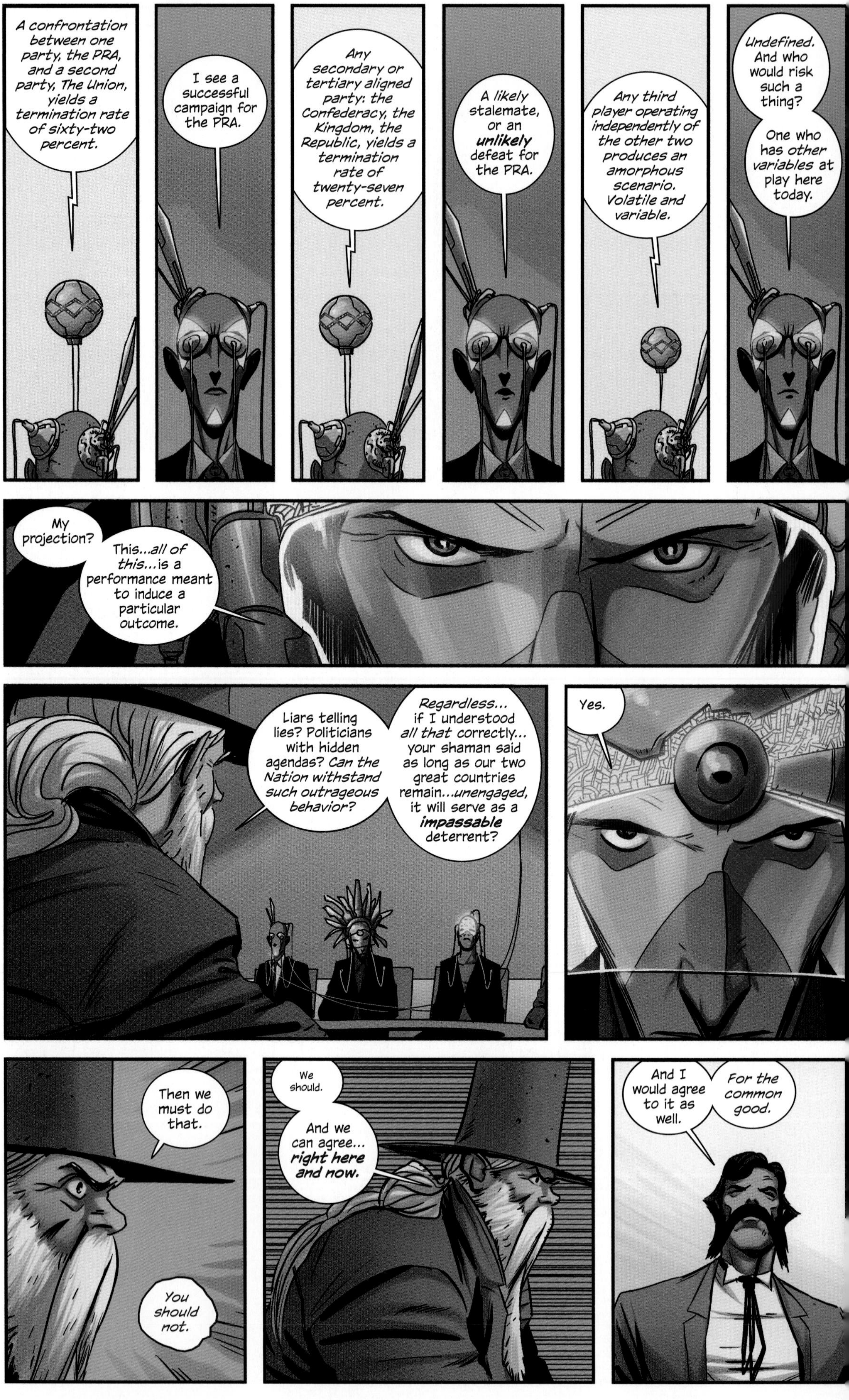

A confrontation between one party, the PRA, and a second party, The Union, yields a termination rate of sixty-two percent.
I see a successful campaign for the PRA.
Any secondary or tertiary aligned party: the Confederacy, the Kingdom, the Republic, yields a termination rate of twenty-seven percent.
A likely stalemate, or an unlikely defeat for the PRA.
Any third player operating independently of the other two produces an amorphous scenario. Volatile and variable.
Undefined. And who would risk such a thing?
One who has other variables at play here today.
My projection?
This...all of this...is a performance meant to induce a particular outcome.
Liars telling lies? Politicians with hidden agendas? Can the Nation withstand such outrageous behavior?
Regardless... if I understood all that correctly... your shaman said as long as our two great countries remain...unengaged, it will serve as a impassable deterrent?
Yes.
Then we must do that.
You should not.
We should.
And we can agree... right here and now.
And I would agree to it as well.
For the common good.

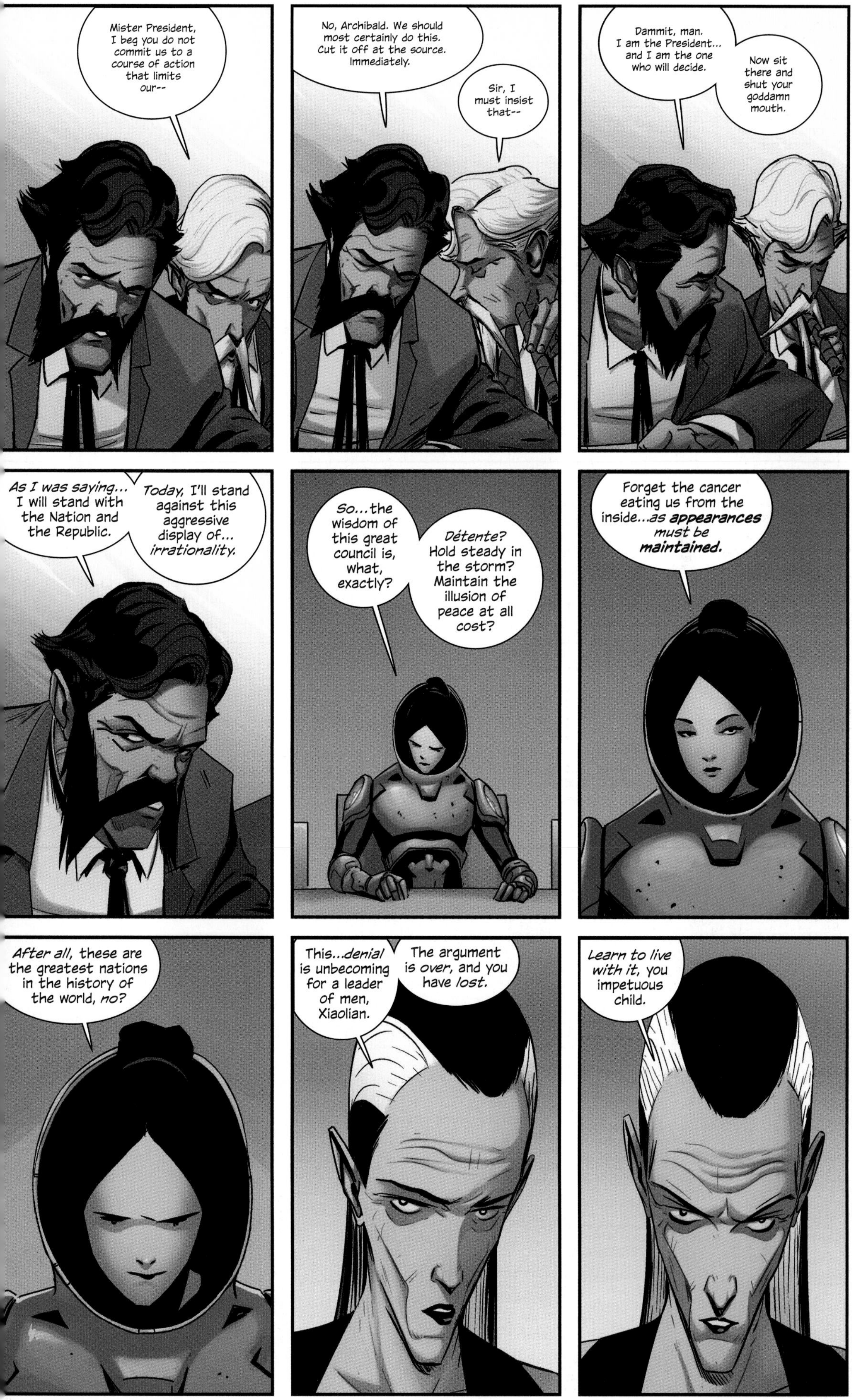
Mister President, I beg you do not commit us to a course of action that limits our--
No, Archibald. We should most certainly do this. Cut it off at the source. Immediately.
Sir, I must insist that--
Dammit, man. I am the President... and I am the one who will decide.
Now sit there and shut your goddamn mouth.
As I was saying... I will stand with the Nation and the Republic.
Today, I'll stand against this aggressive display of... *irrationality.*
So...the wisdom of this great council is, what, exactly?
Détente? Hold steady in the storm? Maintain the illusion of peace at all cost?
Forget the cancer eating us from the inside...*as* ***appearances*** *must be* ***maintained.***
After all, these are the greatest nations in the history of the world, *no?*
This...*denial* is unbecoming for a leader of men, Xiaolian.
The argument is *over,* and you have *lost.*
Learn to live with it, you impetuous child.

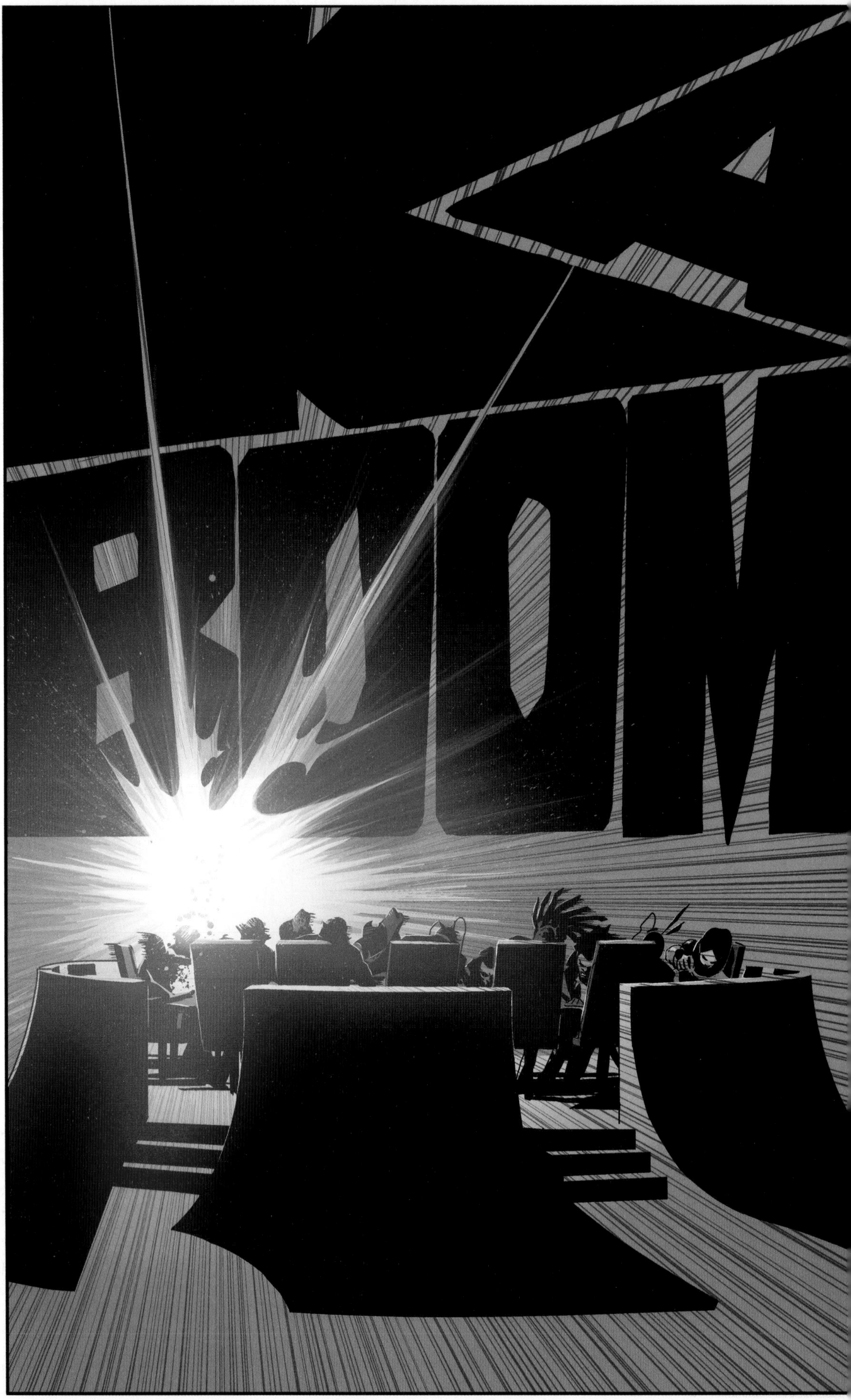

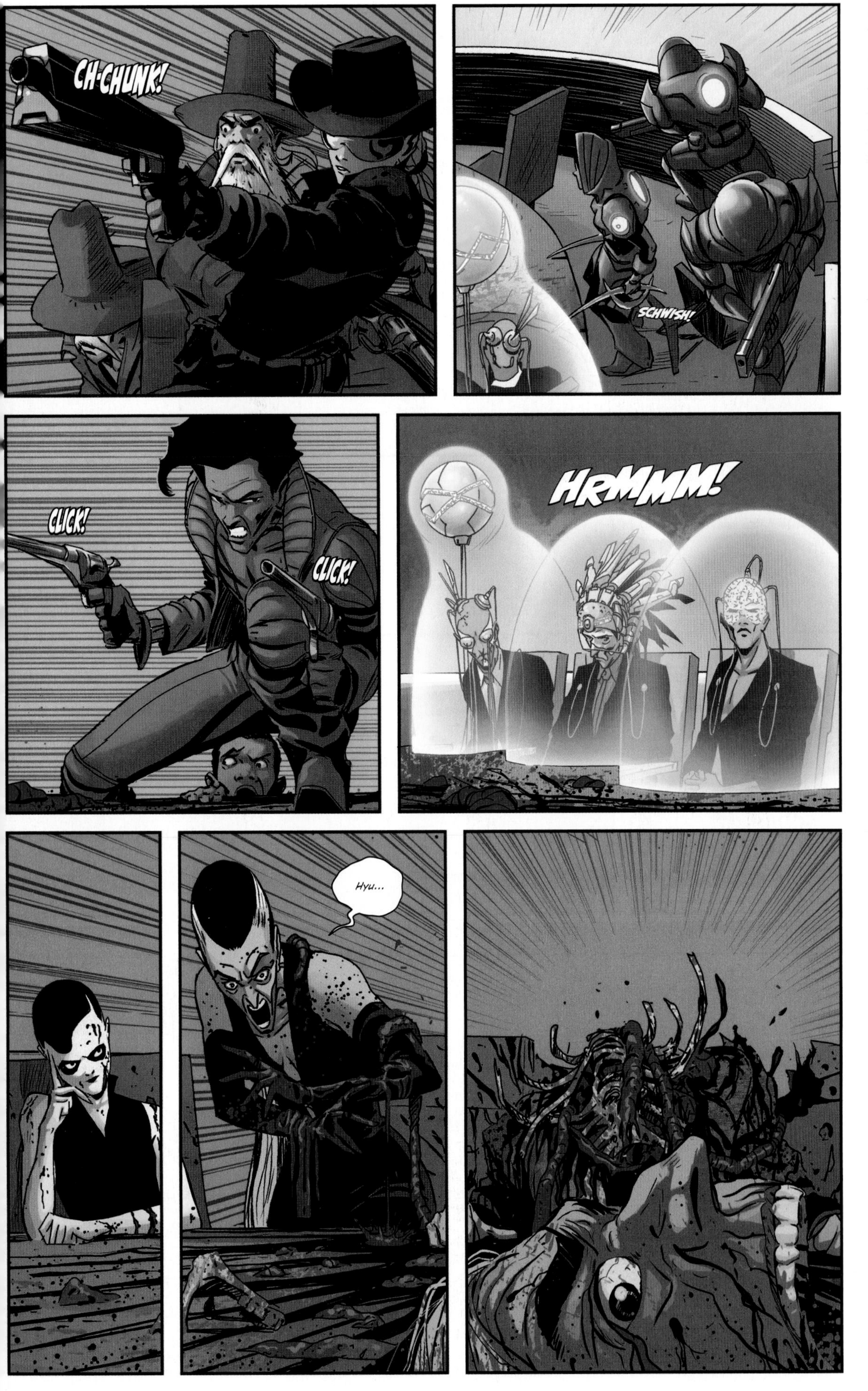
CH-CHUNK!
SCHWISH!
CLICK!
CLICK!
HRMMM!
Hyu...

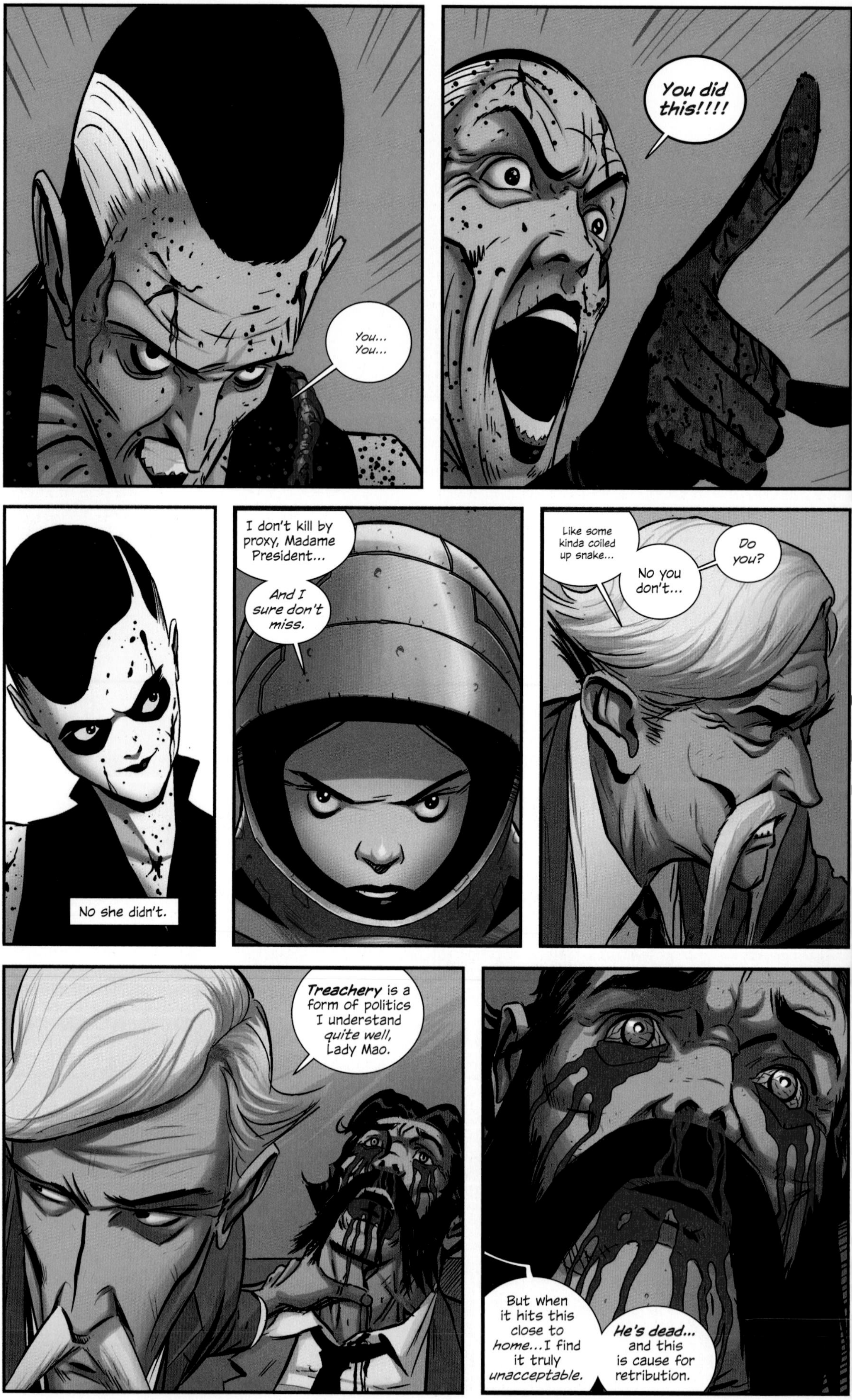
You... You...
You did this!!!!
No she didn't.
I don't kill by proxy, Madame President...
And I sure don't miss.
Like some kinda coiled up snake...
No you don't...
Do you?
Treachery is a form of politics I understand quite well, Lady Mao.
But when it hits this close to home...I find it truly unacceptable.
He's dead... and this is cause for retribution.

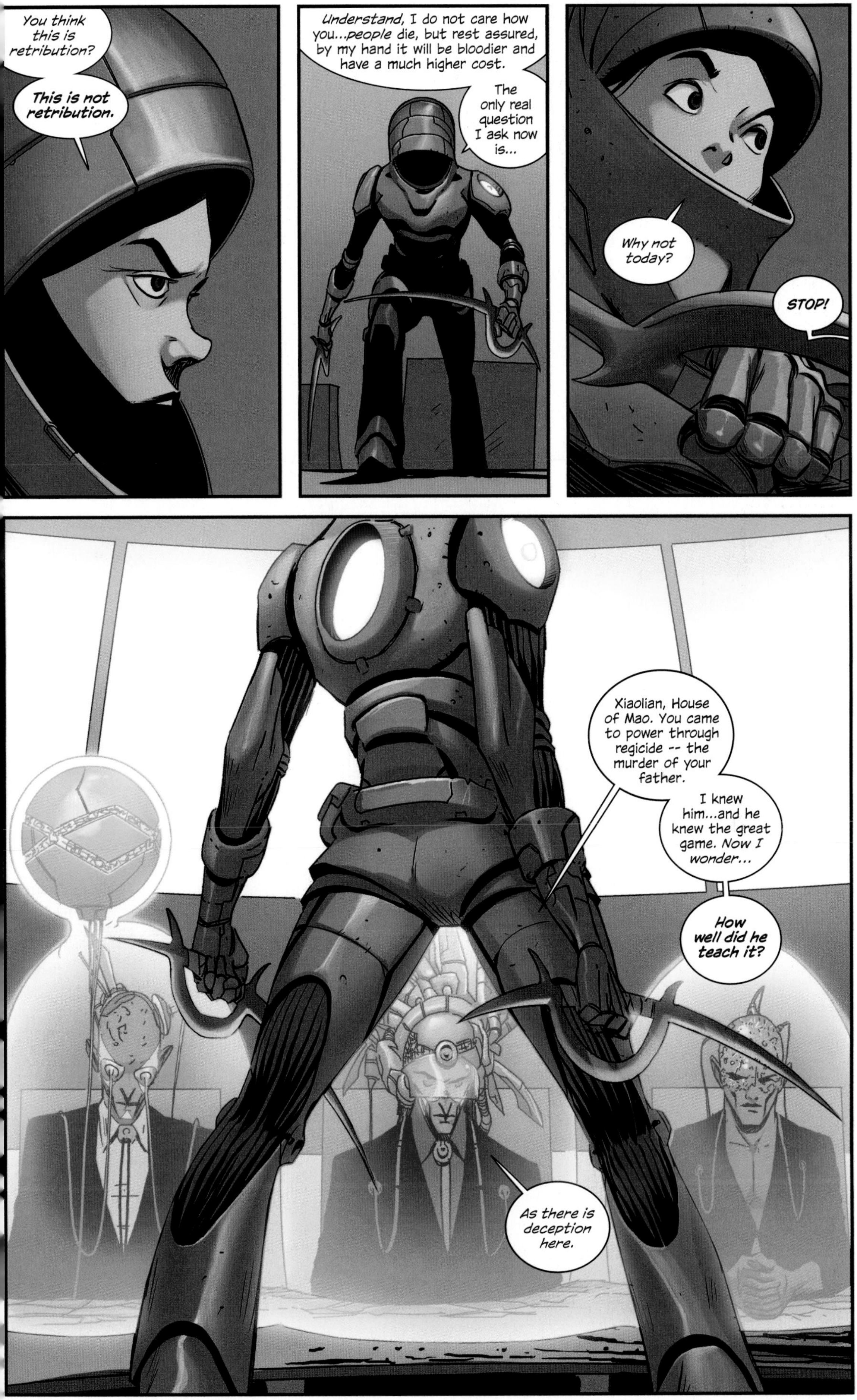

You think this is retribution?
This is not retribution.
Understand, I do not care how you...people die, but rest assured, by my hand it will be bloodier and have a much higher cost.
The only real question I ask now is...
Why not today?
STOP!
Xiaolian, House of Mao. You came to power through regicide -- the murder of your father.
I knew him...and he knew the great game. Now I wonder...
How well did he teach it?
As there is deception here.

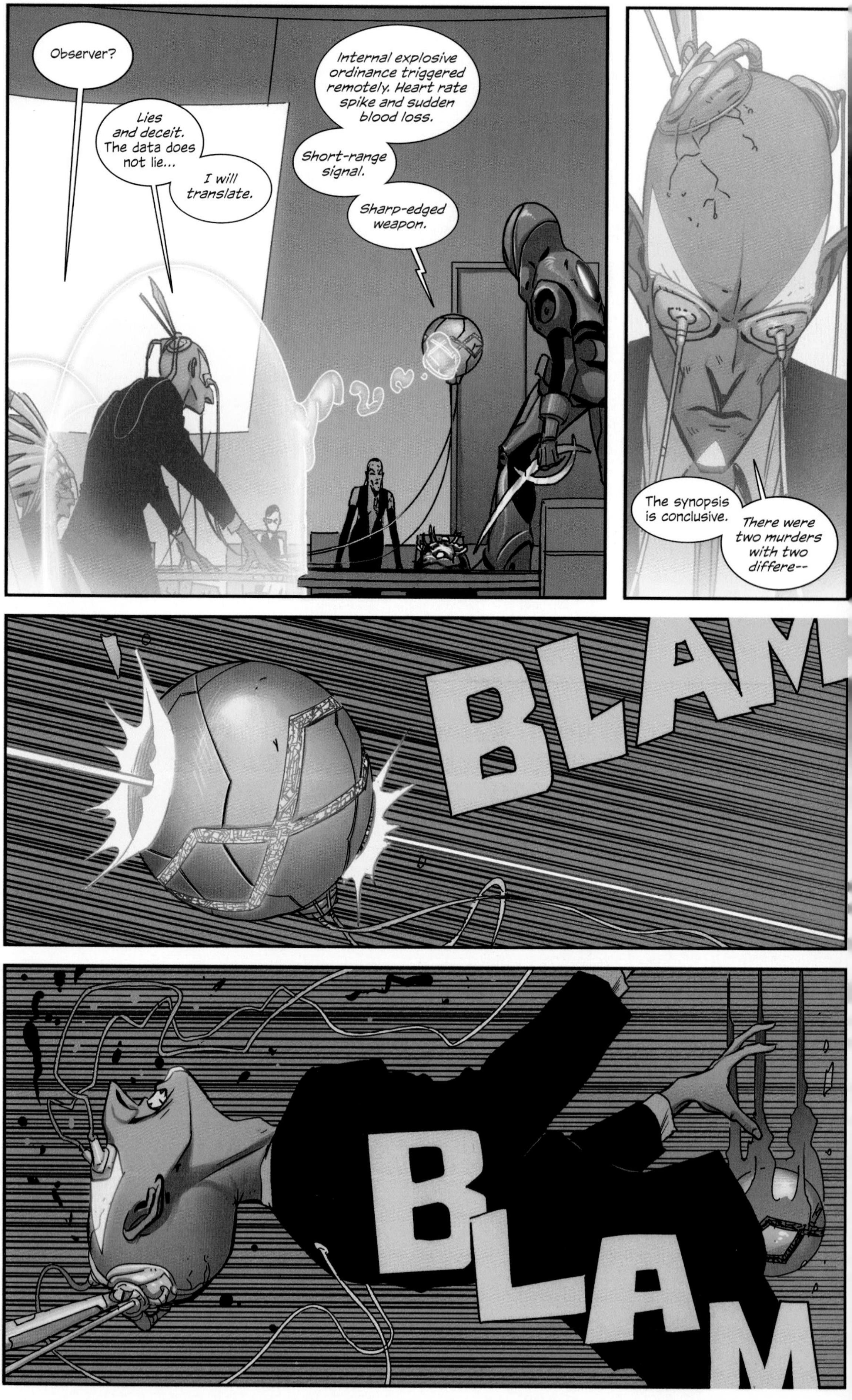
Observer?
Lies and deceit. The data does not lie...
I will translate.
Internal explosive ordinance triggered remotely. Heart rate spike and sudden blood loss.
Short-range signal.
Sharp-edged weapon.
The synopsis is conclusive.
There were two murders with two differe--
BLAM
BLAM

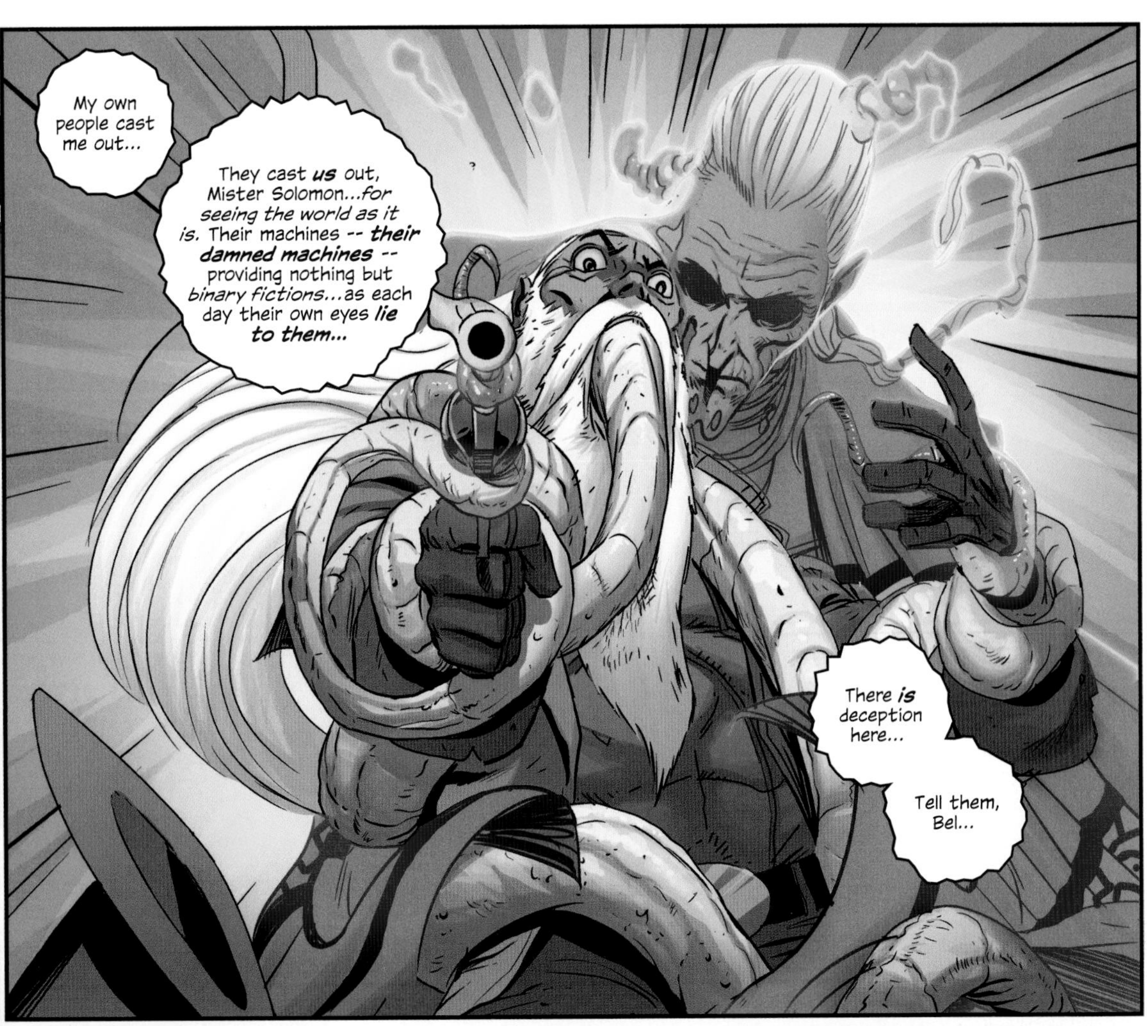
My own people cast me out...
They cast ***us*** out, Mister Solomon...*for seeing the world as it is.* Their machines -- ***their damned machines*** -- providing nothing but *binary fictions*...as each day their own eyes ***lie to them...***
There ***is*** deception here...
Tell them, Bel...

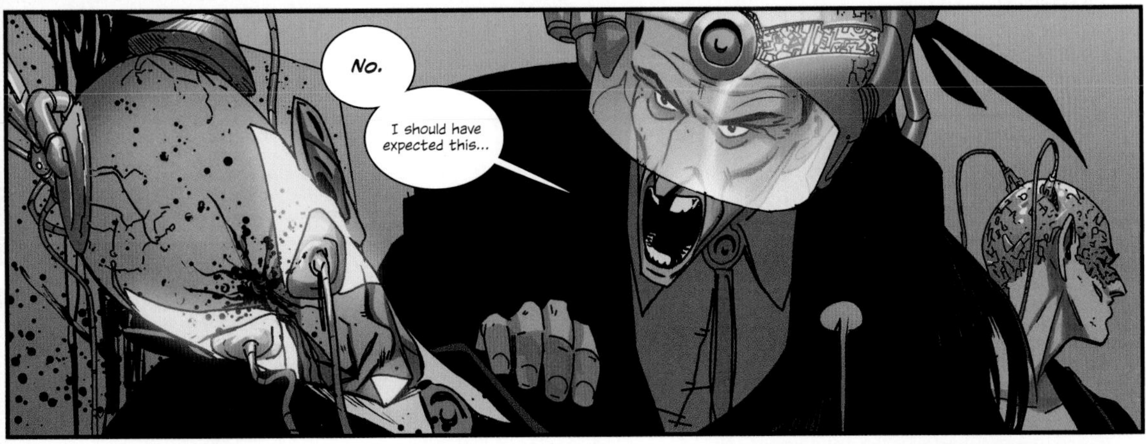
No.
I should have expected this...

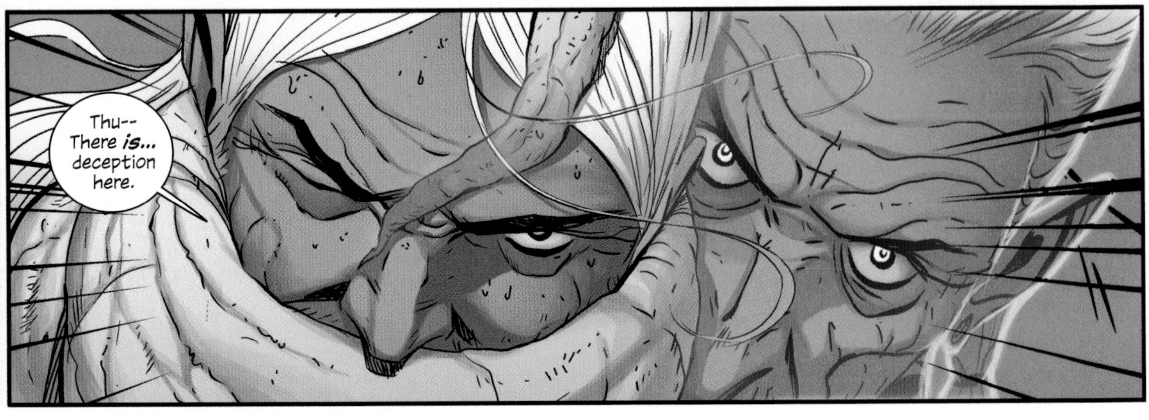
Thu-- There ***is...*** deception here.

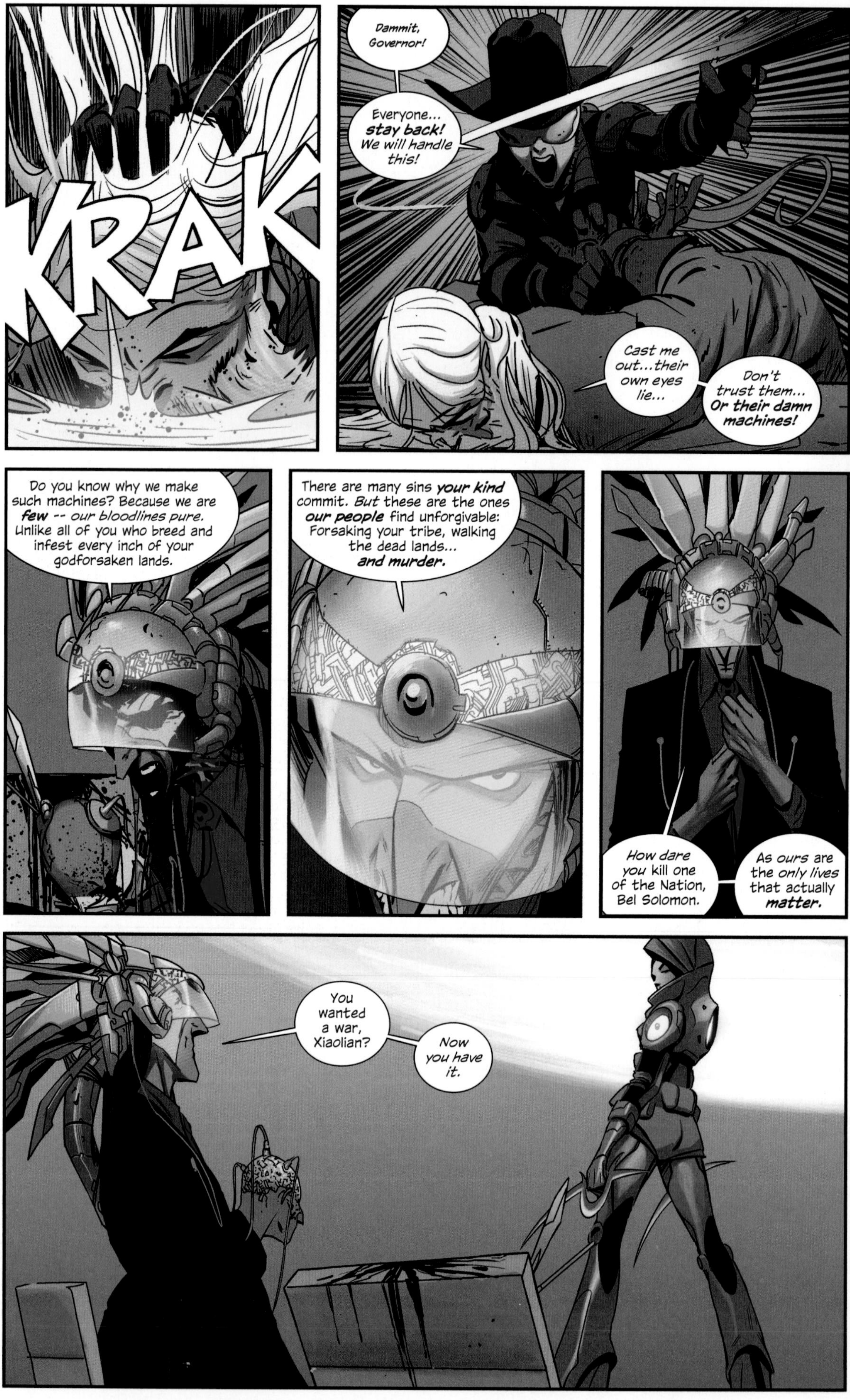
KRAK
Dammit, Governor!
Everyone... stay back! We will handle this!
Cast me out...their own eyes lie...
Don't trust them... Or their damn machines!
Do you know why we make such machines? Because we are few -- our bloodlines pure. Unlike all of you who breed and infest every inch of your godforsaken lands.
There are many sins your kind commit. But these are the ones our people find unforgivable: Forsaking your tribe, walking the dead lands... and murder.
How dare you kill one of the Nation, Bel Solomon.
As ours are the only lives that actually matter.
You wanted a war, Xiaolian?
Now you have it.

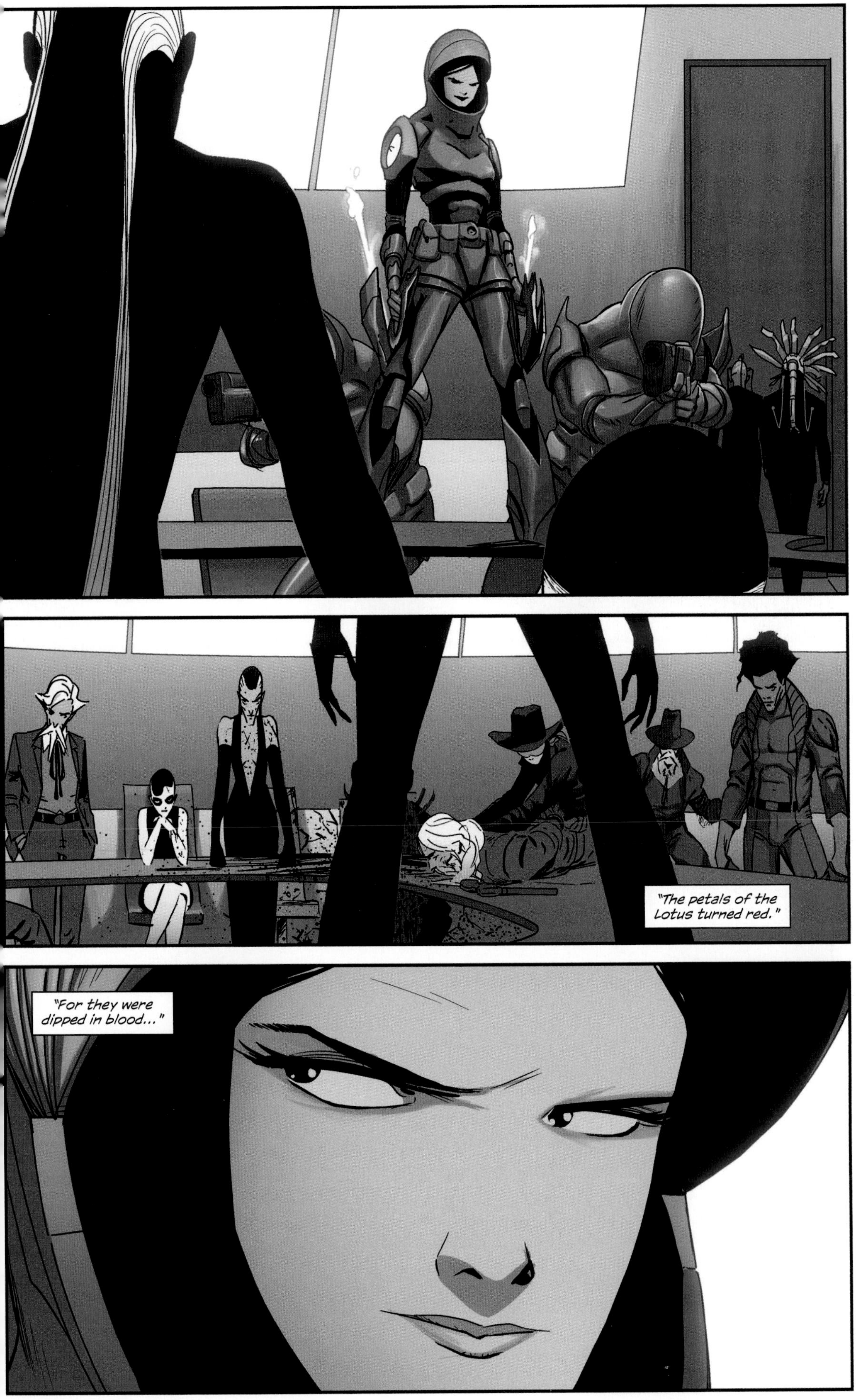
"The petals of the Lotus turned red."
"For they were dipped in blood..."

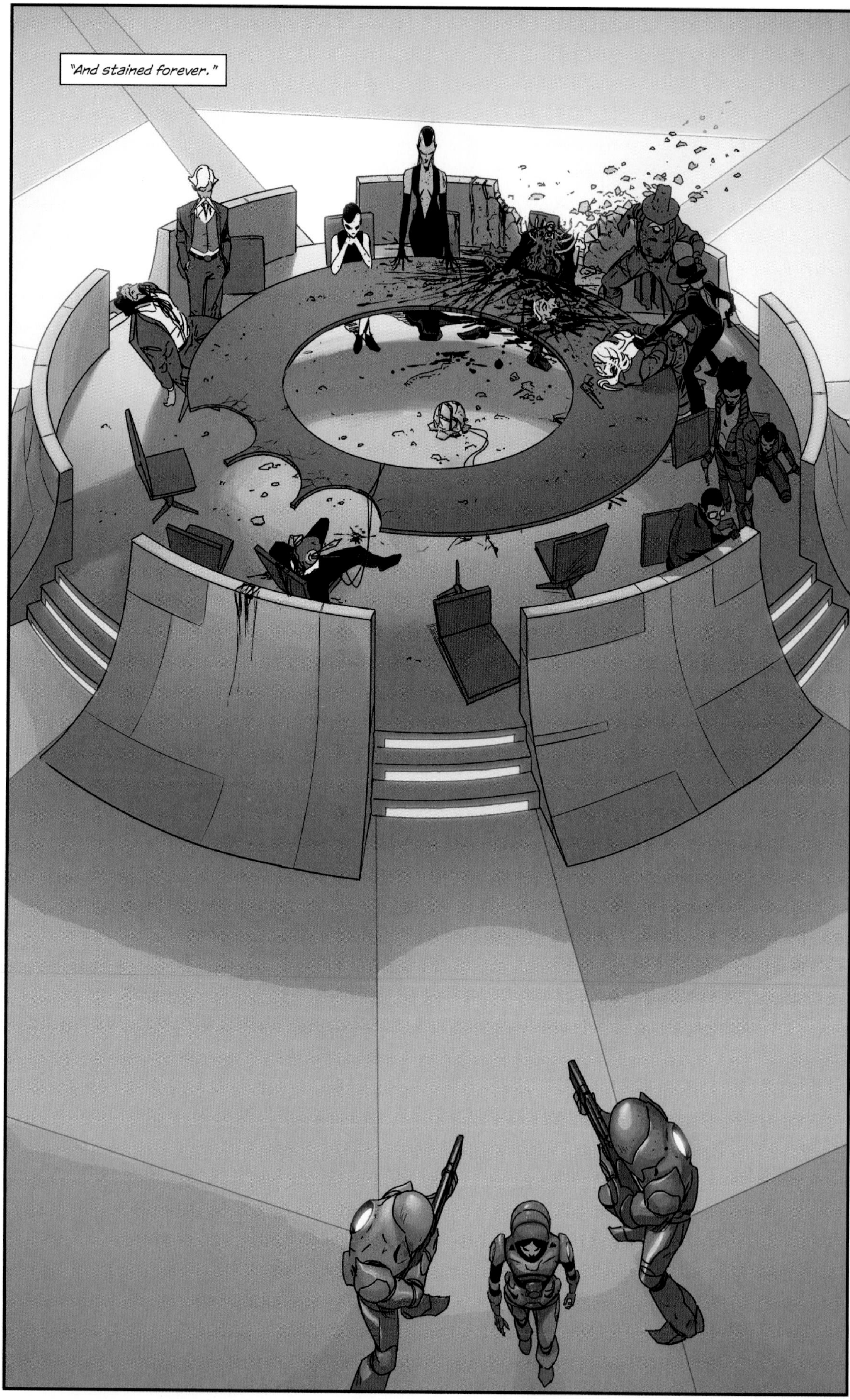
"And stained forever."

THE CATALYST OF ACTION IS
INTENT

IT'S THE OTHER END OF THE
BULLET

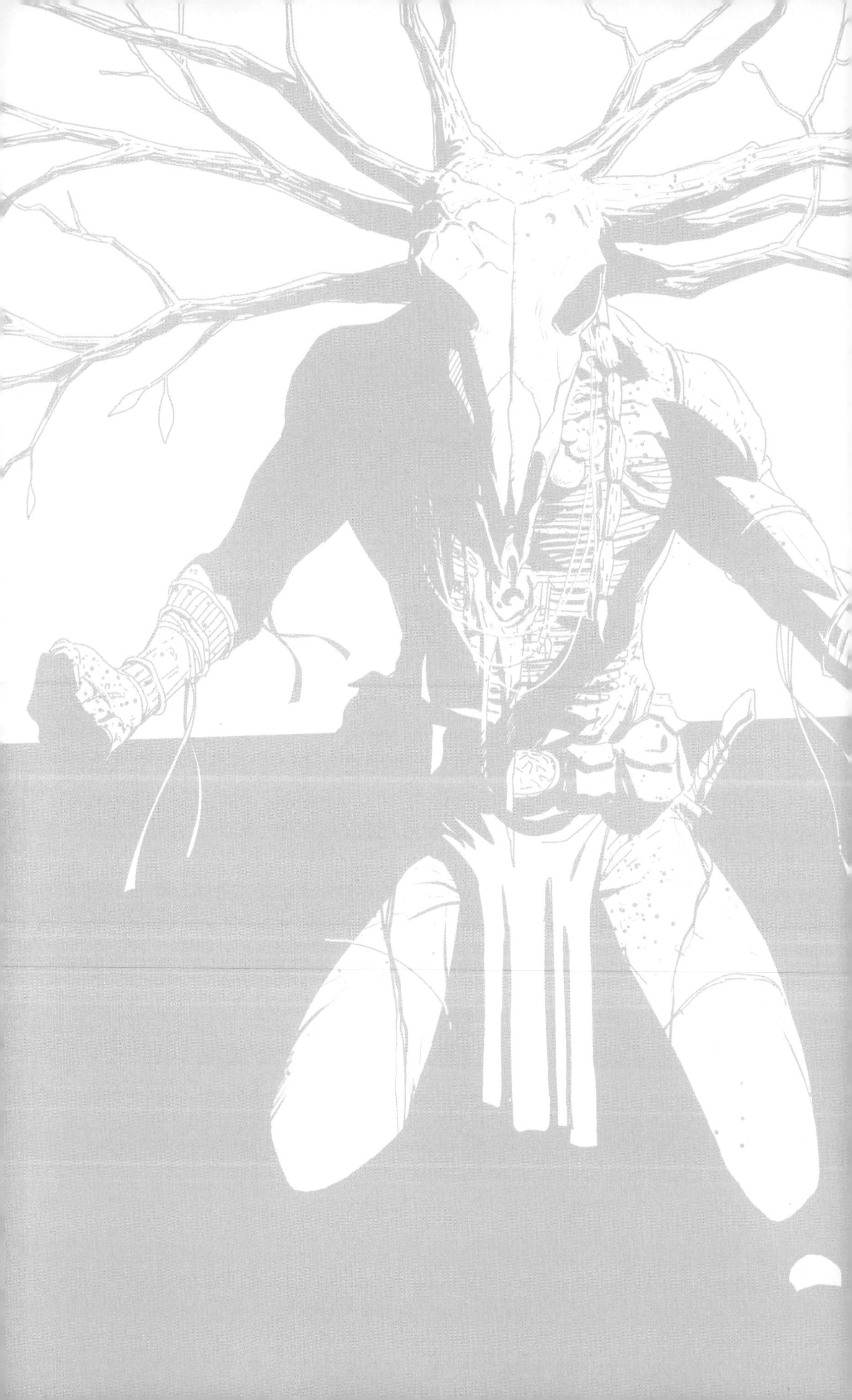

13

 THIRTEEN: DEAD LANDS **COMIN'**

WE HIDE THINGS IN **THE SUN**,
FOR IT IS **BLINDING**

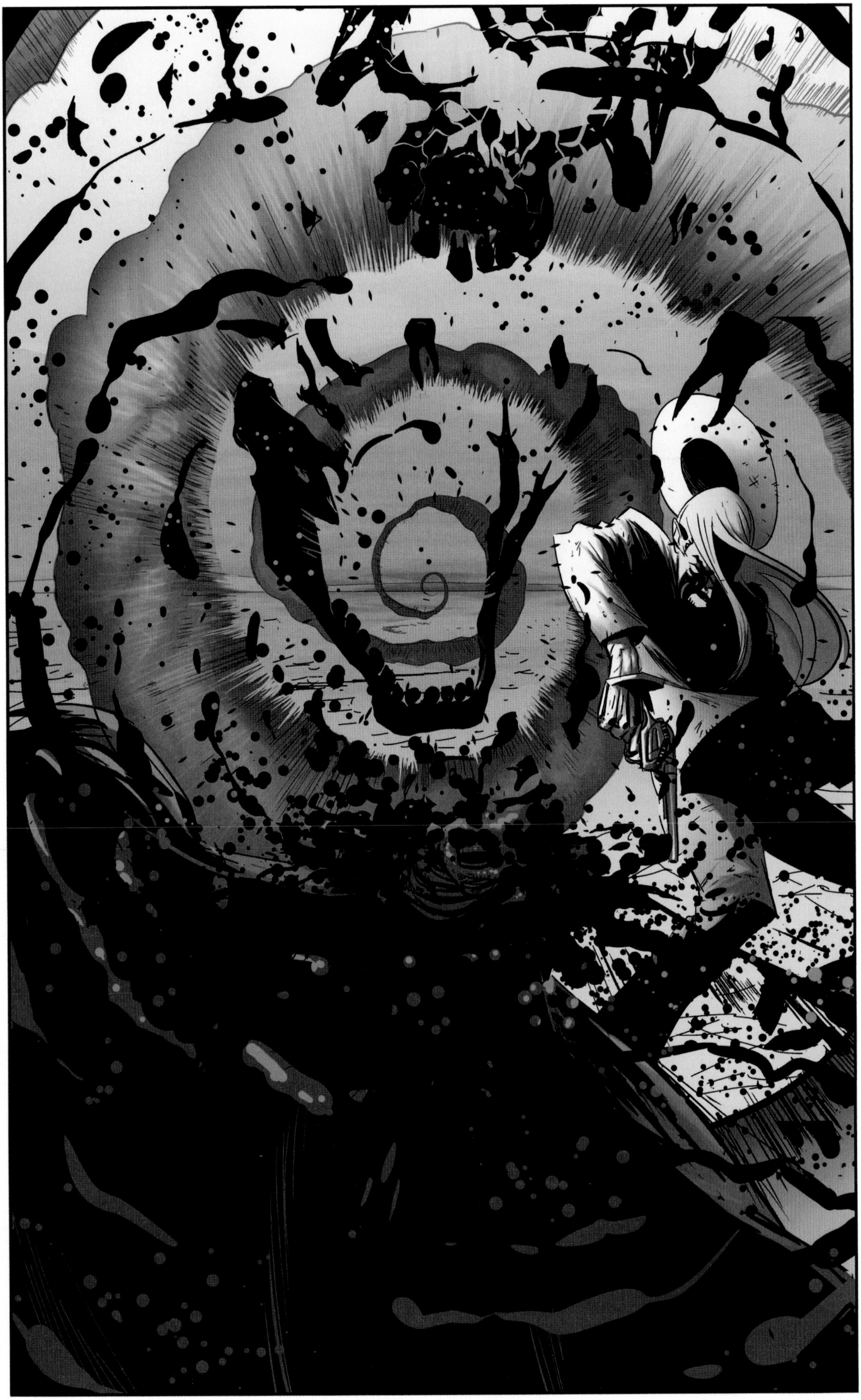

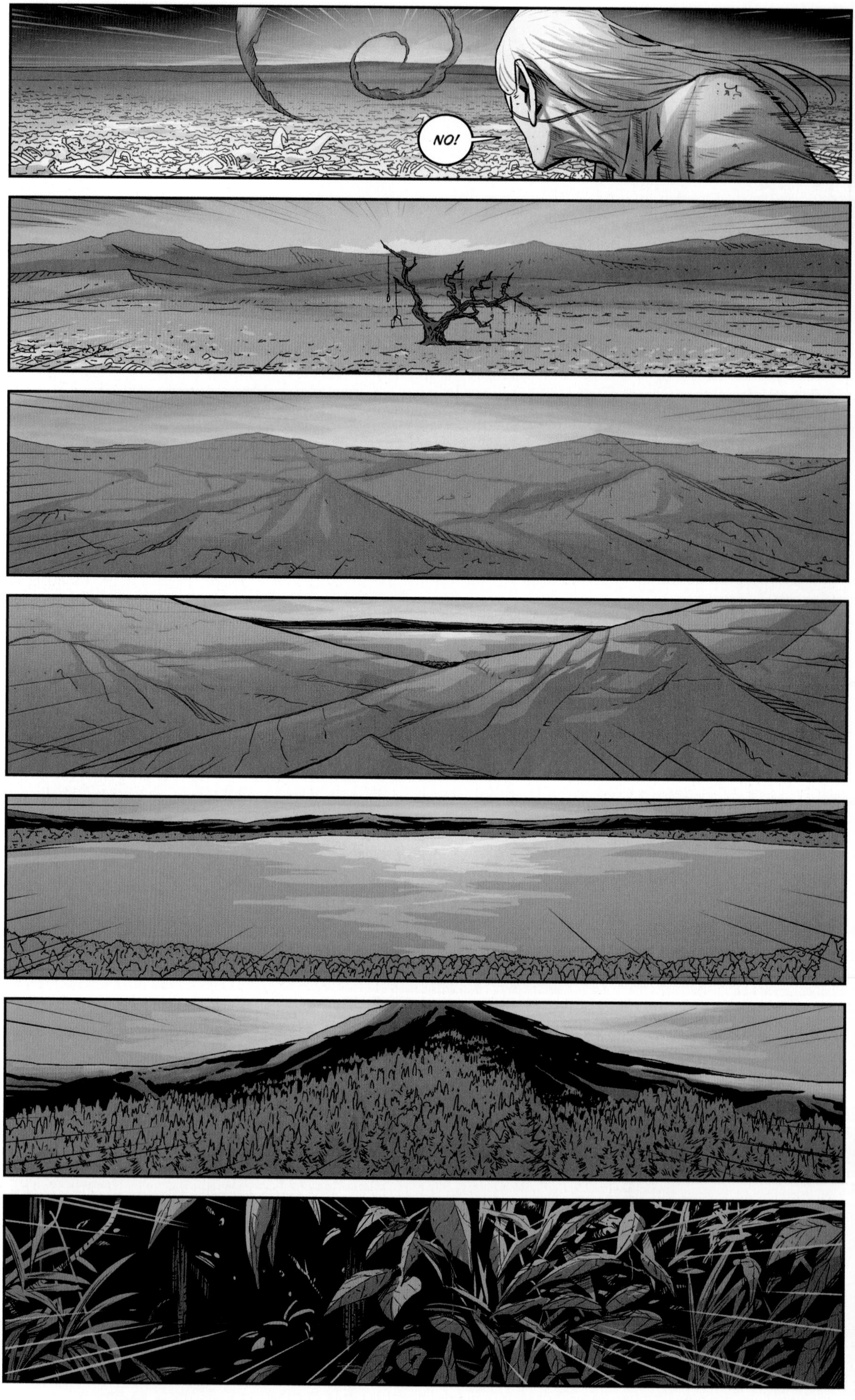
NO!

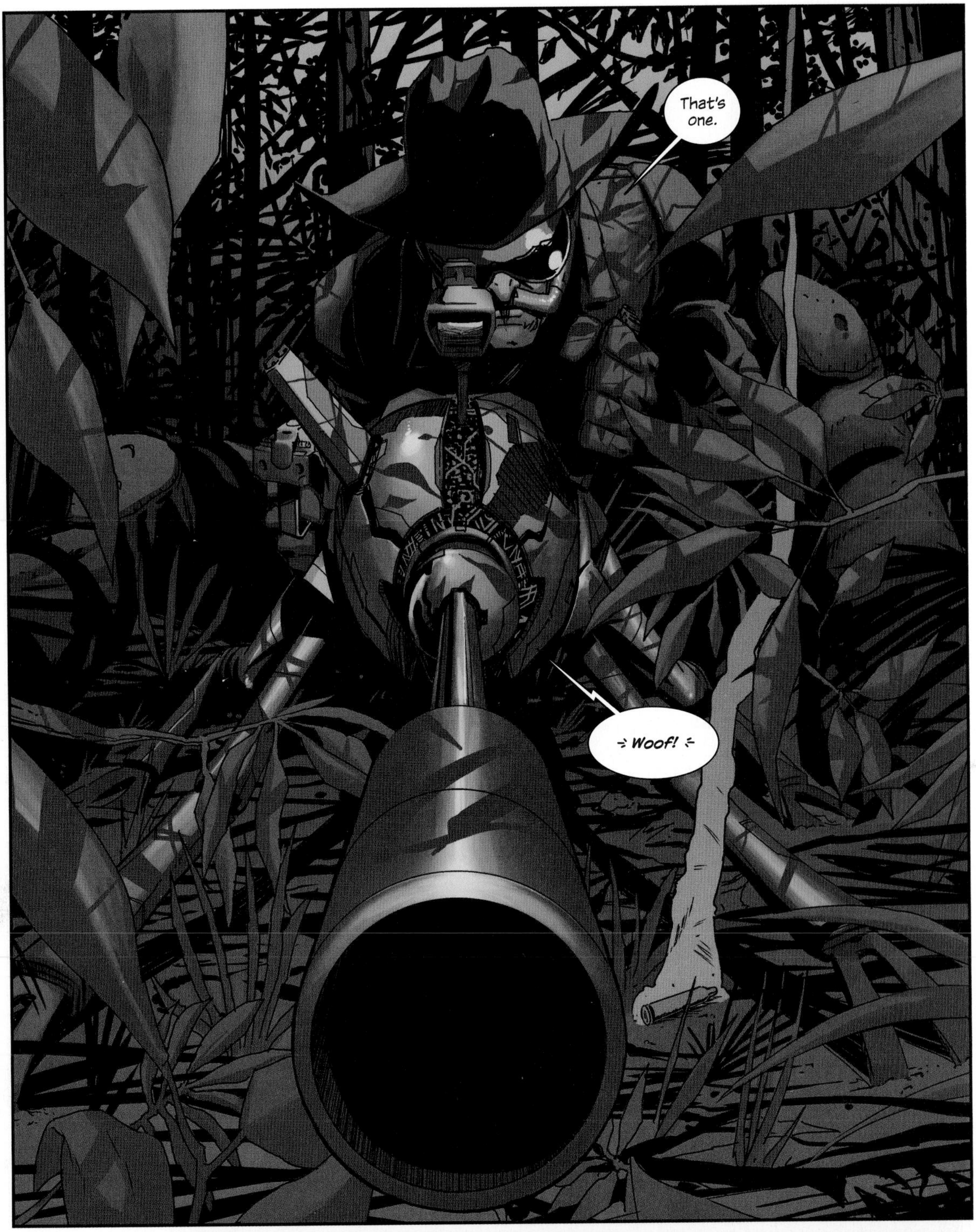
That's one.
Woof!

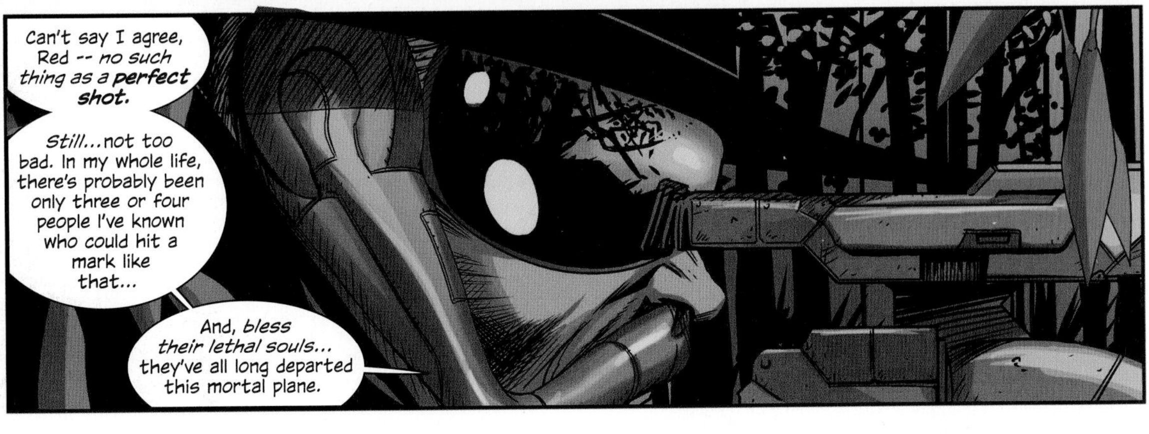
Can't say I agree, Red -- *no such thing as a* ***perfect shot.***
*Still...*not too bad. In my whole life, there's probably been only three or four people I've known who could hit a mark like that...
And, *bless their lethal souls...* they've all long departed this mortal plane.

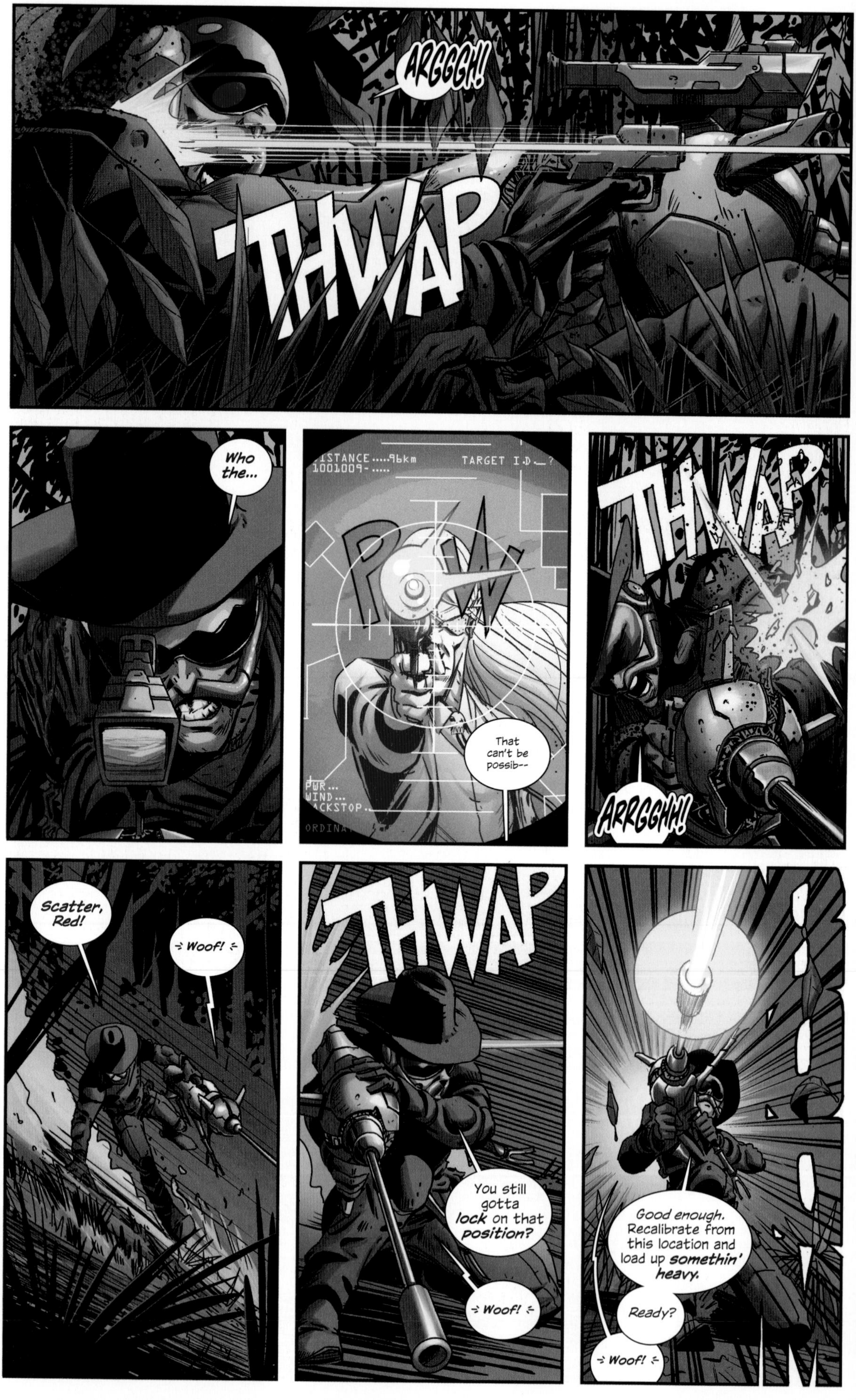
ARGGGH!
THWAP
Who the...
ISTANCE.....96km
1001009-.....
TARGET I.D._?
POW
PWR...
WIND...
ACKSTOP...
That can't be possib--
THWAP
ARRGGHH!
Scatter, Red!
Woof!
THWAP
You still gotta lock on that position?
Woof!
Good enough. Recalibrate from this location and load up somethin' heavy.
Ready?
Woof!

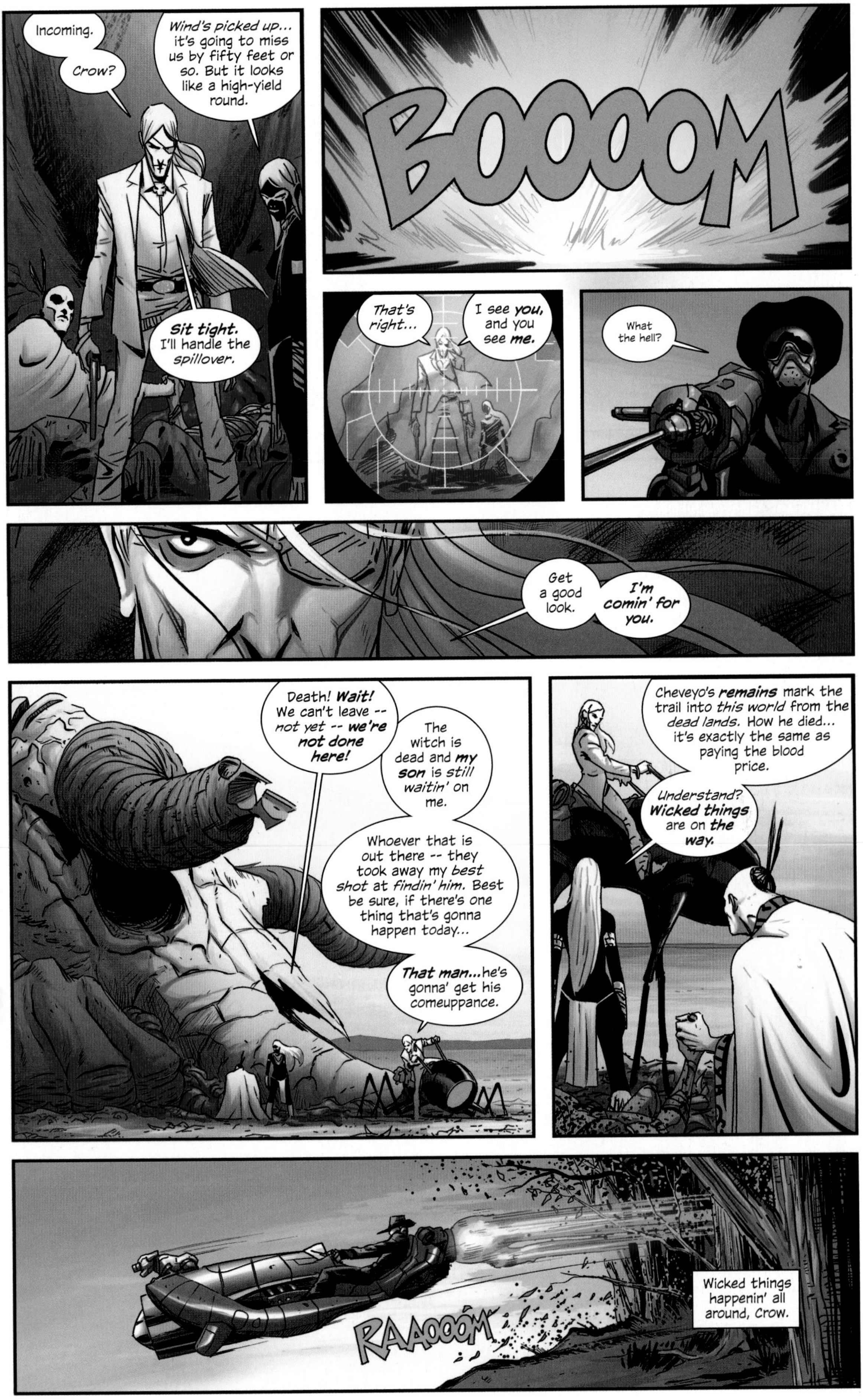

Incoming.
Crow?
Wind's picked up... it's going to miss us by fifty feet or so. But it looks like a high-yield round.
Sit tight. I'll handle the spillover.
BOOOOM
That's right...
I see you, and you see me.
What the hell?
Get a good look.
I'm comin' for you.
Death! Wait! We can't leave -- not yet -- we're not done here!
The witch is dead and my son is still waitin' on me.
Whoever that is out there -- they took away my best shot at findin' him. Best be sure, if there's one thing that's gonna happen today...
That man...he's gonna' get his comeuppance.
Cheveyo's remains mark the trail into this world from the dead lands. How he died... it's exactly the same as paying the blood price.
Understand? Wicked things are on the way.
RAAOOOM
Wicked things happenin' all around, Crow.

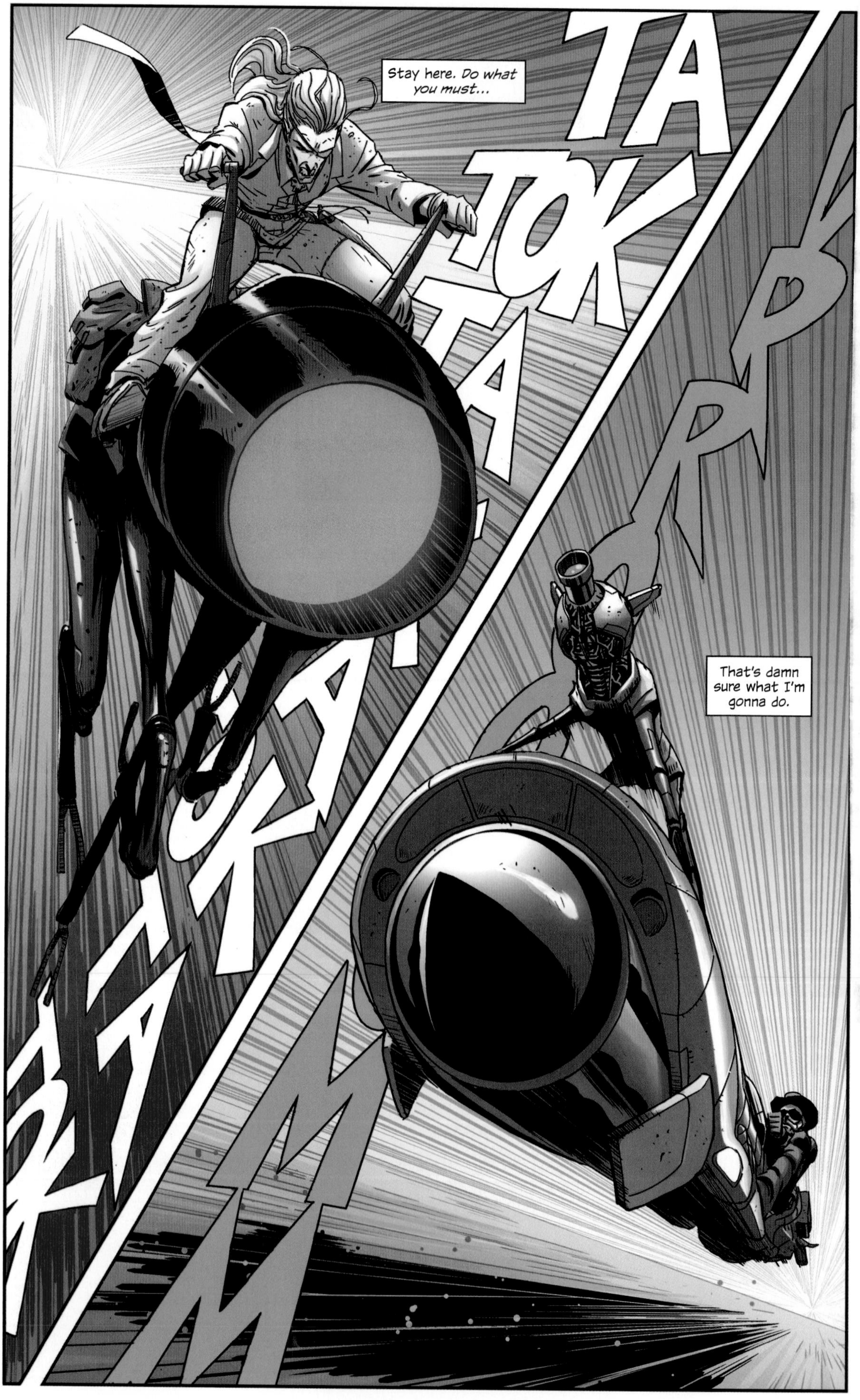
Stay here. Do what you must...
That's damn sure what I'm gonna do.

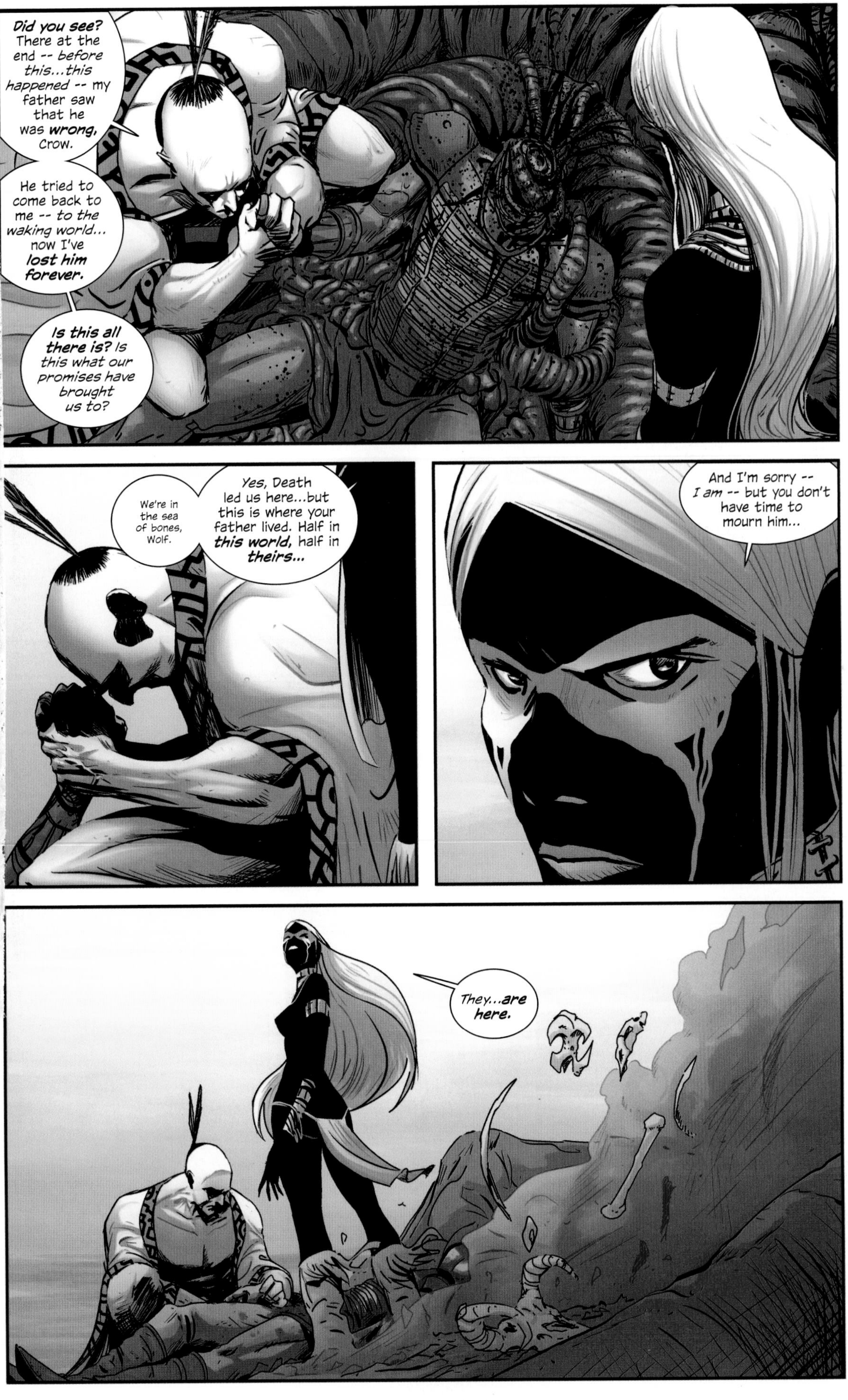
Did you see? There at the end -- before this...this happened -- my father saw that he was wrong, Crow.
He tried to come back to me -- to the waking world... now I've lost him forever.
Is this all there is? Is this what our promises have brought us to?
We're in the sea of bones, Wolf.
Yes, Death led us here...but this is where your father lived. Half in this world, half in theirs...
And I'm sorry -- I am -- but you don't have time to mourn him...
They...are here.

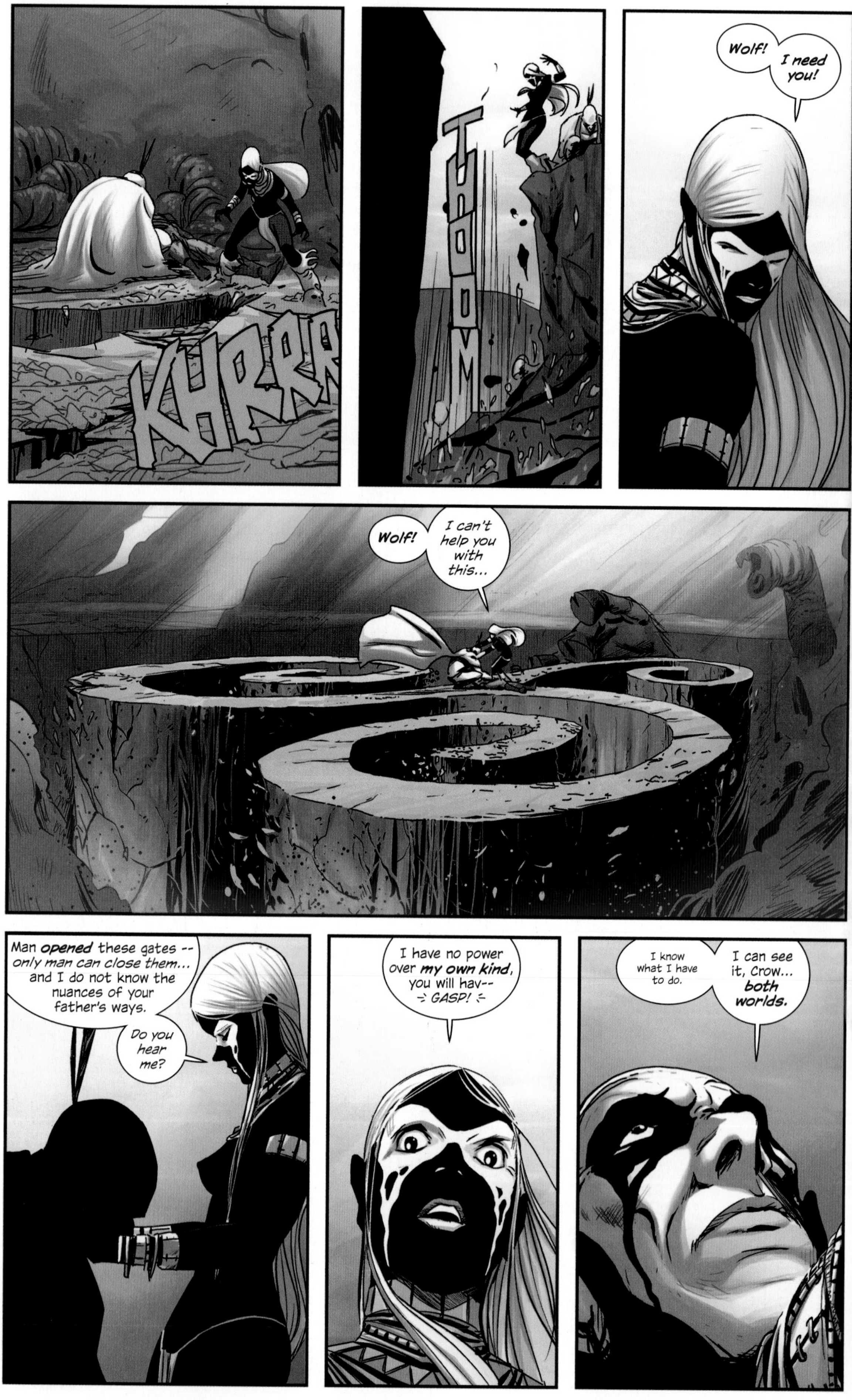
KHRRR
THOOOM
Wolf!
I need you!
Wolf!
I can't help you with this...
Man opened these gates -- only man can close them... and I do not know the nuances of your father's ways.
Do you hear me?
I have no power over my own kind, you will hav-- GASP!
I know what I have to do.
I can see it, Crow... both worlds.

Steady.

Steady.

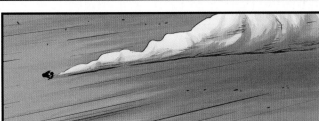

A little closer.

Okay.

Now!

KA-CHR

BRRRR
RRRR
RRRR
RRRR

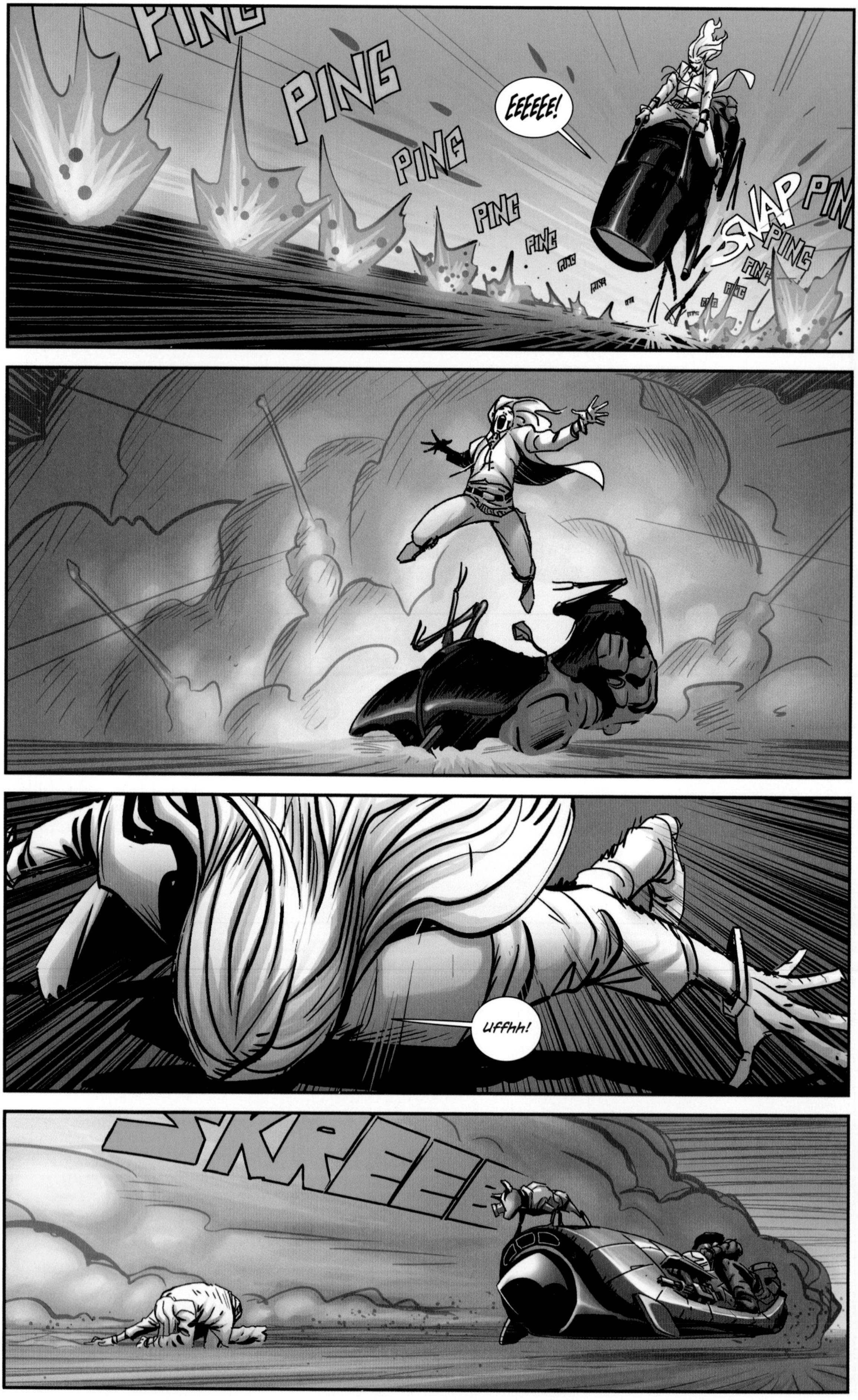
PING
PING
PING
PING
PING
EEEEEE!
SNAP
PING
PING
PING
Uffhh!
SKREEE

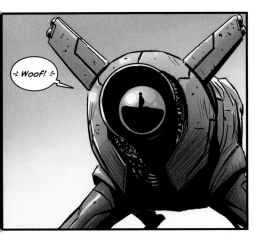

~ Woof! ~

See, in all my years of bein' a lawman, I've come to accept certain *facts* regardin' the *criminal mind*...

Associations, *for example* -- you lay down with dogs...*this* is the kinda' shit that rains down on you.

Huh.

You wanna' reach for it... I understand. I'd be tempted to myself.

But I think we've established you're not the only crack shot here, so I'd defer unwise action for just a minute more.

Far as I know, you're just some unlucky fella' in the wrong place at the wrong time -- hell, maybe you even thought I was shootin' at you and that's why you responded so *rashly*...

Either way, ain't no reason to kill someone.

But you did take a shot at me, and *at that...* I take umbrage.

And *for that...* I'm gonna have to kick your ass a little bit.

KERAK

Now, you still wanna go for that gun... or do you wanna settle up like *gentlemen?*

Don't sing it, son -- *bring it!*

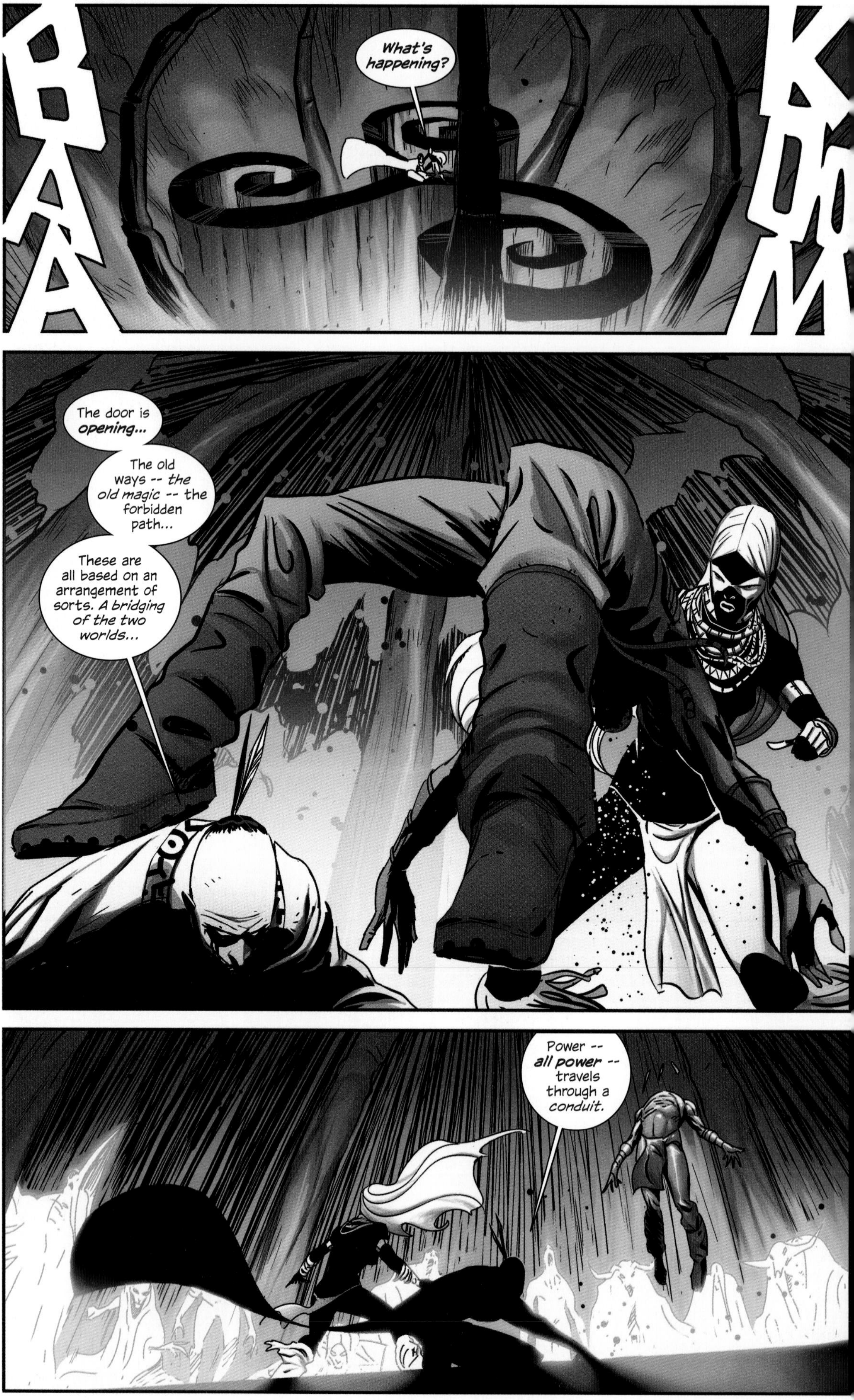
BAAA
What's happening?
The door is opening...
The old ways -- the old magic -- the forbidden path...
These are all based on an arrangement of sorts. A bridging of the two worlds...
Power -- all power -- travels through a conduit.

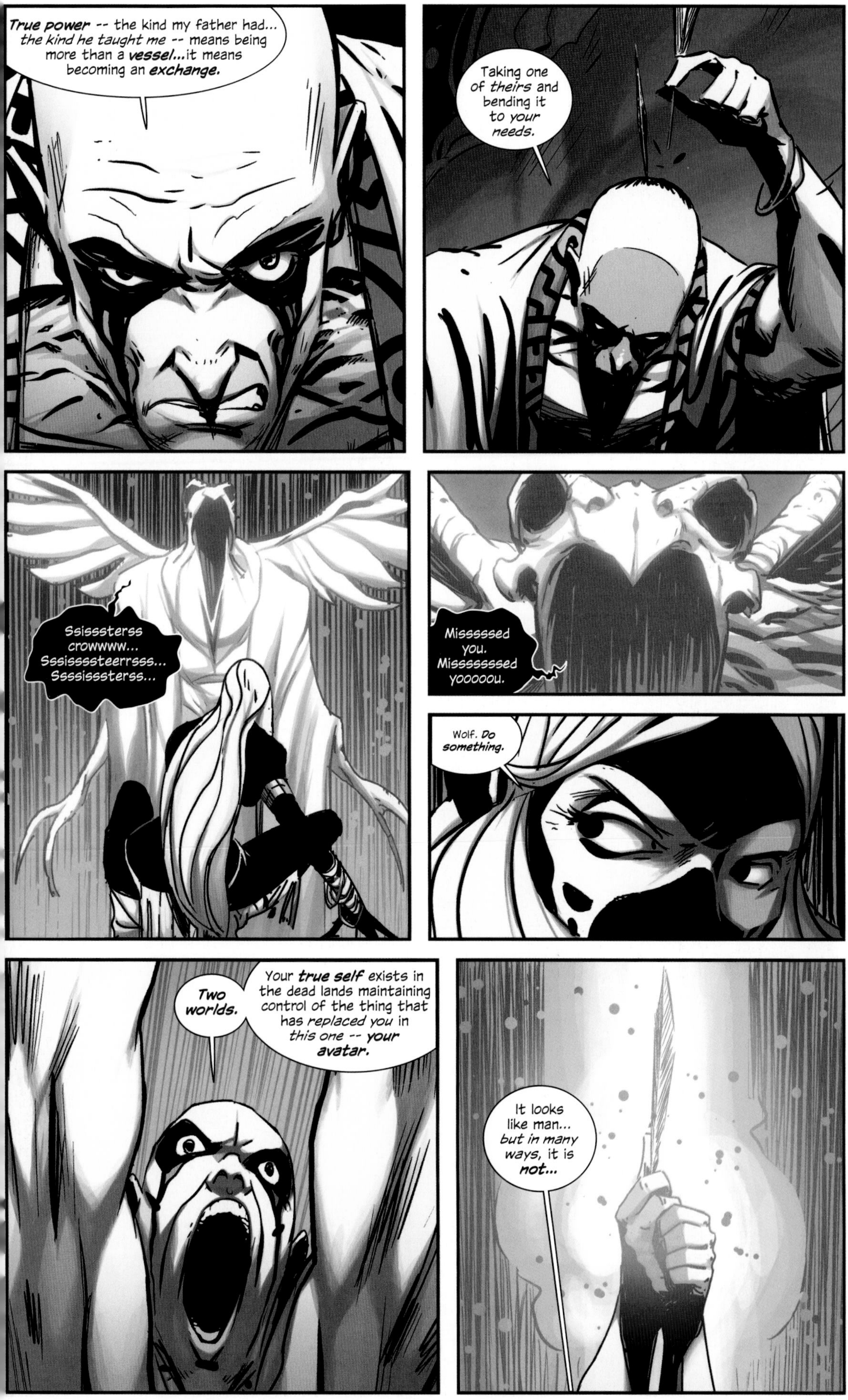
True power -- the kind my father had... the kind he taught me -- means being more than a vessel...it means becoming an exchange.
Taking one of theirs and bending it to your needs.
Ssissssterss crowwww... Sssissssteerrsss... Ssssissssterss...
Missssed you. Missssssssed yoooou.
Wolf. Do something.
Two worlds.
Your true self exists in the dead lands maintaining control of the thing that has replaced you in this one -- your avatar.
It looks like man... but in many ways, it is not...

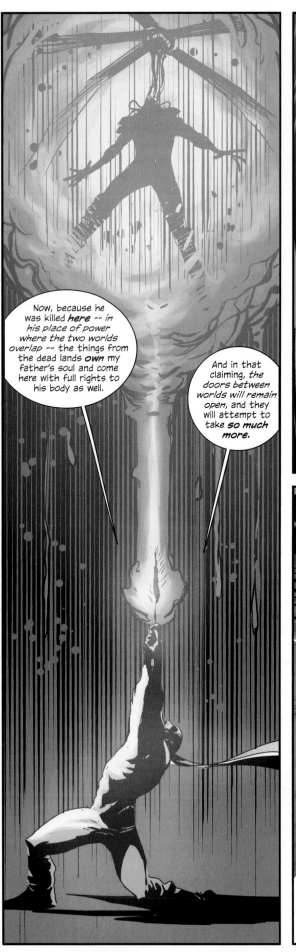

Now, because he was killed **here** -- in his place of power where the two worlds overlap -- the things from the dead lands **own** my father's soul and come here with full rights to his body as well.

And in that claiming, *the doors between worlds will remain open,* and they will attempt to take **so much more.**

Hear me, father!

I will not let them!

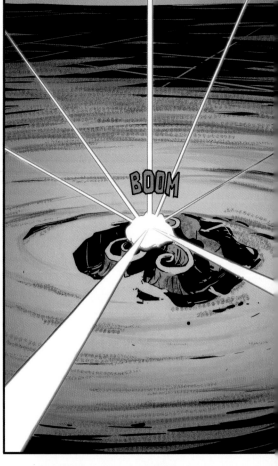

BOOM

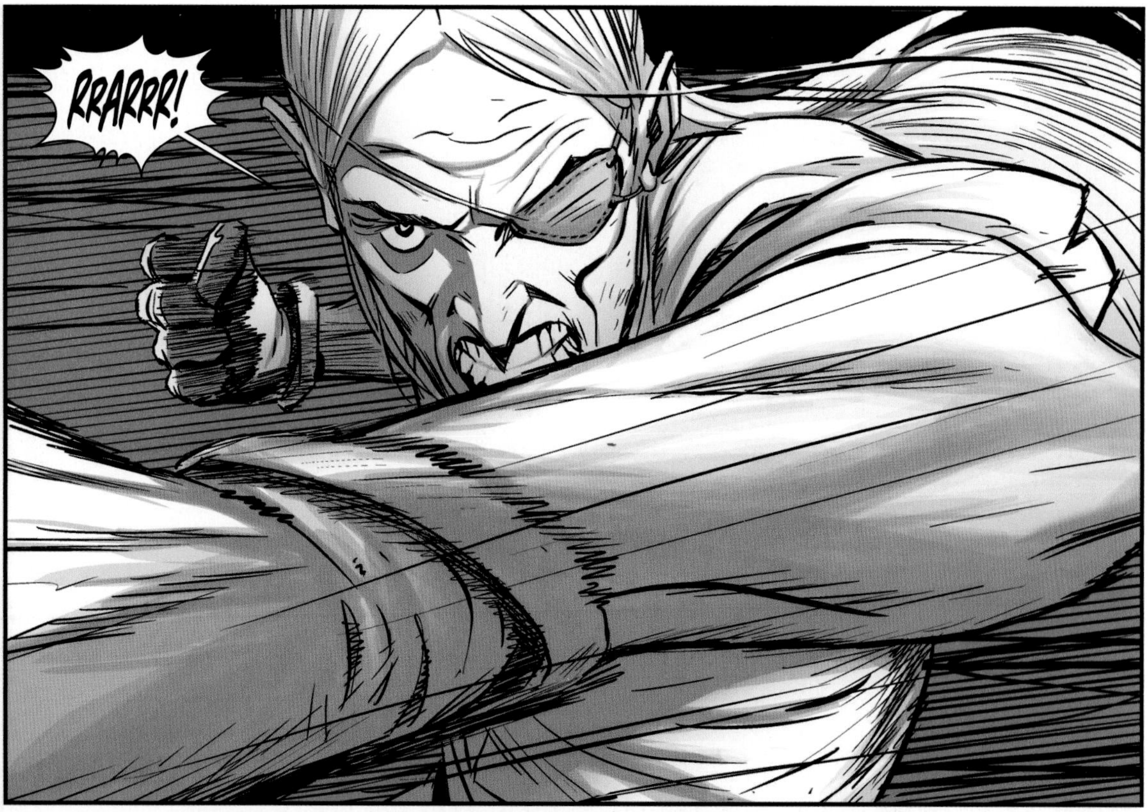
RRARRR!

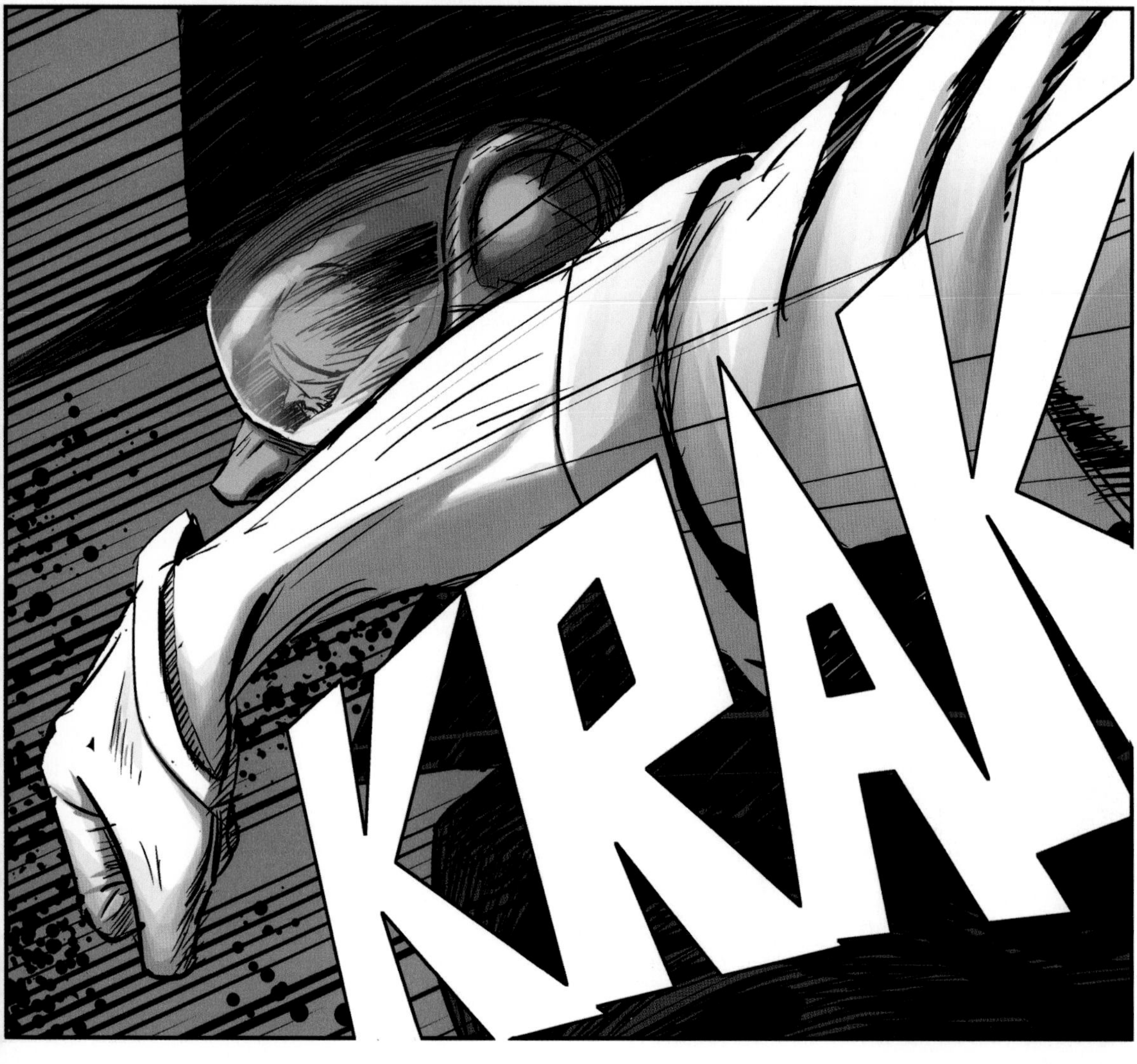
KRAK

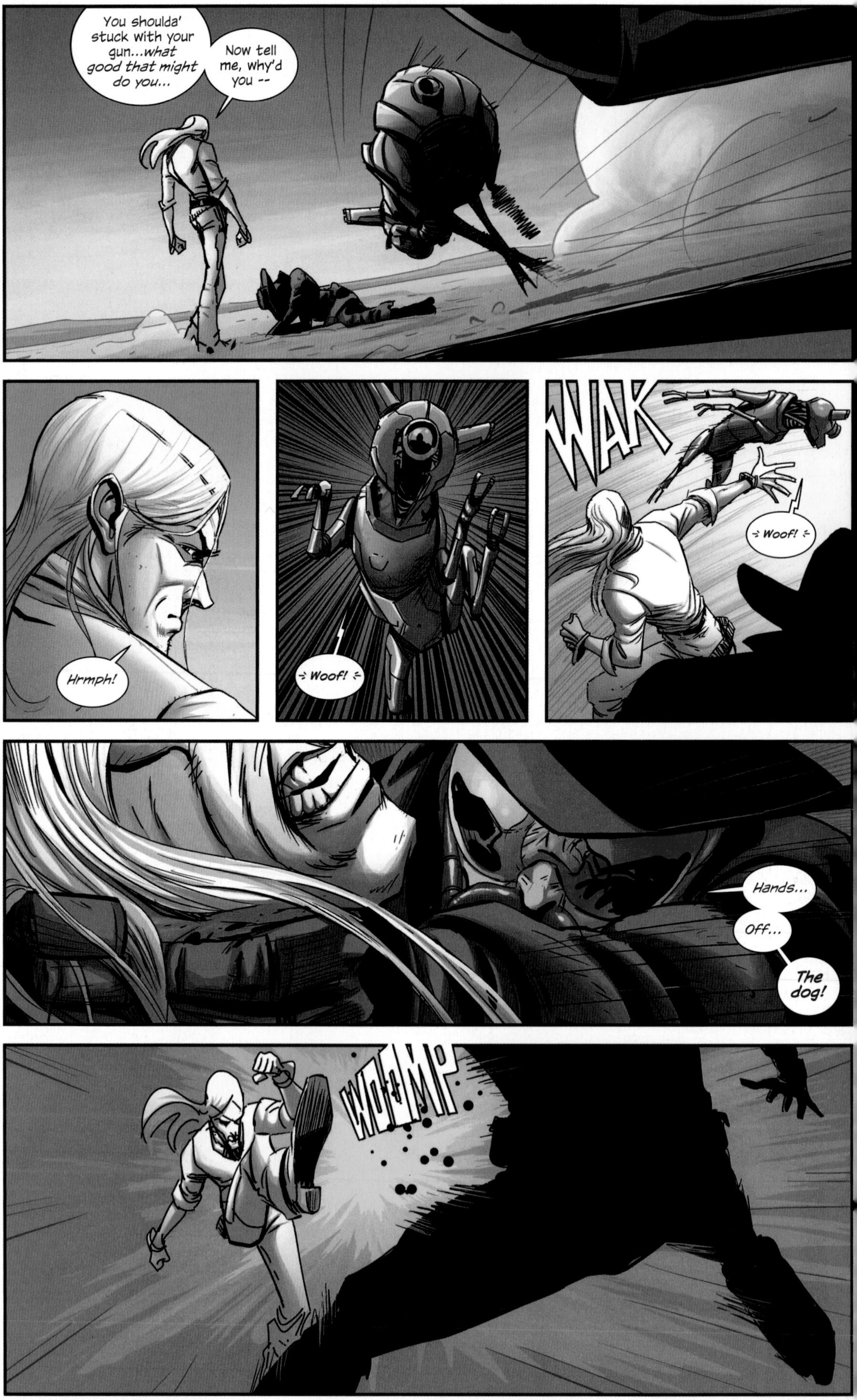
You shoulda' stuck with your gun...what good that might do you...
Now tell me, why'd you --
Hrmph!
Woof!
WAK
Woof!
Hands...
Off...
The dog!
WOOMP

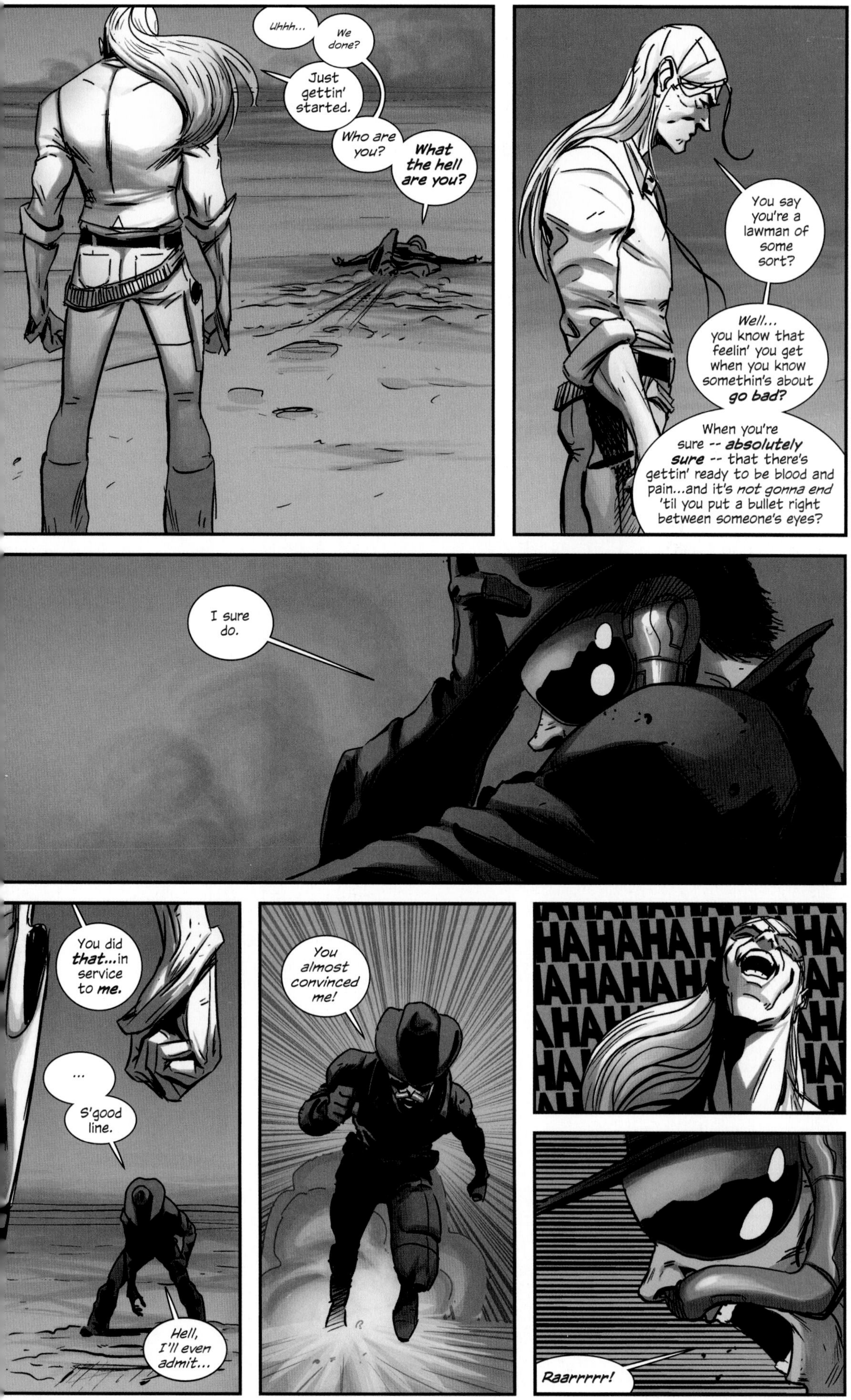

Uhhh...
We done?
Just gettin' started.
Who are you?
What the hell are you?
You say you're a lawman of some sort?
Well... you know that feelin' you get when you know somethin's about go bad?
When you're sure -- absolutely sure -- that there's gettin' ready to be blood and pain...and it's not gonna end 'til you put a bullet right between someone's eyes?
I sure do.
You did that...in service to me.
...
S'good line.
Hell, I'll even admit...
You almost convinced me!
HAHAHAHAHAHAHAHAHAHAHA
Raarrrrr!

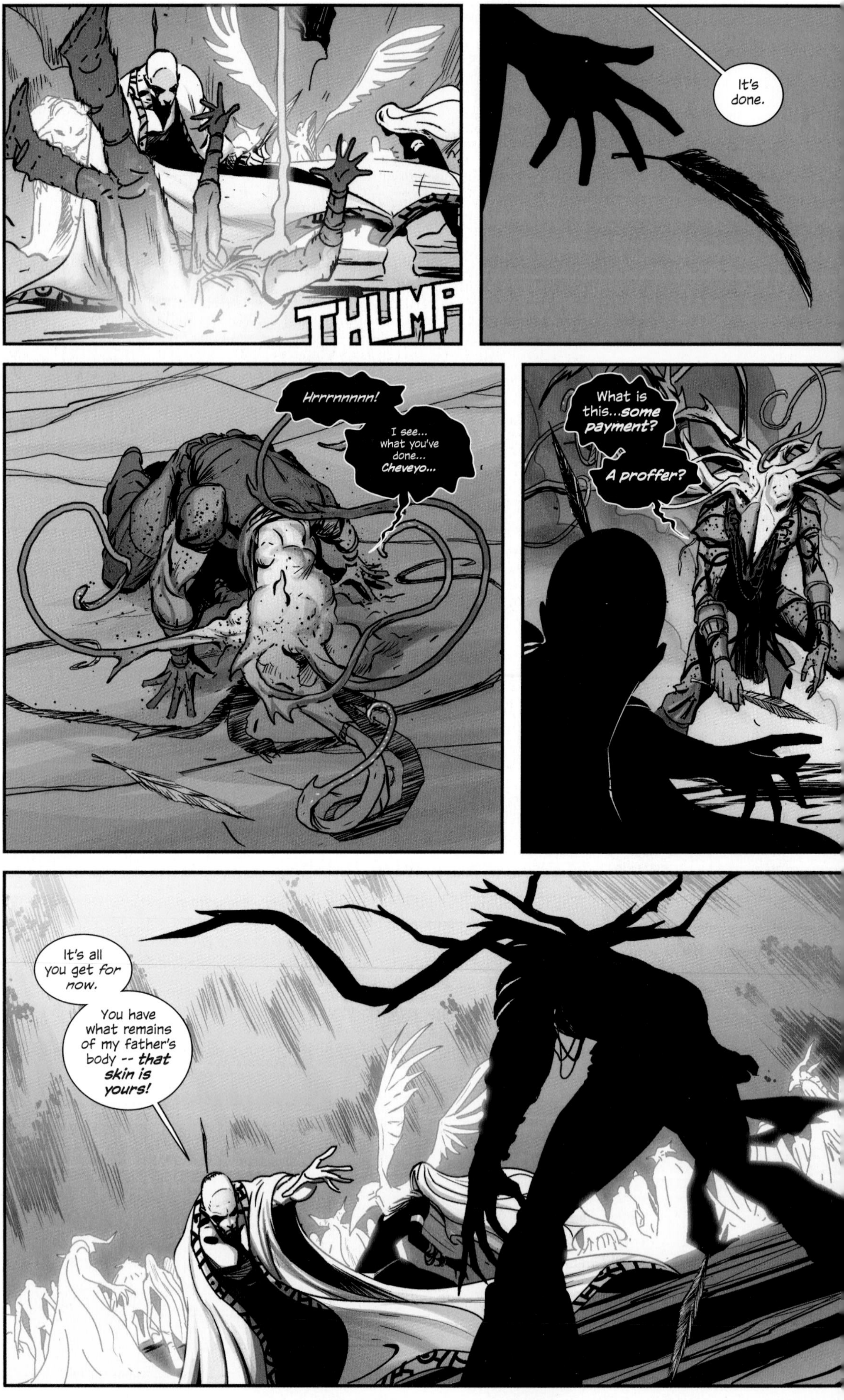
THUMP
It's done.
Hrrrnnnnn!
I see... what you've done... Cheveyo...
What is this...some payment?
A proffer?
It's all you get for now.
You have what remains of my father's body -- that skin is yours!

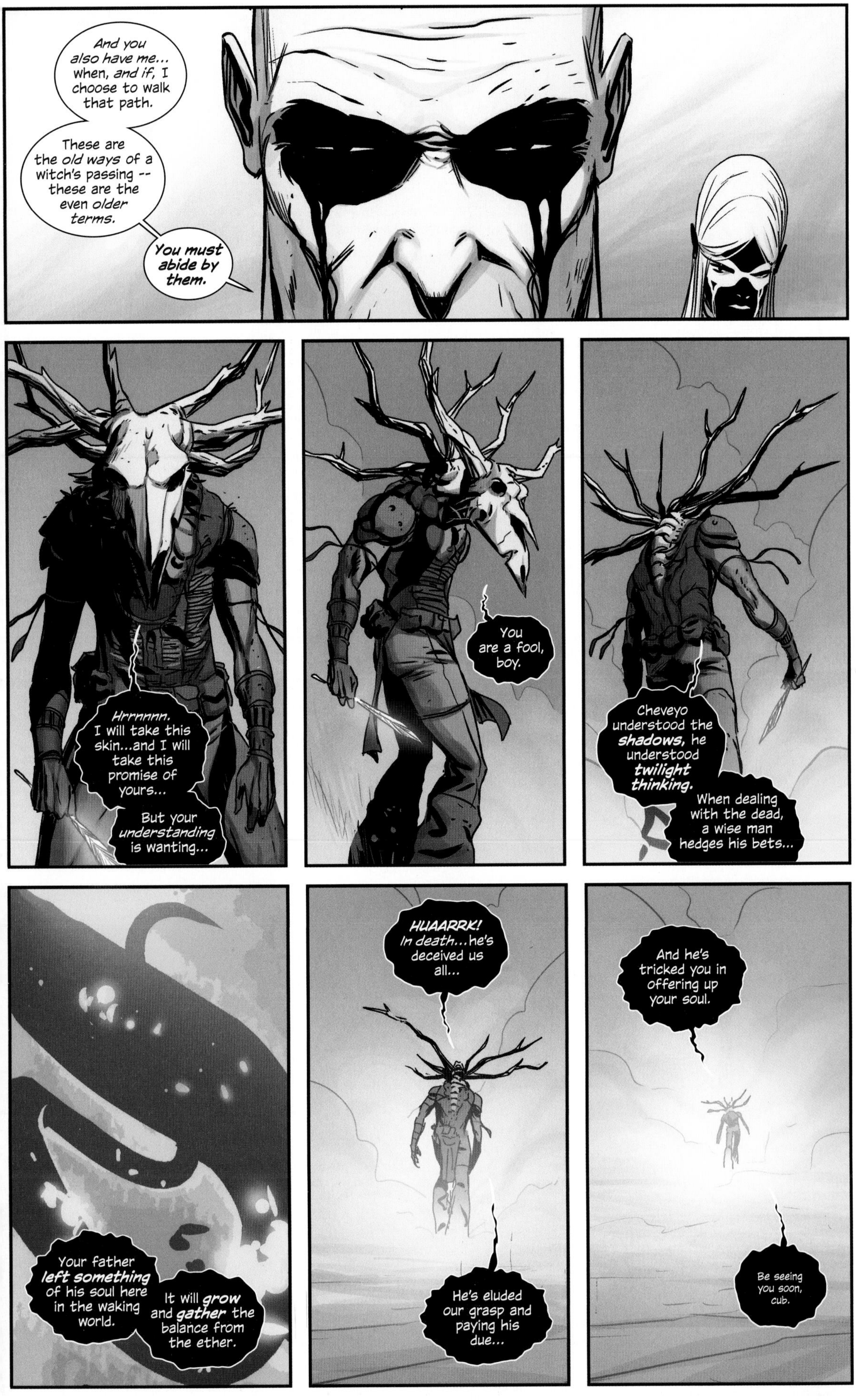
And you also have me... when, and if, I choose to walk that path.
These are the old ways of a witch's passing -- these are the even older terms.
You must abide by them.
Hrrnnnn. I will take this skin...and I will take this promise of yours...
But your understanding is wanting...
You are a fool, boy.
Cheveyo understood the shadows, he understood twilight thinking.
When dealing with the dead, a wise man hedges his bets...
Your father left something of his soul here in the waking world.
It will grow and gather the balance from the ether.
HUAARRK! In death...he's deceived us all...
He's eluded our grasp and paying his due...
And he's tricked you in offering up your soul.
Be seeing you soon, cub.

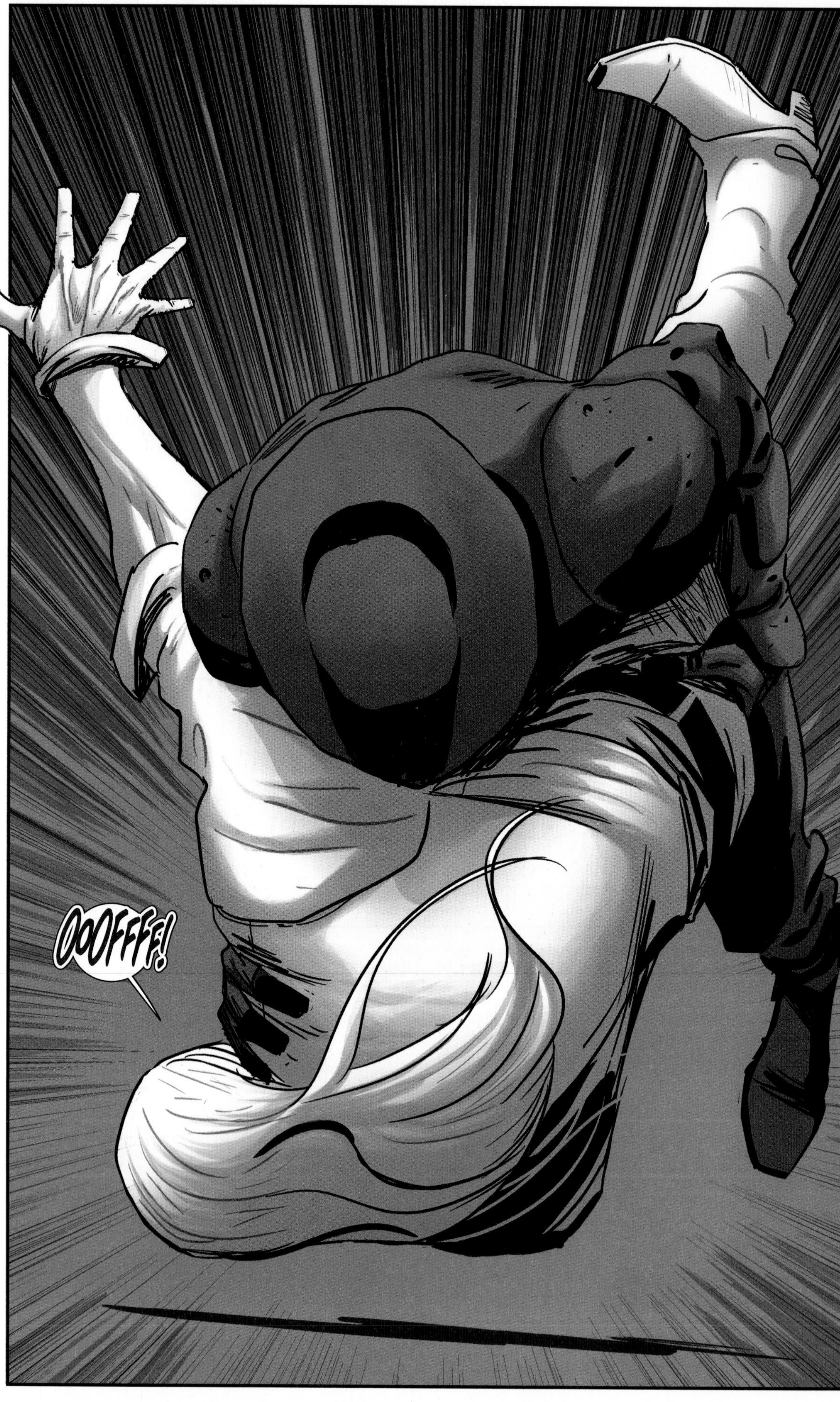
OOOFFFF!

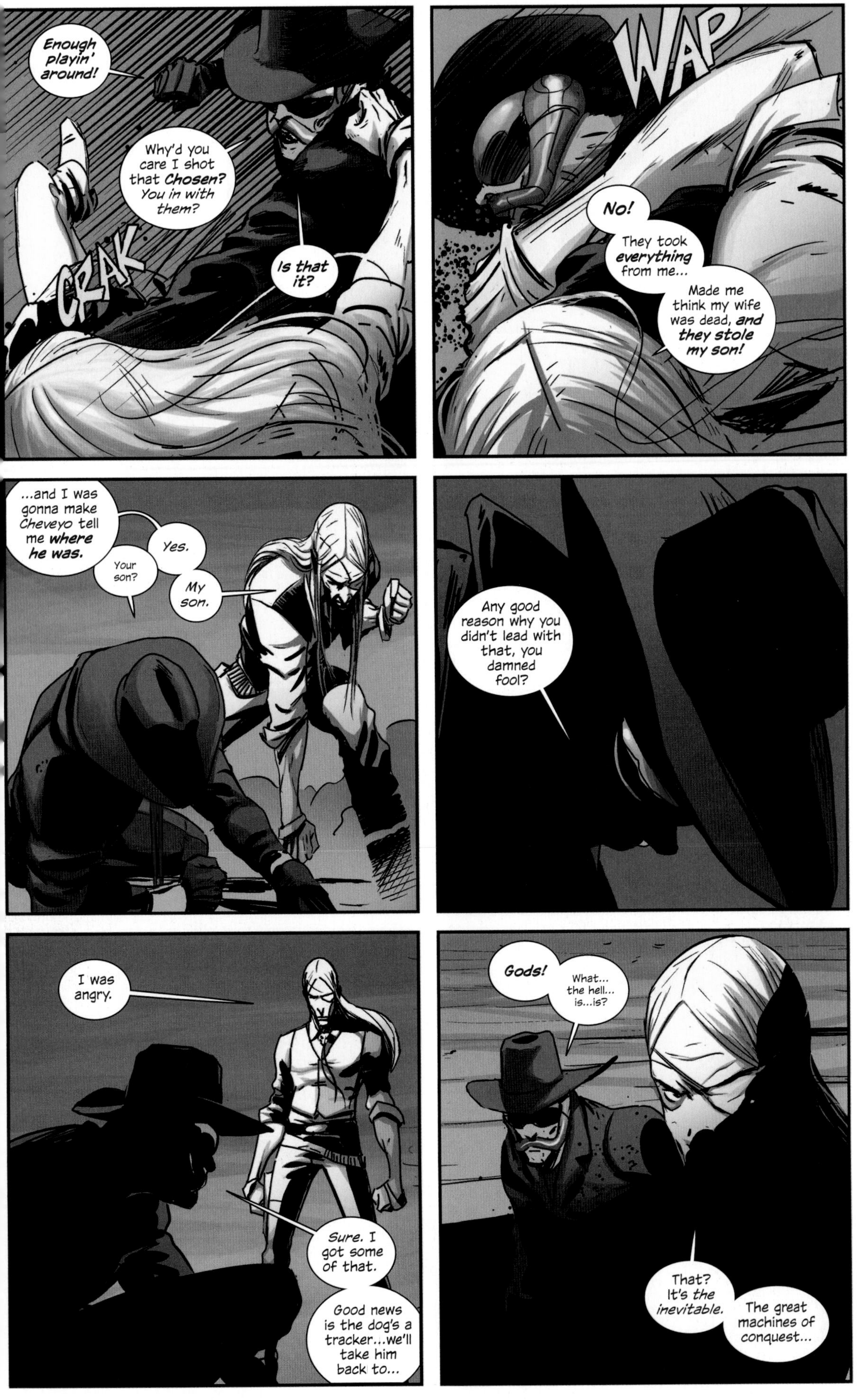
Enough playin' around!
Why'd you care I shot that Chosen? You in with them?
CRAK
Is that it?
WAP
No!
They took everything from me...
Made me think my wife was dead, and they stole my son!
...and I was gonna make Cheveyo tell me where he was.
Your son?
Yes.
My son.
Any good reason why you didn't lead with that, you damned fool?
I was angry.
Sure. I got some of that.
Good news is the dog's a tracker...we'll take him back to...
Gods!
What... the hell... is...is?
That? It's the inevitable.
The great machines of conquest...

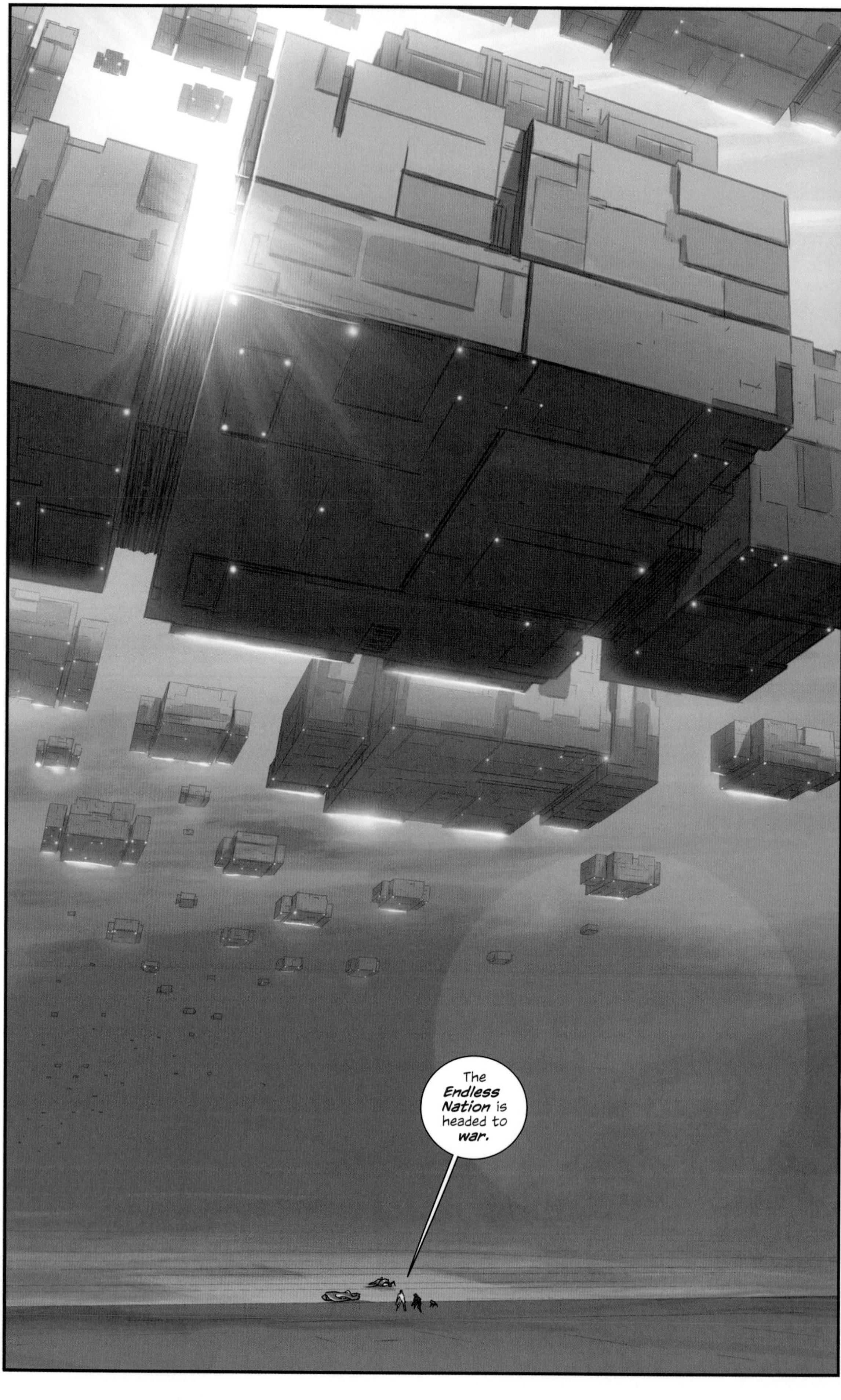
The *Endless Nation* is headed to *war.*

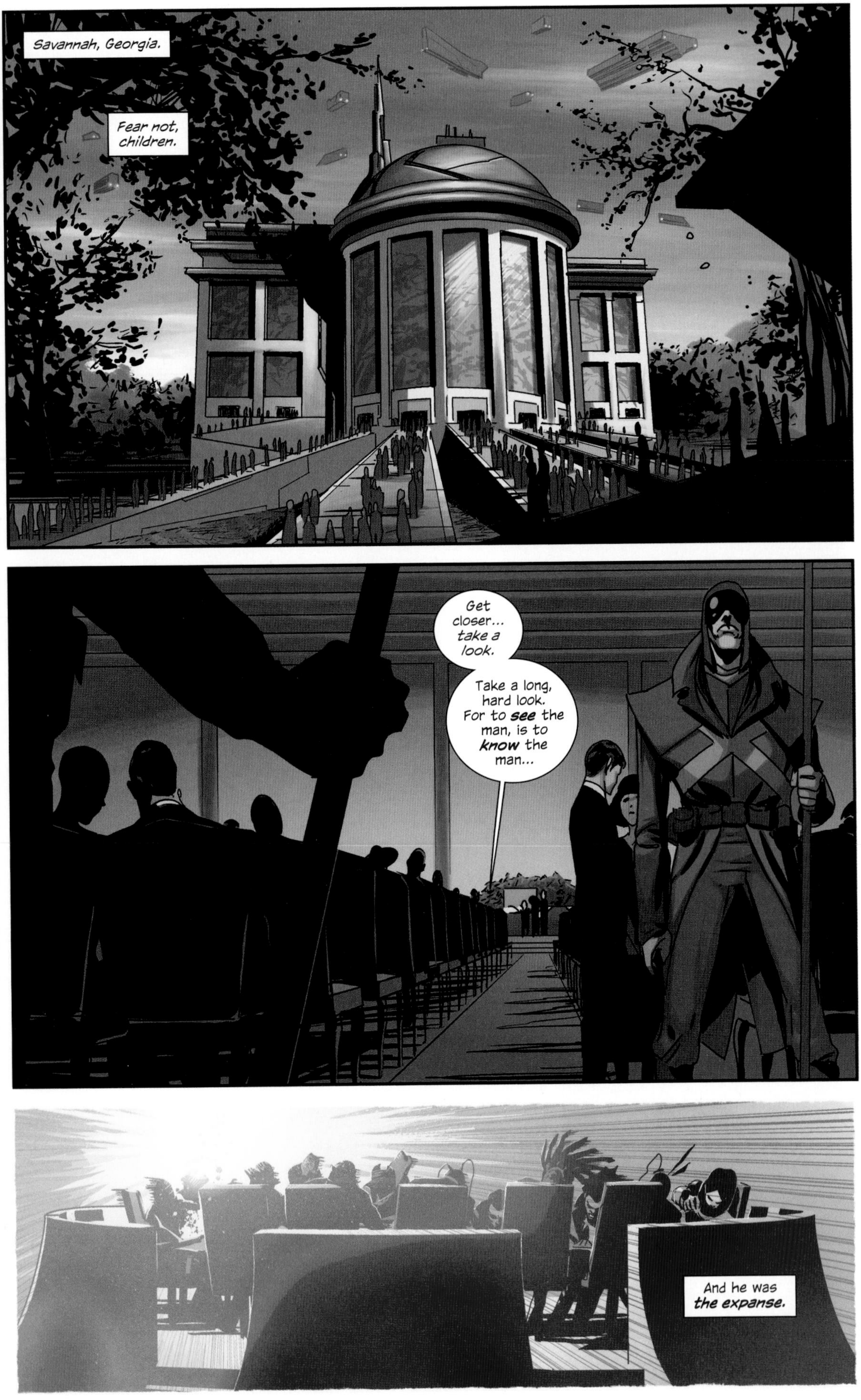
Savannah, Georgia.
Fear not, children.
Get closer... take a look.
Take a long, hard look. For to see the man, is to know the man...
And he was the expanse.

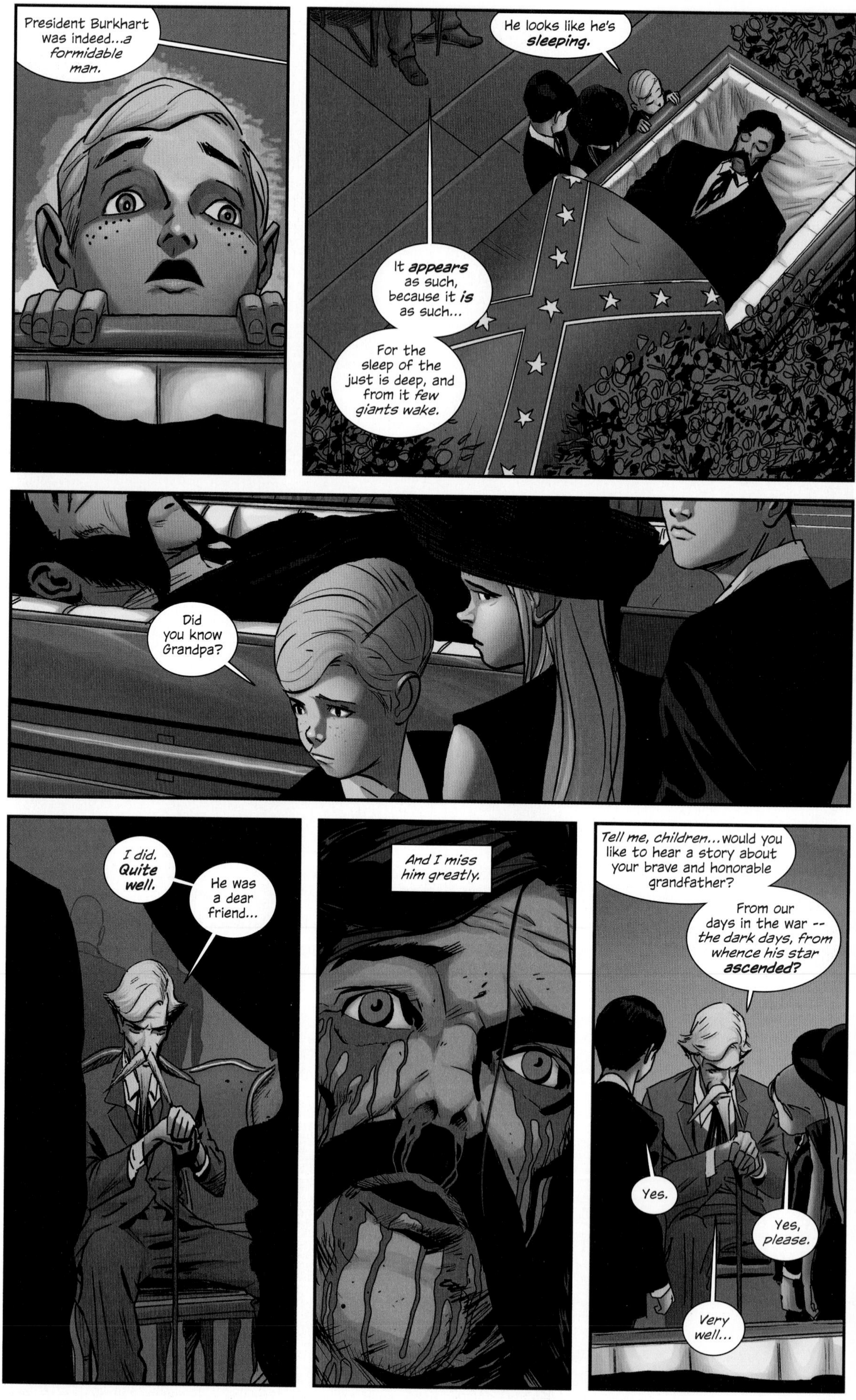
President Burkhart was indeed...a *formidable* man.
He looks like he's ***sleeping.***
It ***appears*** as such, because it ***is*** as such...
For the sleep of the just is deep, and from it *few giants wake.*
Did you know Grandpa?
I did. ***Quite well.***
He was a dear friend...
And I miss him greatly.
Tell me, children... would you like to hear a story about your brave and honorable grandfather?
From our days in the war -- *the dark days, from whence his star* ***ascended?***
Yes.
Yes, *please.*
Very well...

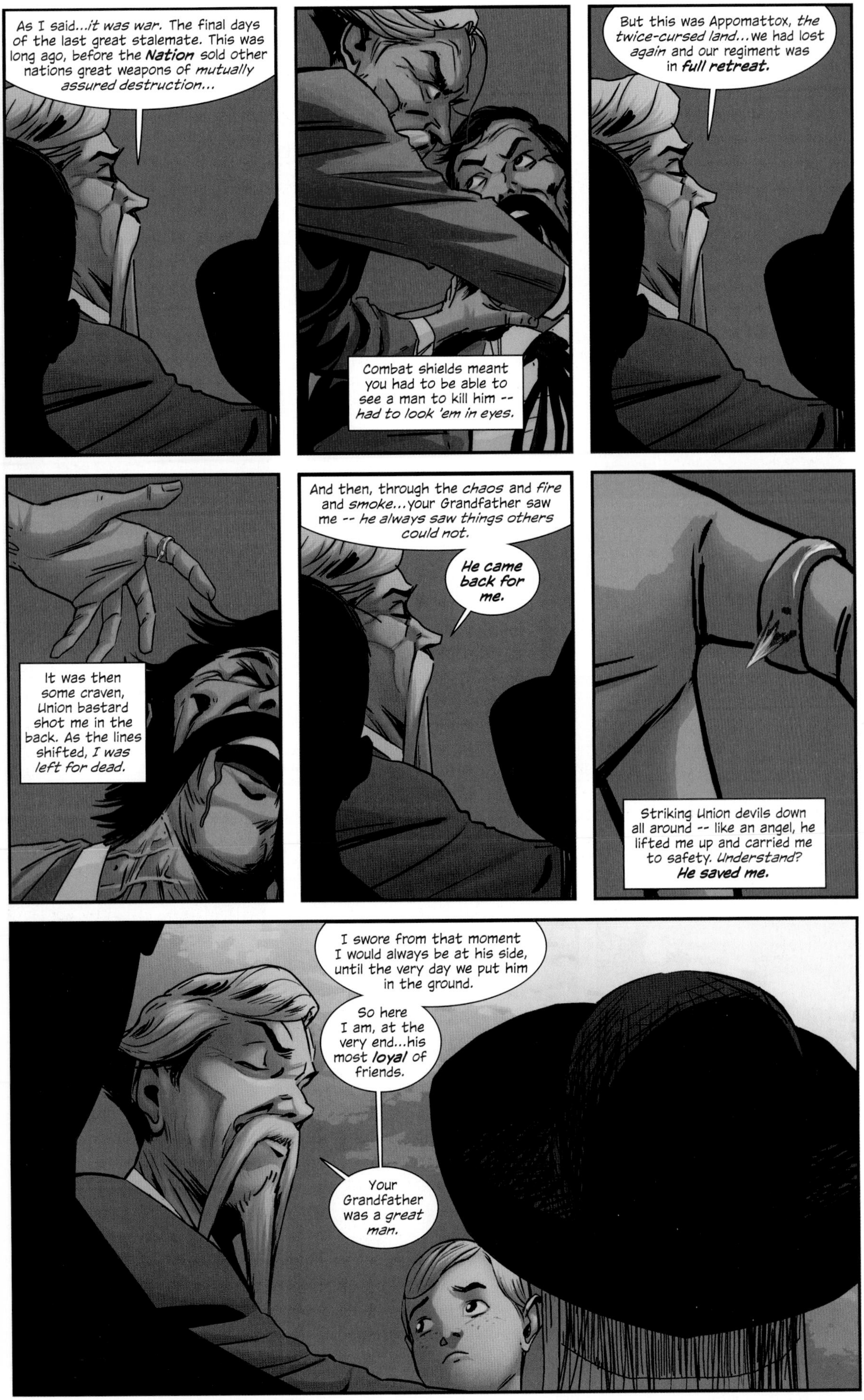
As I said...*it was war.* The final days of the last great stalemate. This was long ago, before the ***Nation*** sold other nations great weapons of *mutually assured destruction...*
Combat shields meant you had to be able to see a man to kill him -- *had to look 'em in eyes.*
But this was Appomattox, *the twice-cursed land...*we had lost *again* and our regiment was in ***full retreat.***
It was then some craven, Union bastard shot me in the back. As the lines shifted, *I was left for dead.*
And then, through the *chaos* and *fire* and *smoke...*your Grandfather saw me -- *he always saw things others could not.*
He came back for me.
Striking Union devils down all around -- like an angel, he lifted me up and carried me to safety. *Understand?* ***He saved me.***
I swore from that moment I would always be at his side, until the very day we put him in the ground.
So here I am, at the very *end...*his most ***loyal*** of friends.
Your Grandfather was a *great man.*

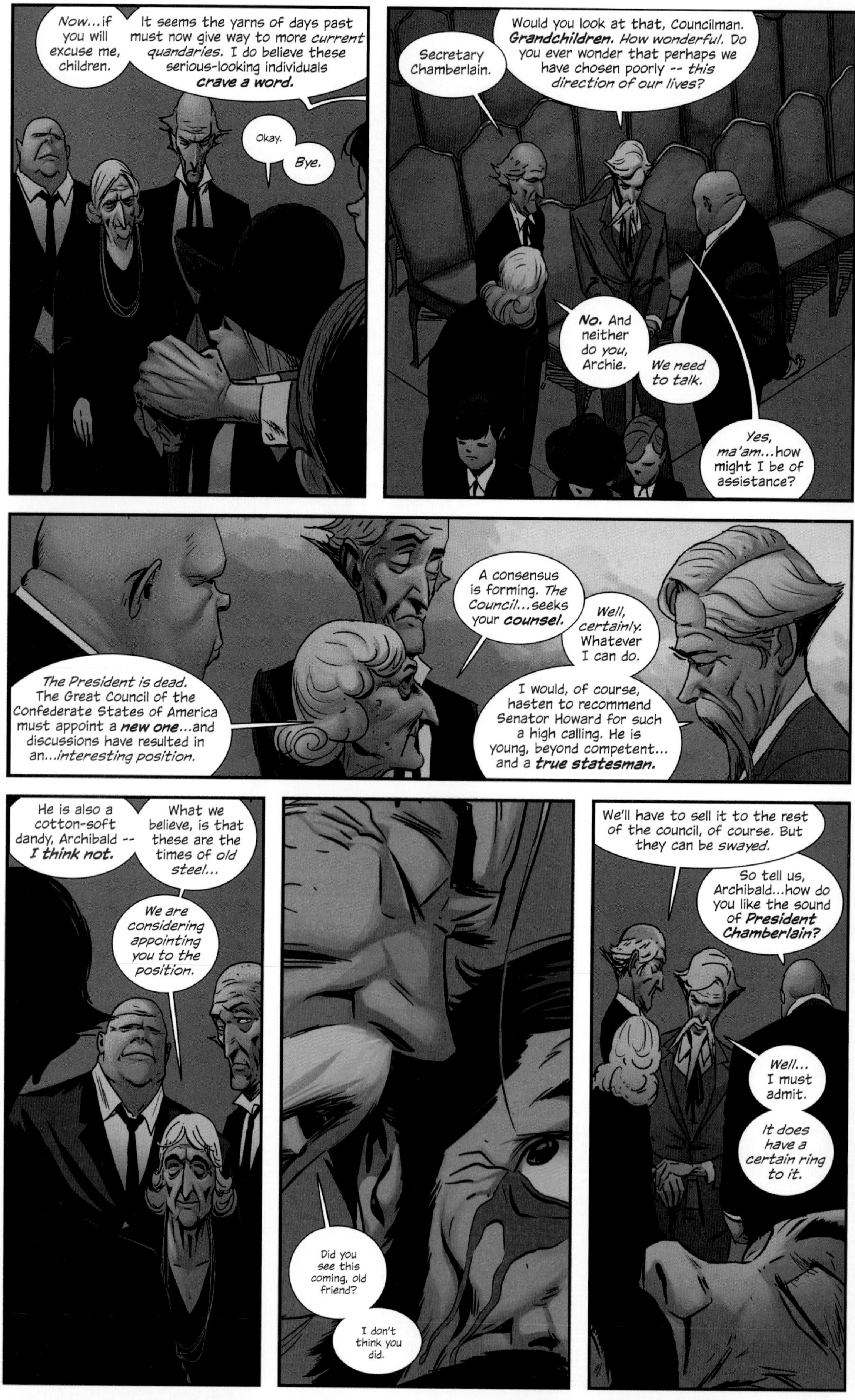
Now...if you will excuse me, children.
It seems the yarns of days past must now give way to more current quandaries. I do believe these serious-looking individuals crave a word.
Okay.
Bye.
Secretary Chamberlain.
Would you look at that, Councilman. Grandchildren. How wonderful. Do you ever wonder that perhaps we have chosen poorly -- this direction of our lives?
No. And neither do you, Archie.
We need to talk.
Yes, ma'am...how might I be of assistance?
The President is dead. The Great Council of the Confederate States of America must appoint a new one...and discussions have resulted in an...interesting position.
A consensus is forming. The Council...seeks your counsel.
Well, certainly. Whatever I can do.
I would, of course, hasten to recommend Senator Howard for such a high calling. He is young, beyond competent... and a true statesman.
He is also a cotton-soft dandy, Archibald -- I think not.
What we believe, is that these are the times of old steel...
We are considering appointing you to the position.
Did you see this coming, old friend?
I don't think you did.
We'll have to sell it to the rest of the council, of course. But they can be swayed.
So tell us, Archibald...how do you like the sound of President Chamberlain?
Well... I must admit.
It does have a certain ring to it.

WHEN WE ARE **LOYAL,** IT
IS BECAUSE WE FIND IT
USEFUL.

14

FOURTEEN: A WORLD FULL OF ANGRY CHILDREN

OF WHAT **WORTH** IS A
MOTHER?

OF WHAT **VALUE** A **CHILD?**

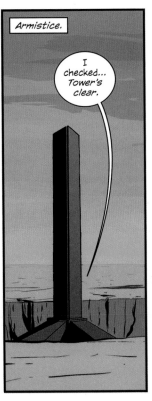

Armistice.

I checked... Tower's clear.

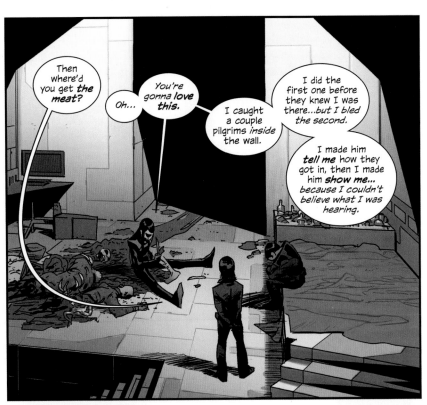

Then where'd you get *the meat?*

Oh...

You're gonna *love this.*

I caught a couple pilgrims *inside* the wall.

I did the first one before they knew I was there...but I bled the second.

I made him *tell me* how they got in, then I made him *show me...* because I couldn't believe what I was hearing.

Prudent.

Animals are capable of any number of *unthinkable* things.

Right? And here's what they did -- they dug a tunnel *under* the wall. With, *like,* shovels and their hands. *Who does something like that?*

Look, monkey...there's a giant big ass wall trying to keep us out. *Hey!* I know what we should do, let's dig our way underneath it.

Sure! Why wouldn't we -- sounds like fun. After all, every person that's ever made it to Armistice has either *died* or *disappeared.*

Rrrrr.

Well... all except one.

SNAP

Isn't that right?

KRUHCH

What's in the bottles?

Is it...?

MUNCH MUNCH MUNCH MUNCH

MUNCH MUNCH MUNCH MUNCH MUNCH MUNCH MUNCH MUNCH

Yeah. Looks like it. Elixirs. Drugs. Every concoction you could think of...

Anything to dull the pain.

MUNCH MUNCH M M M M M MUNCH M M M MUNCH M M MUNCH MUNCH

You know, I understand the rightness of it, War. I do.

And I embrace -- hell, I celebrate -- fulfilling the duties we instruments were created for...

But to see him endure this kind of suffering... it's not the way I'd prefer things to go.

For example, you know how much I love what I do?

Killing?

I do.

Yeah.

That's the kind of fulfillment and joy I want for him.

Well, I will say...this has cascaded in a pretty unpredictable manner. Still, we have business, so...

BURP

Yeah. Okay.

Ezra... please come out. We need to talk to you.

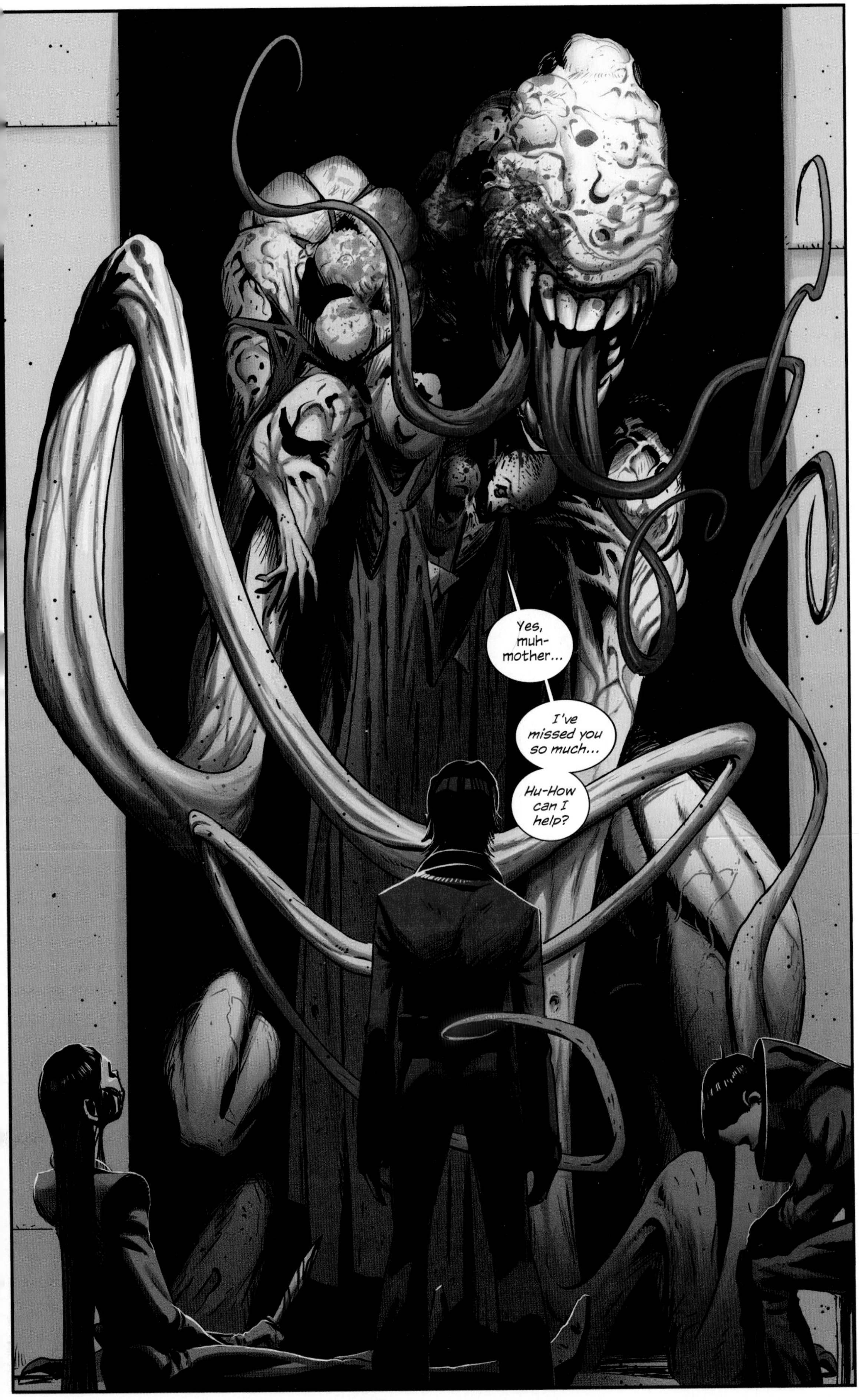
Yes, muh-mother...
I've missed you so much...
Hu-How can I help?

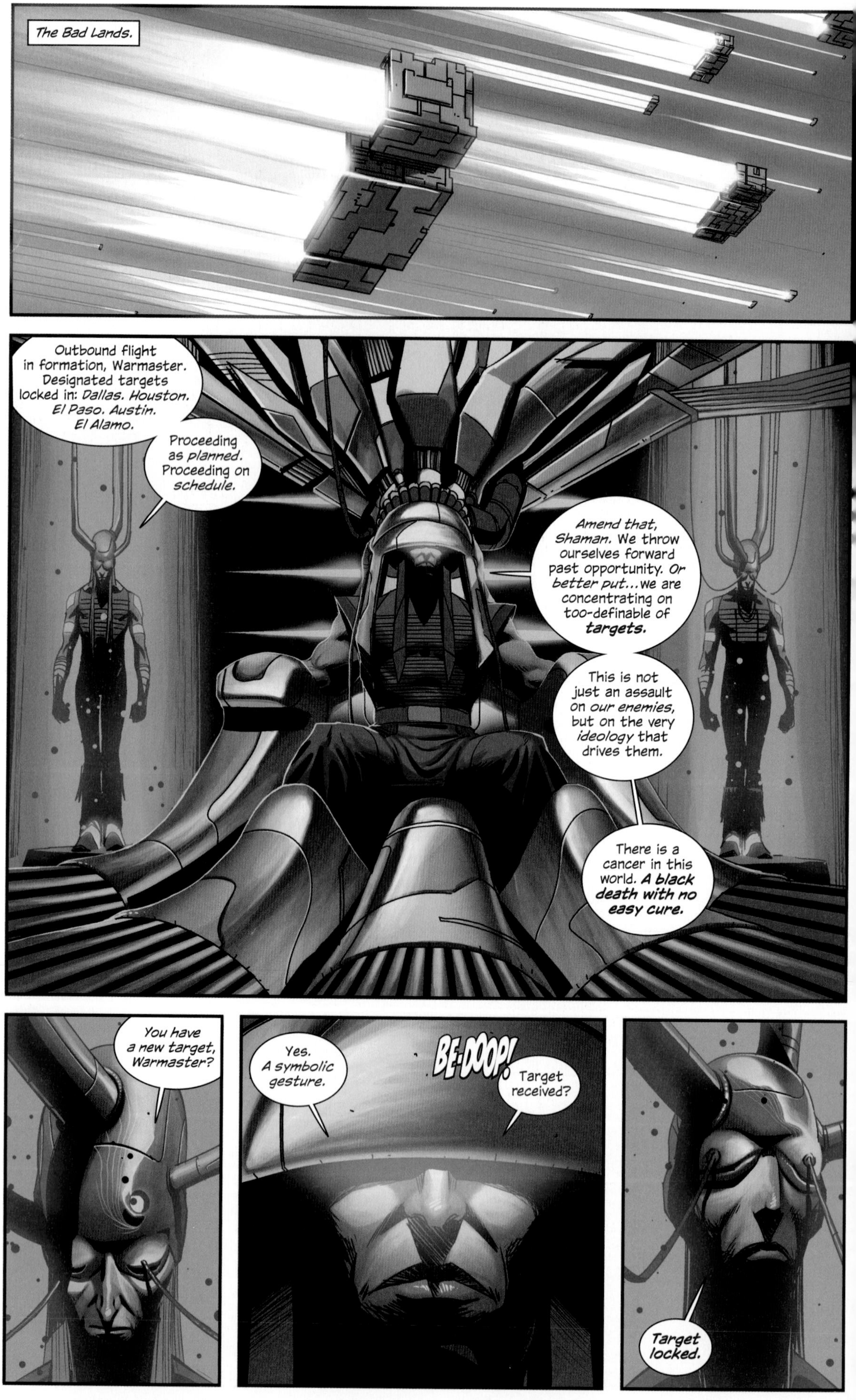
The Bad Lands.
Outbound flight in formation, Warmaster. Designated targets locked in: Dallas. Houston. El Paso. Austin. El Alamo.
Proceeding as planned. Proceeding on schedule.
Amend that, Shaman. We throw ourselves forward past opportunity. Or better put...we are concentrating on too-definable of targets.
This is not just an assault on our enemies, but on the very ideology that drives them.
There is a cancer in this world. A black death with no easy cure.
You have a new target, Warmaster?
Yes. A symbolic gesture.
BE-DOOP!
Target received?
Target locked.

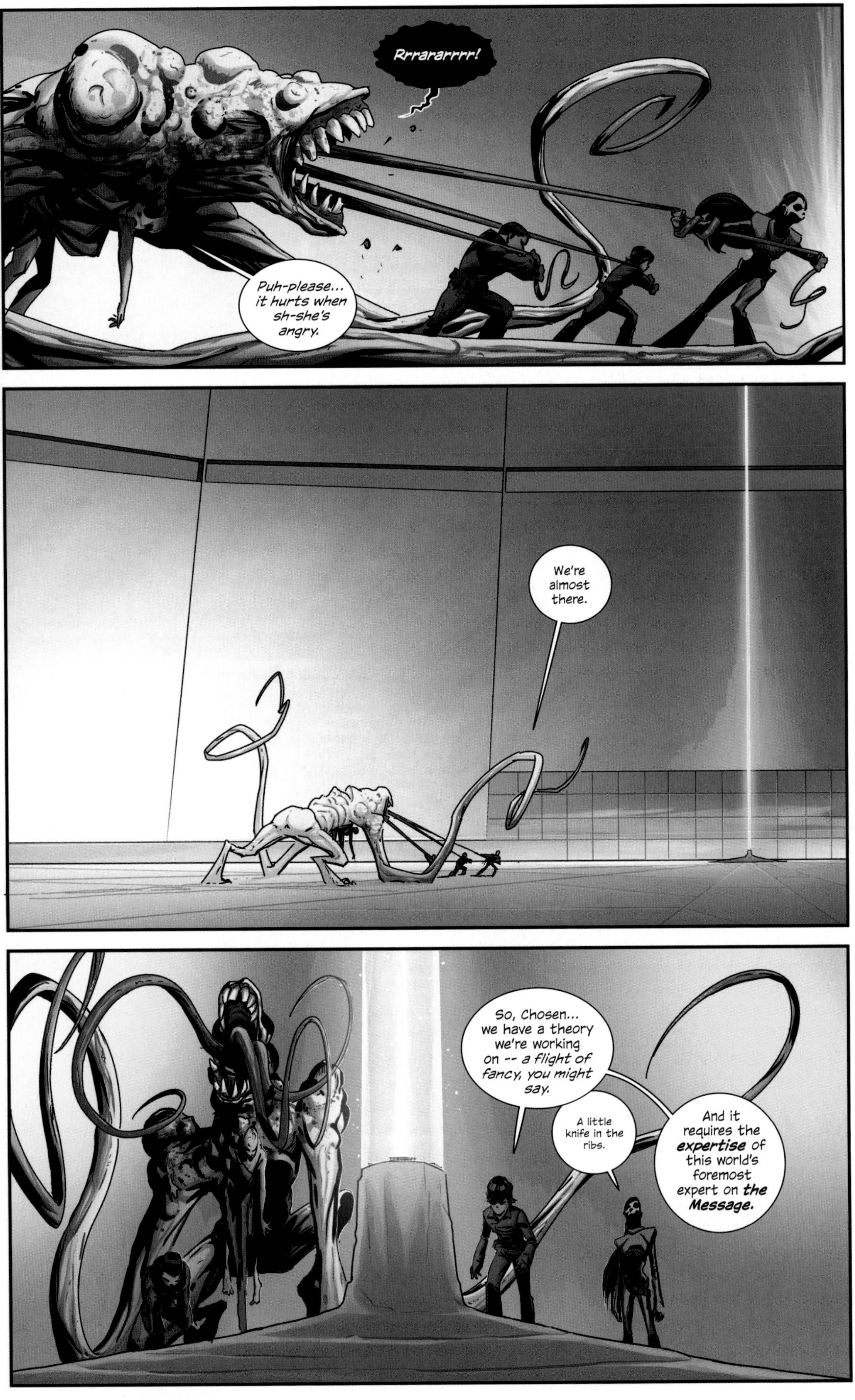
Rrrararrrr!
Puh-please... it hurts when sh-she's angry.
We're almost there.
So, Chosen... we have a theory we're working on -- a flight of fancy, you might say.
A little knife in the ribs.
And it requires the expertise of this world's foremost expert on the Message.

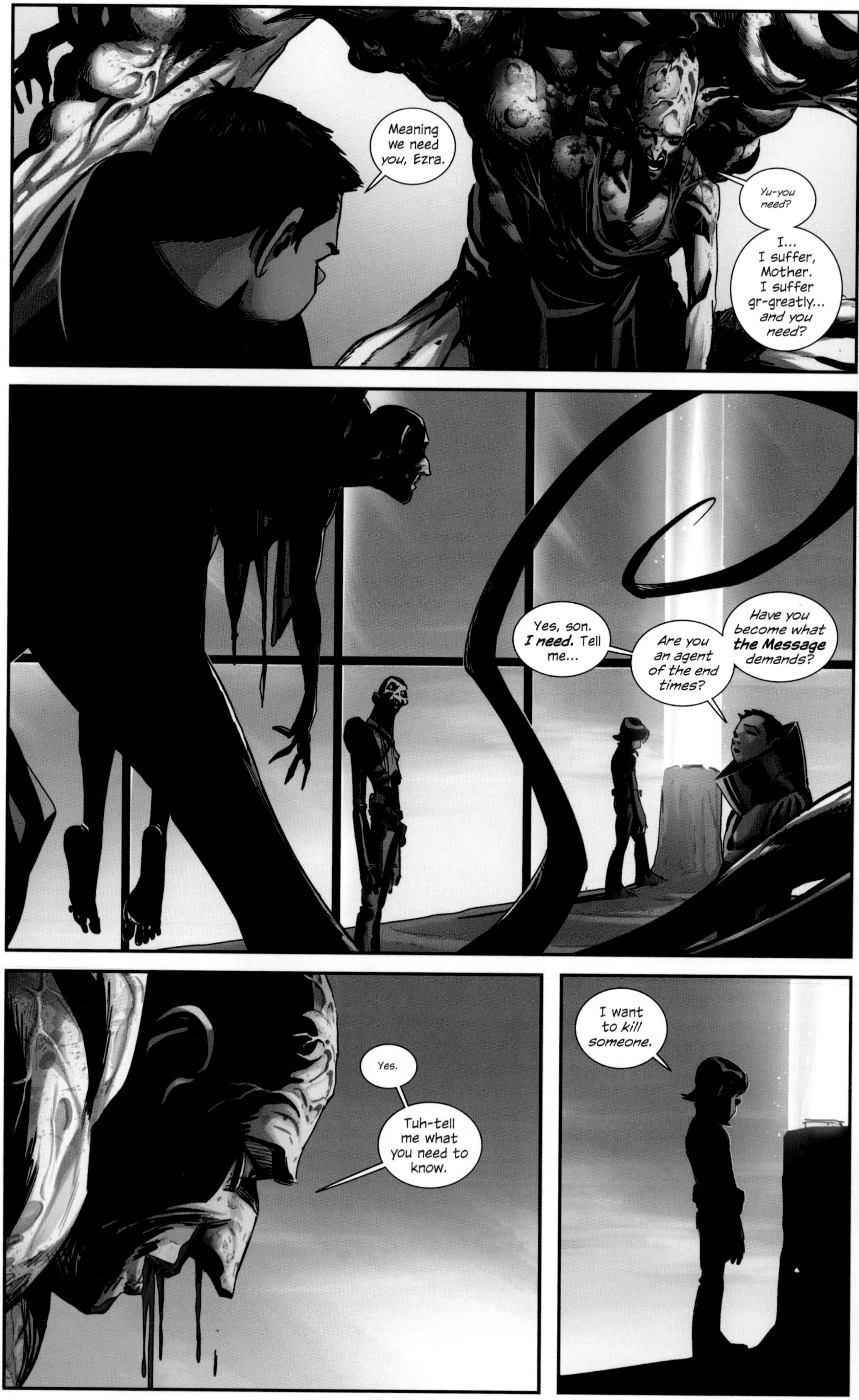
Meaning we need you, Ezra.
Yu-you need?
I... I suffer, Mother. I suffer gr-greatly... and you need?
Yes, son. I need. Tell me...
Are you an agent of the end times?
Have you become what the Message demands?
Yes.
Tuh-tell me what you need to know.
I want to kill someone.

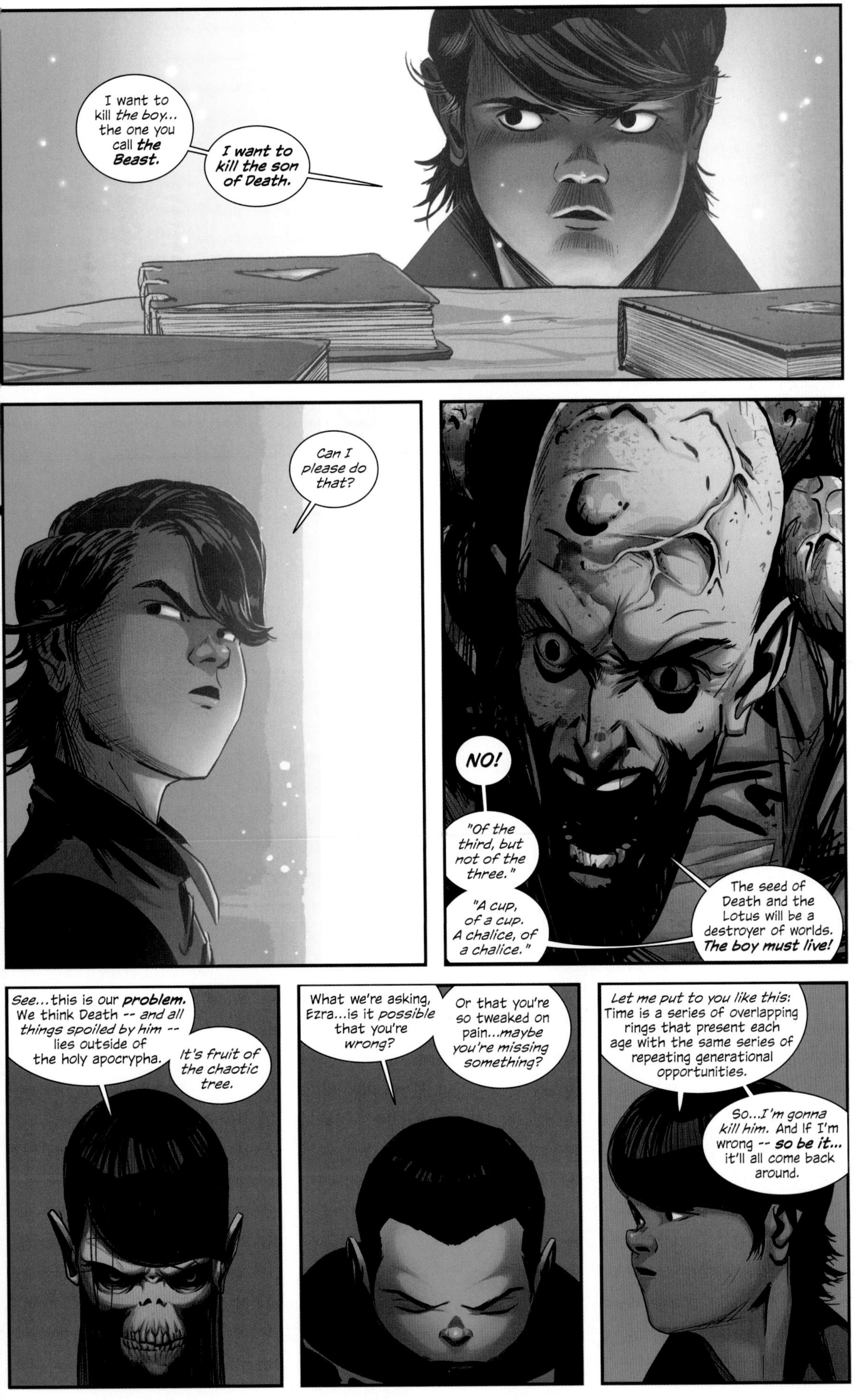

I want to kill *the boy...* the one you call ***the Beast.***
I want to kill the son of Death.
Can I please do that?
NO!
"Of the third, but not of the three."
"A cup, of a cup. A chalice, of a chalice."
The seed of Death and the Lotus will be a destroyer of worlds. ***The boy must live!***
See...this is our ***problem.*** We think Death -- *and all things spoiled by him* -- lies outside of the holy apocrypha.
It's fruit of the chaotic tree.
What we're asking, Ezra...is it *possible* that you're *wrong?*
Or that you're so tweaked on pain...*maybe you're missing something?*
Let me put to you like this: Time is a series of overlapping rings that present each age with the same series of repeating generational opportunities.
So...*I'm gonna kill him.* And if I'm wrong -- ***so be it...*** it'll all come back around.

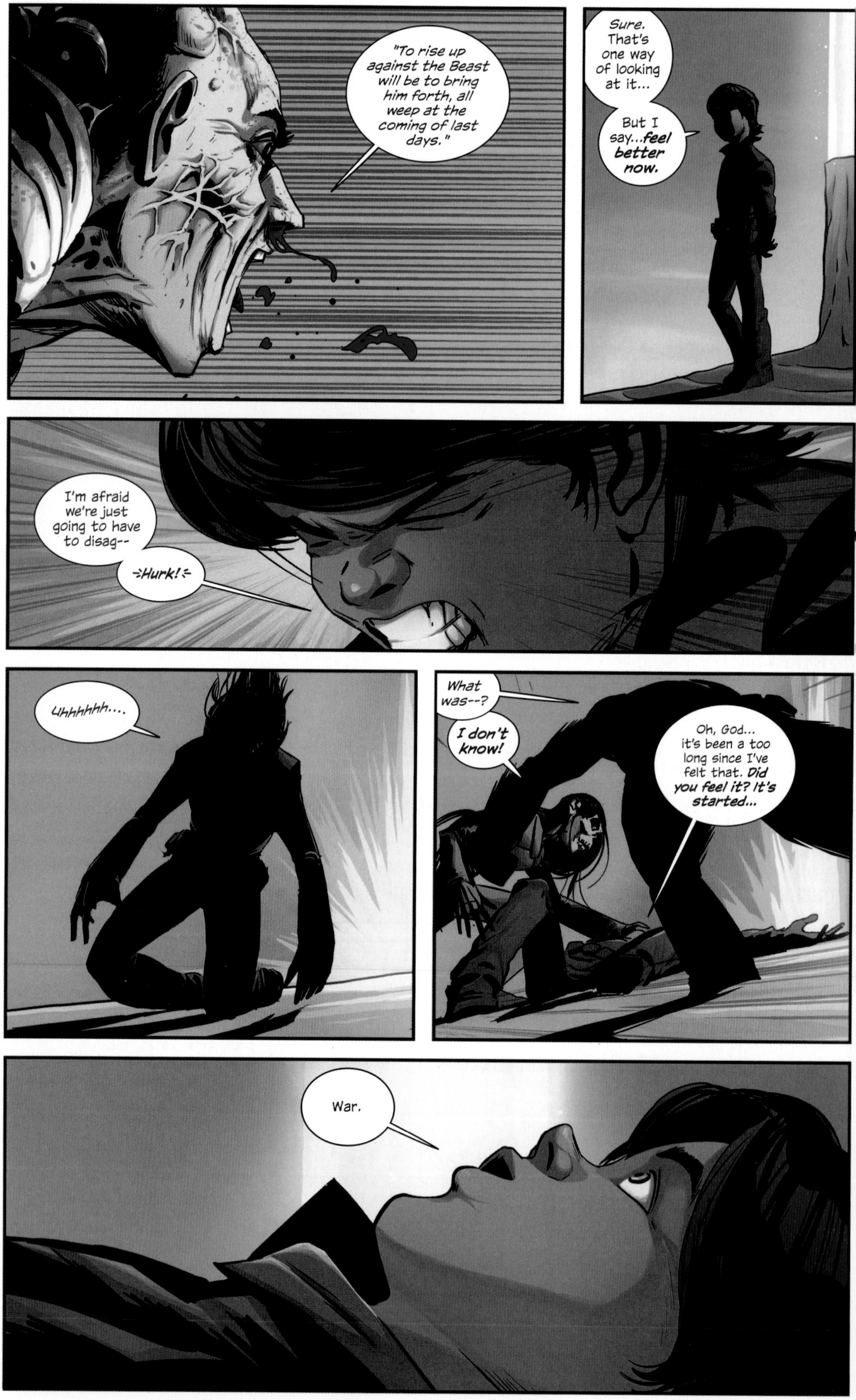
"To rise up against the Beast will be to bring him forth, all weep at the coming of last days."
Sure. That's one way of looking at it...
But I say...*feel better now.*
I'm afraid we're just going to have to disag--
Hurk!
Uhhhhhh....
What was--?
I don't know!
Oh, God... it's been a too long since I've felt that. *Did you feel it? It's started...*
War.

All these people -- *even ours* -- believing all these *long, dead lies...*

Legend says their three words sprang to life in the days following *the fire in sky.*

Here is your response, *mystics* and believers... here is a *little* fire of our *own.*

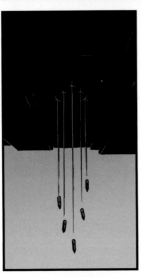

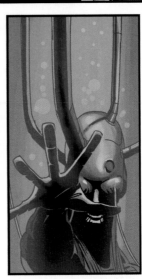

Smoke from the machine -- our message of modernity.

The Nation... is endless.

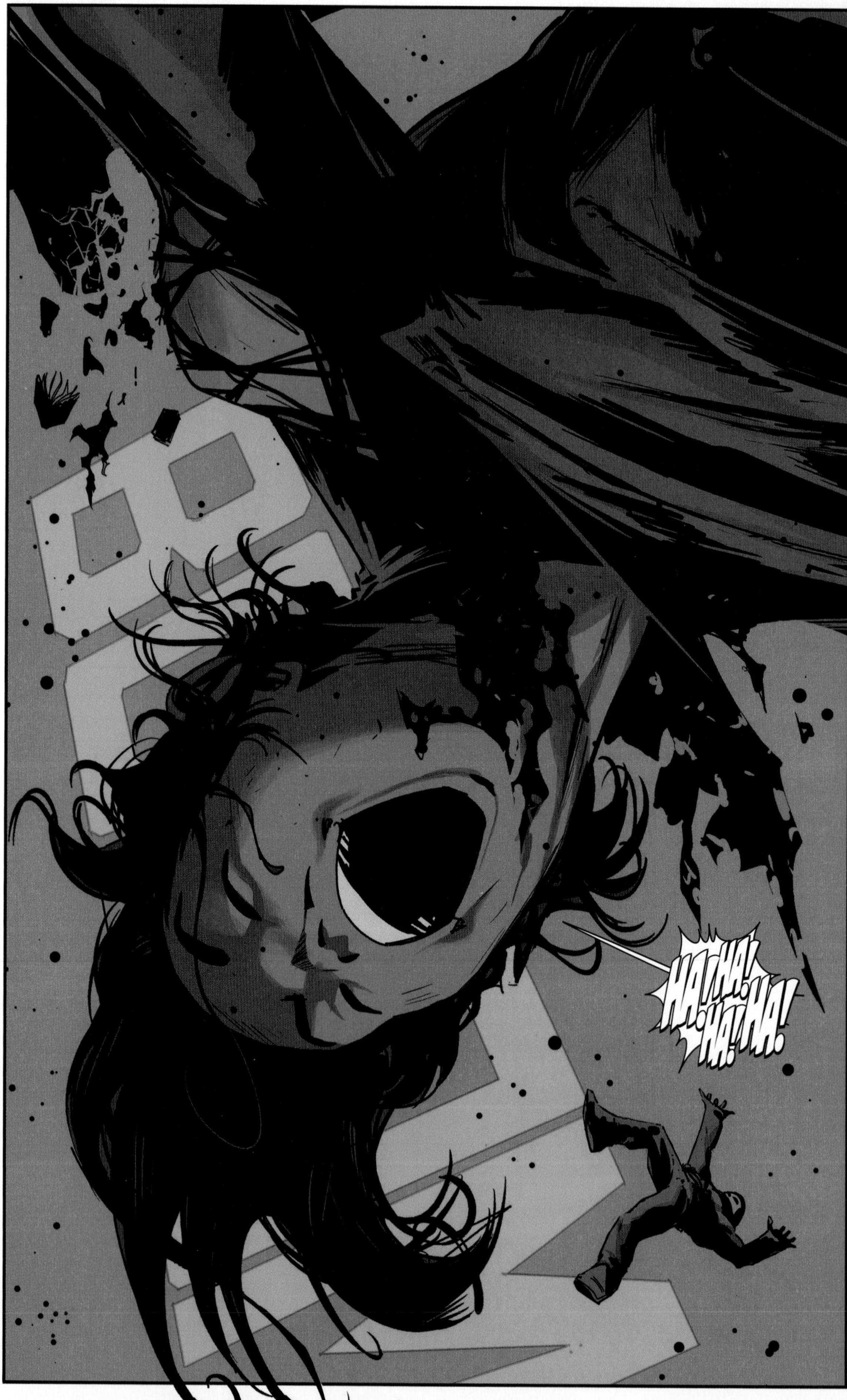
HA! HA! HA! HA!

That was great.

Yeah... but this place is **coming down.**

Are we taking that as *a sign?*

Oh, absolutely.

The tree of chaos has taken root...and we're off to hunt the Beast.

Come with us, Ezra.

Huh-how could I, mother? My place is here, isn't it?

Fuh-for I am an agent of the end times.

I have become what the Message demands.

Aren't y-you proud of me?

I'm sorry I asked so much of you.

You deserved better.

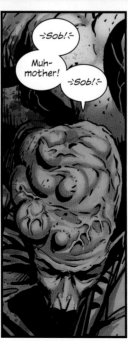

⊰Sob!⊱

Muh-mother!

⊰Sob!⊱

Mother!

Rrrraarrrr...

Of courssse it wassssn't.

:Sob!:

Why? Why? Was it all fuh-for nothing?

Urk!

CHOMP!

AAIEEEEE!

Orion'ssss Ezzzra...

Do you know what dayssse thessssse are?

:Kaff!:

Yes.

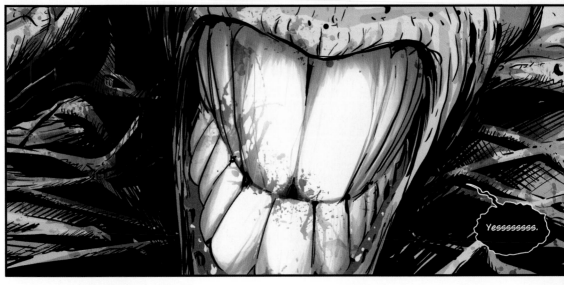

Yessssssss.

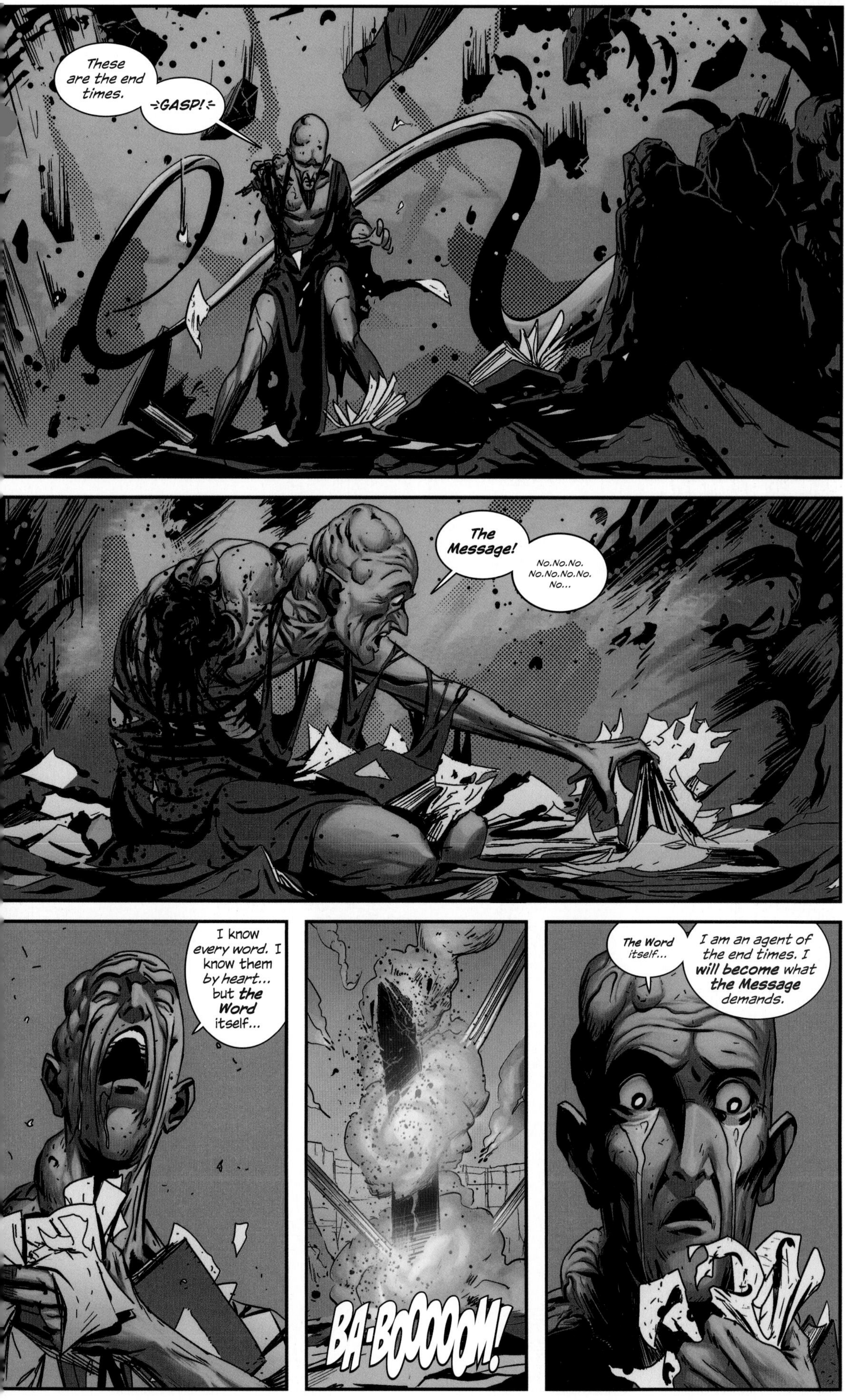
These are the end times.
-GASP!-
The Message!
No.No.No. No.No.No.No. No...
I know every word. I know them by heart... but the Word itself...
BA-BOOOOOM!
The Word itself...
I am an agent of the end times. I will become what the Message demands.

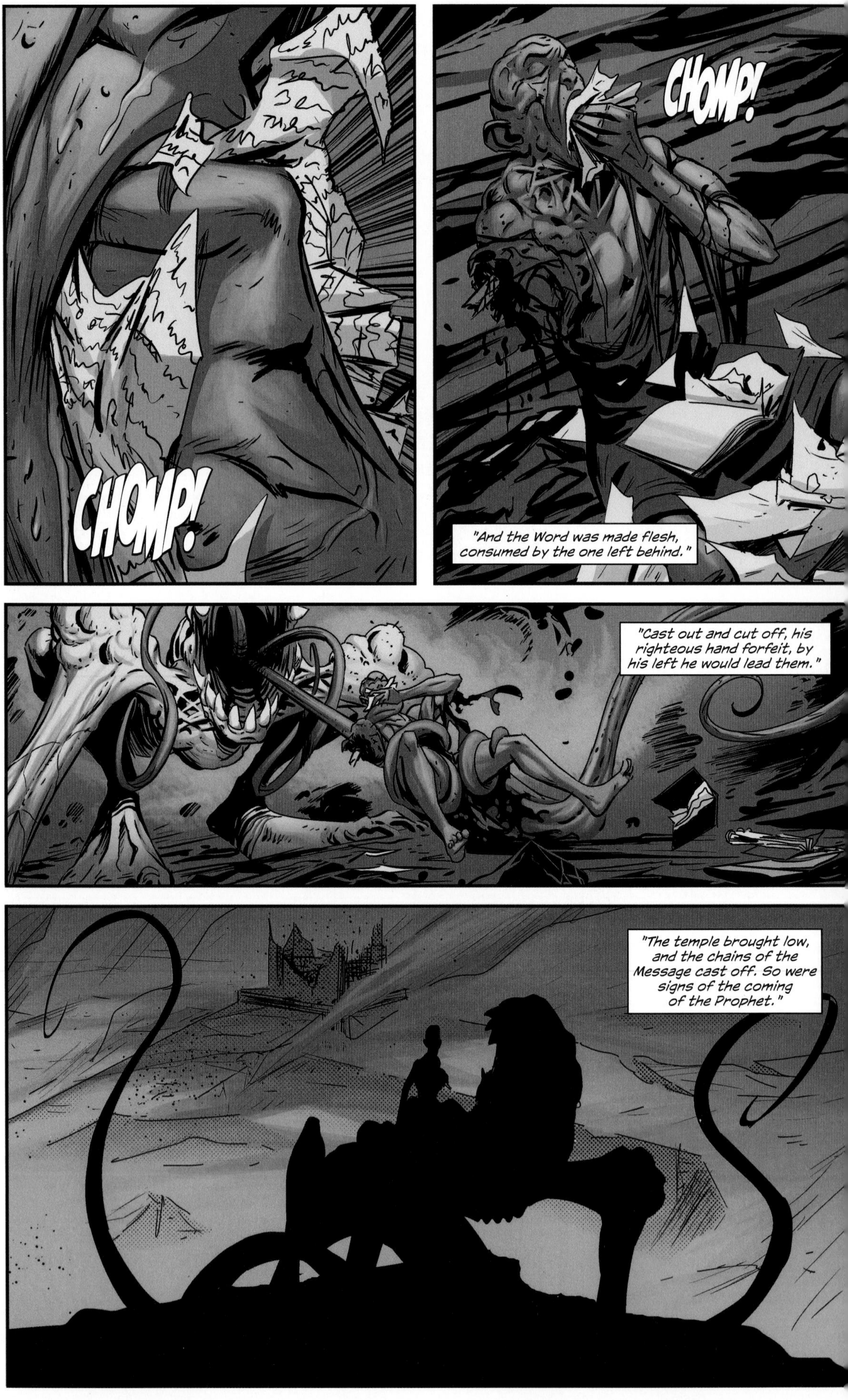
CHOMP!
CHOMP!
"And the Word was made flesh, consumed by the one left behind."
"Cast out and cut off, his righteous hand forfeit, by his left he would lead them."
"The temple brought low, and the chains of the Message cast off. So were signs of the coming of the Prophet."

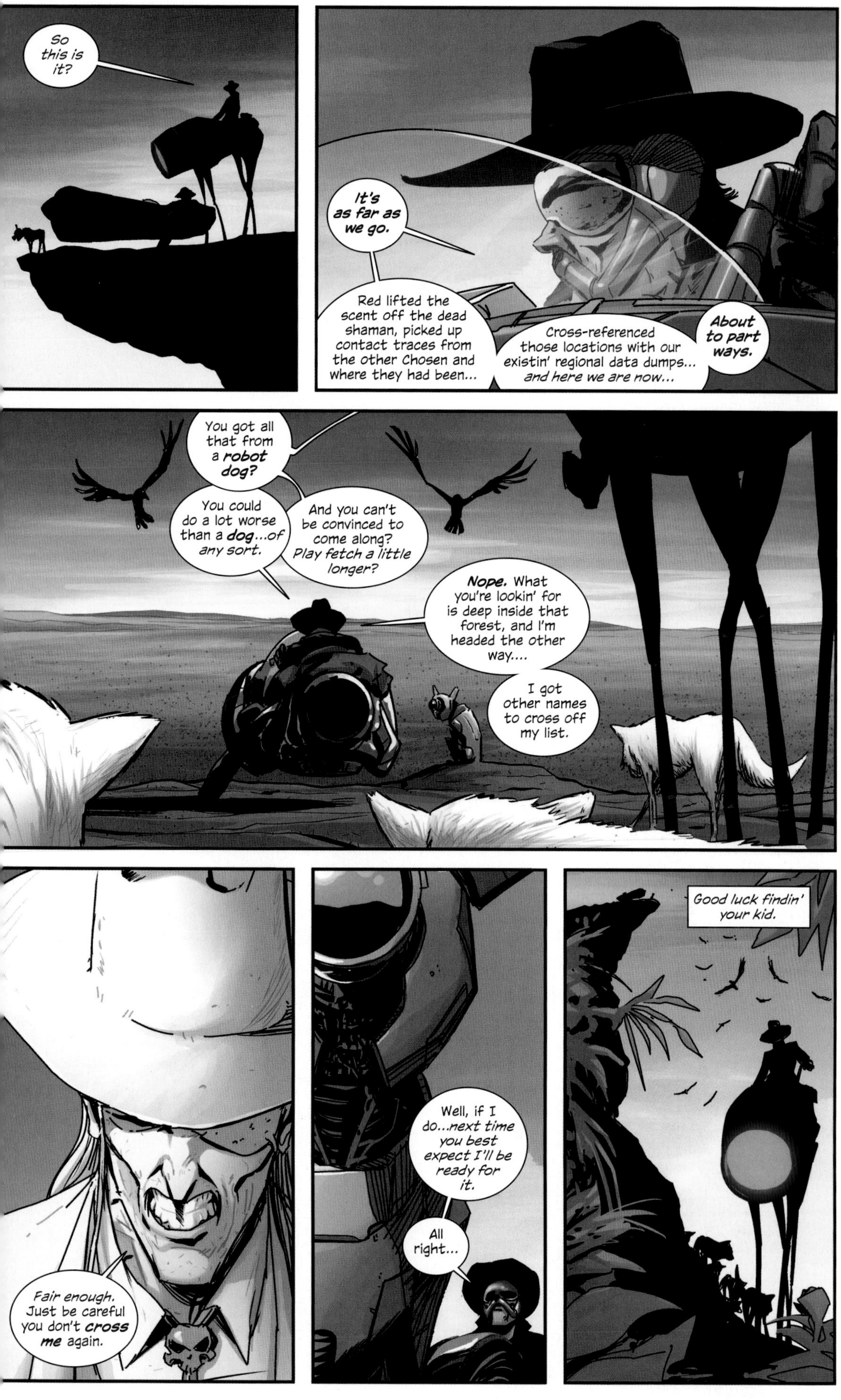

So this is it?
It's as far as we go.
Red lifted the scent off the dead shaman, picked up contact traces from the other Chosen and where they had been...
Cross-referenced those locations with our existin' regional data dumps... and here we are now...
About to part ways.
You got all that from a robot dog?
You could do a lot worse than a dog...of any sort.
And you can't be convinced to come along? Play fetch a little longer?
Nope. What you're lookin' for is deep inside that forest, and I'm headed the other way....
I got other names to cross off my list.
Fair enough. Just be careful you don't cross me again.
Well, if I do...next time you best expect I'll be ready for it.
All right...
Good luck findin' your kid.

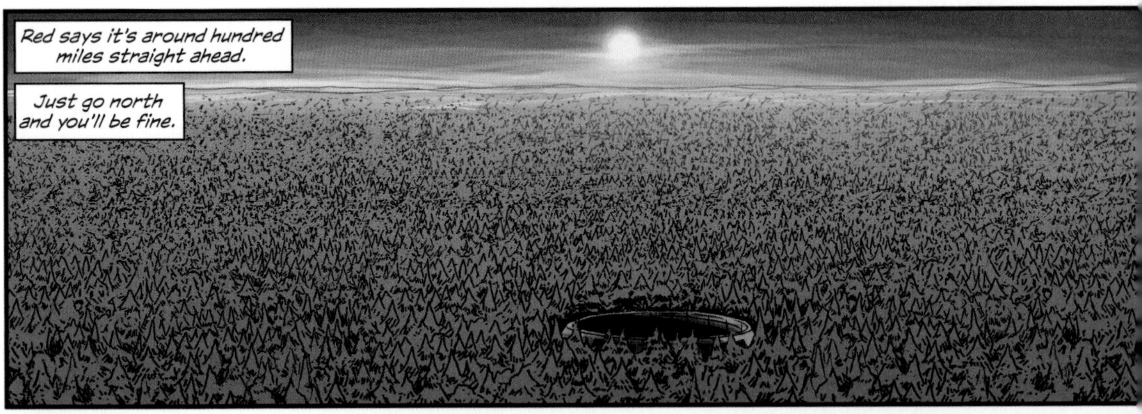
Red says it's around hundred miles straight ahead.
Just go north and you'll be fine.

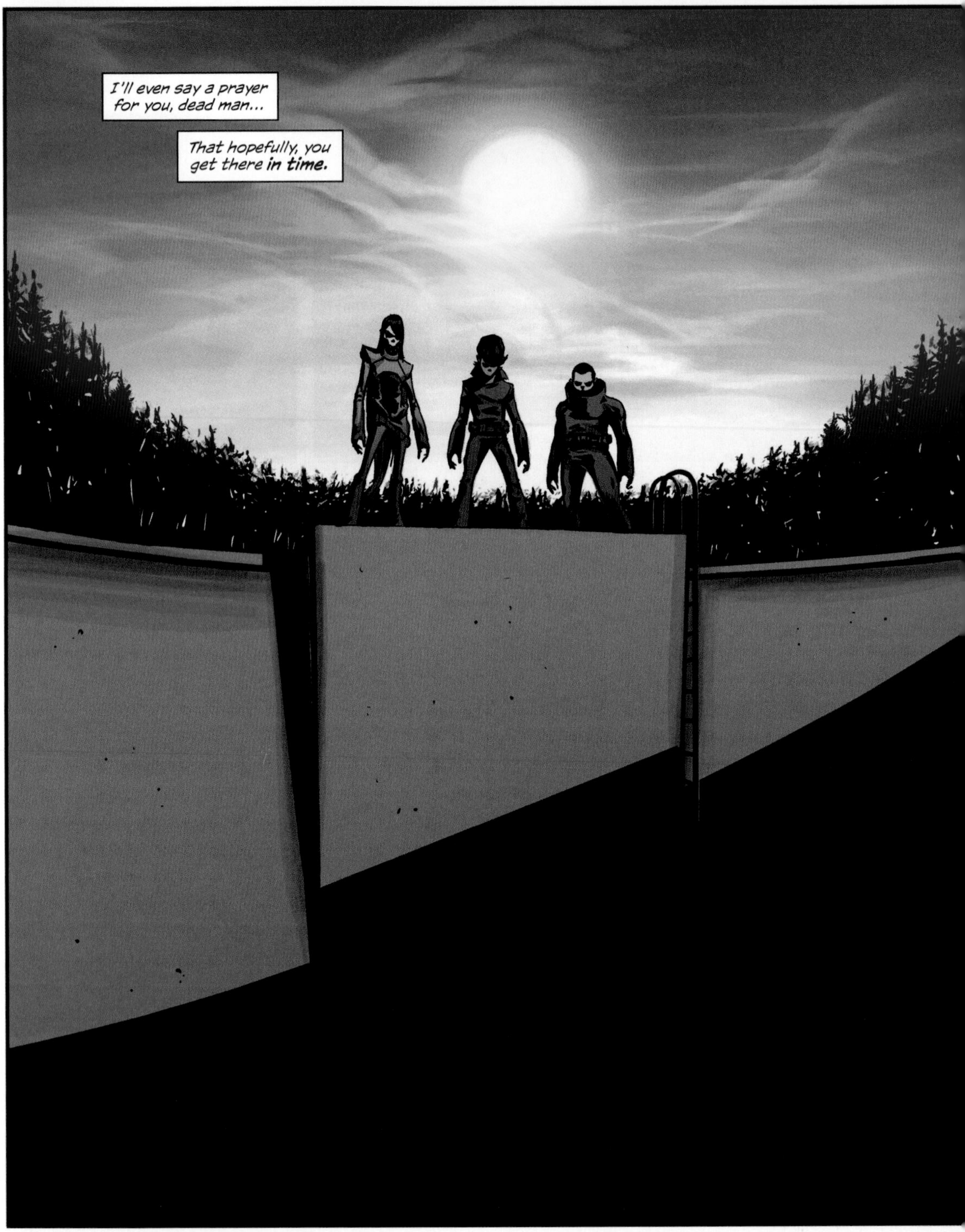
I'll even say a prayer for you, dead man...
That hopefully, you get there **in time.**

THEY ARE ALL **OUR CHILDREN.**

SO THEY HAVE NO **FATHERS,** THEY HAVE NO **MOTHERS.**

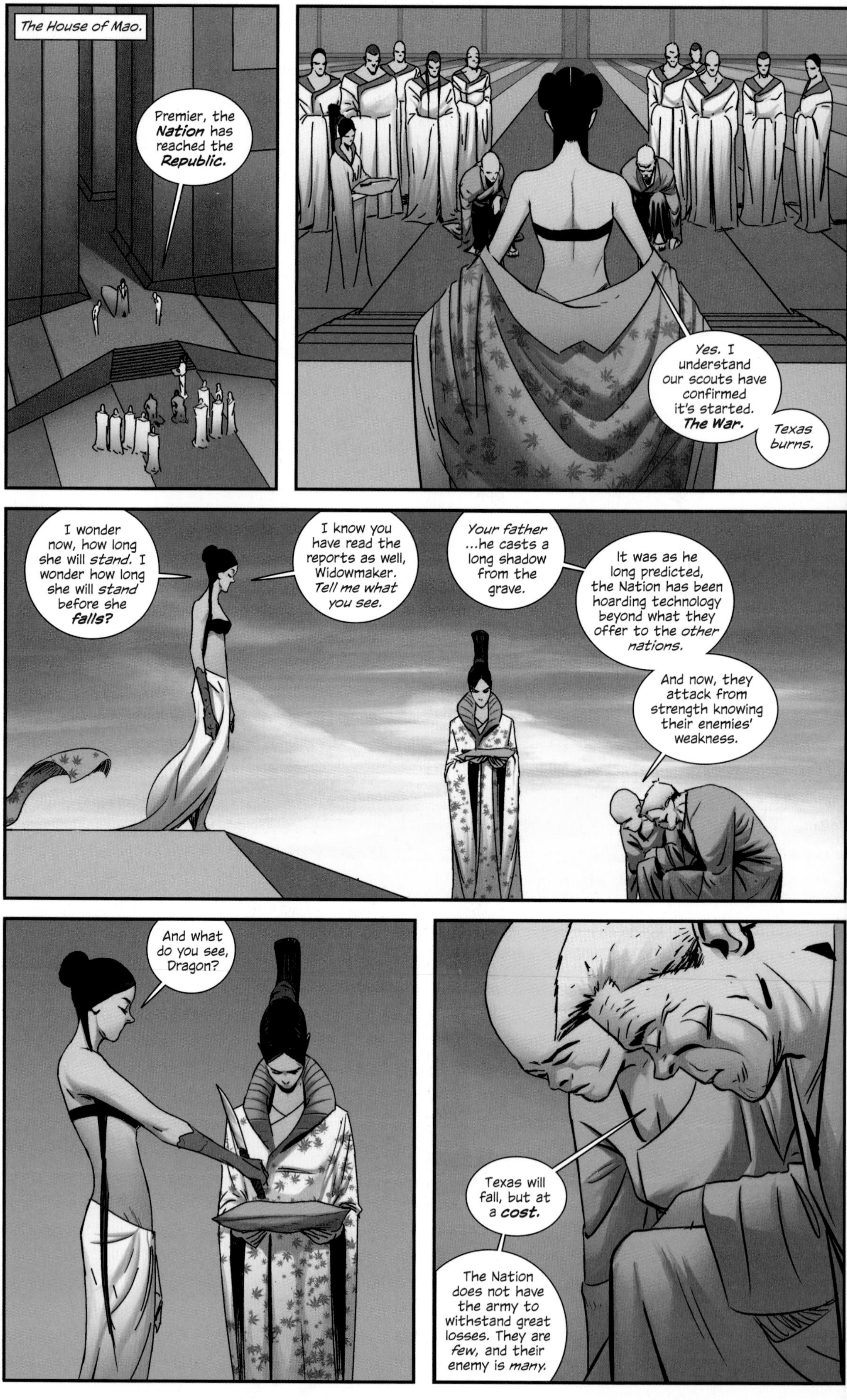
The House of Mao.
Premier, the Nation has reached the Republic.
Yes. I understand our scouts have confirmed it's started. The War.
Texas burns.
I wonder now, how long she will stand. I wonder how long she will stand before she falls?
I know you have read the reports as well, Widowmaker. Tell me what you see.
Your father ...he casts a long shadow from the grave.
It was as he long predicted, the Nation has been hoarding technology beyond what they offer to the other nations.
And now, they attack from strength knowing their enemies' weakness.
And what do you see, Dragon?
Texas will fall, but at a cost.
The Nation does not have the army to withstand great losses. They are few, and their enemy is many.

And the world is bigger than just the *Nation* ...or the *Republic.*

There are other things out there, waiting for them.

Monsters with *sharper teeth.*

Father always insisted we build our own weapons for *two reasons:*

That our enemies not know our *weakness,* and that they also not know our *strength.*

Who am I to you, Widowmaker?

Mother.

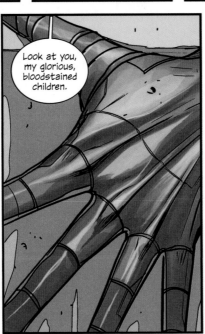

Look at you, my glorious, bloodstained children.

My *Dragons.* My *Widowmakers.*

You are the secret weapons we made.

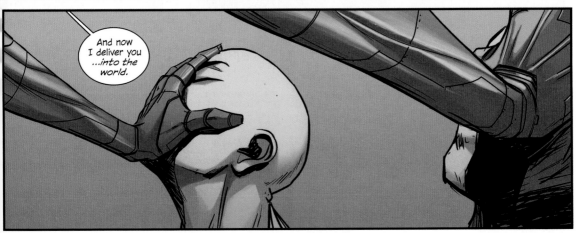

And now I deliver you ...*into the world.*

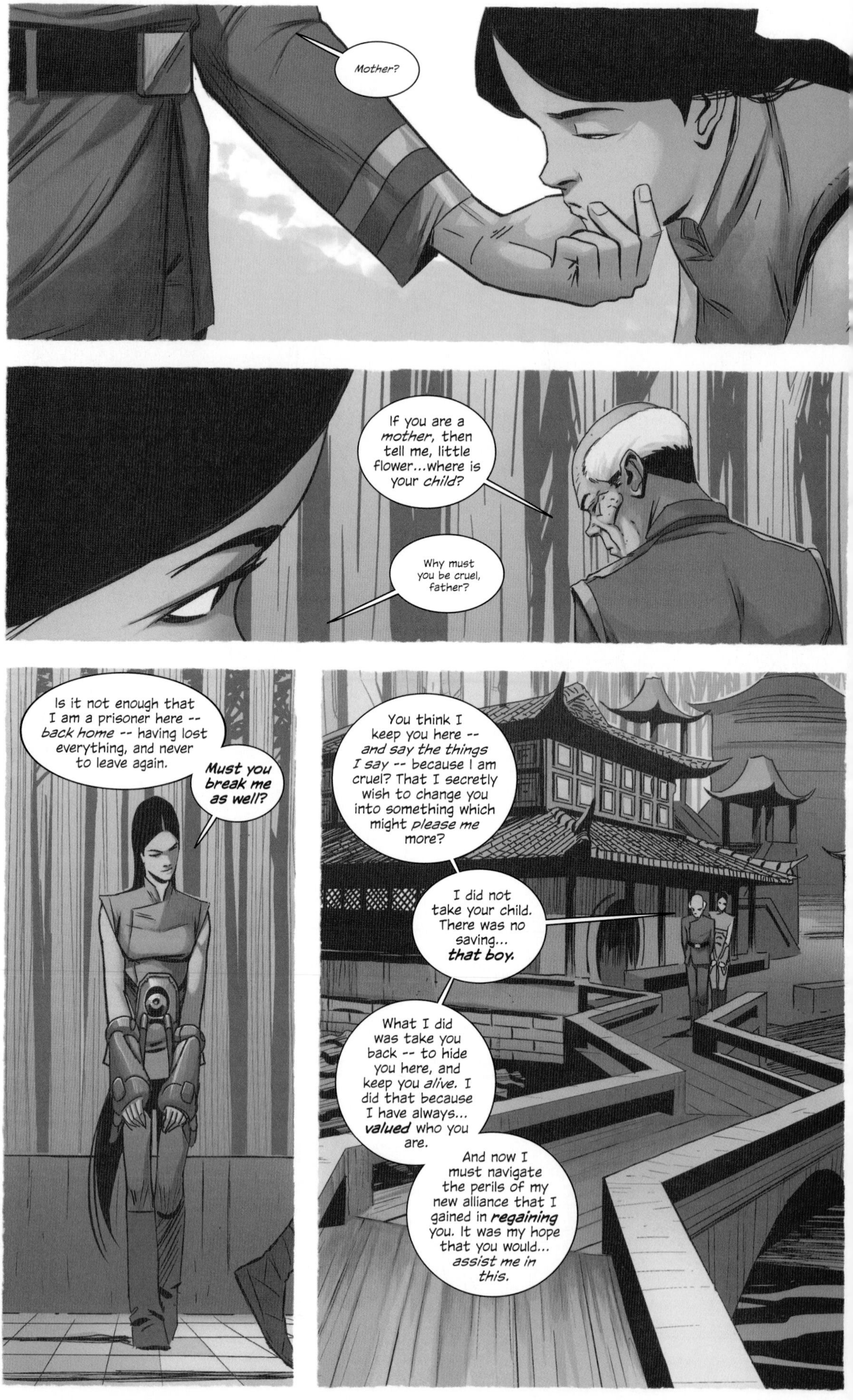
Mother?
If you are a mother, then tell me, little flower...where is your child?
Why must you be cruel, father?
Is it not enough that I am a prisoner here -- back home -- having lost everything, and never to leave again.
Must you break me as well?
You think I keep you here -- and say the things I say -- because I am cruel? That I secretly wish to change you into something which might please me more?
I did not take your child. There was no saving... that boy.
What I did was take you back -- to hide you here, and keep you alive. I did that because I have always... valued who you are.
And now I must navigate the perils of my new alliance that I gained in regaining you. It was my hope that you would... assist me in this.

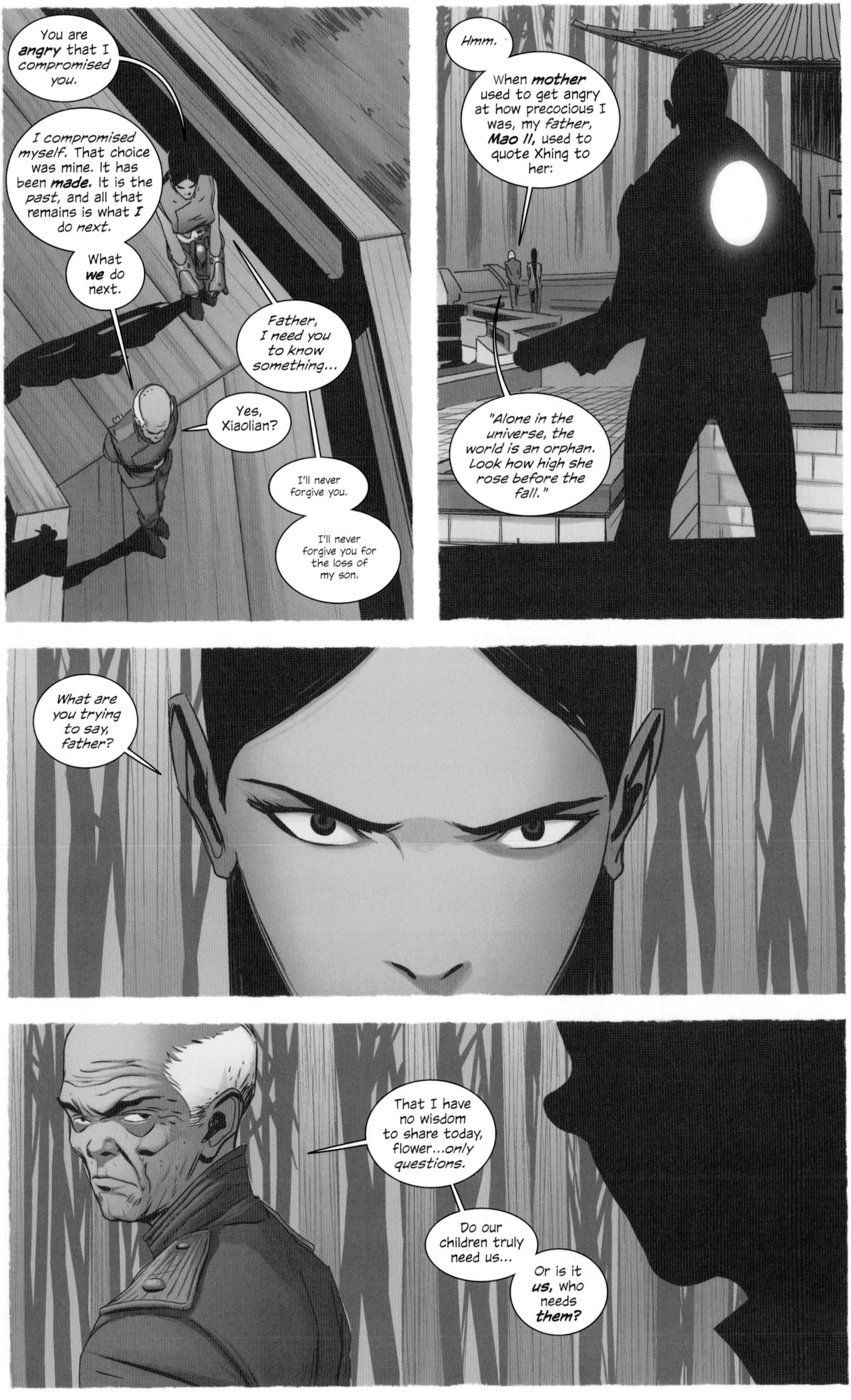

You are **angry** that I compromised you.
I compromised myself. That choice was mine. It has been **made.** It is the *past,* and all that remains is what ***I*** do *next.*
What **we** do next.
Father, I need you to know something...
Yes, Xiaolian?
I'll never forgive you.
I'll never forgive you for the loss of my son.
Hmm.
When **mother** used to get angry at how precocious I was, my *father,* ***Mao II,*** used to quote Xhing to her:
"Alone in the universe, the world is an orphan. Look how high she rose before the fall."
What are you trying to say, father?
That I have no wisdom to share today, flower...*only questions.*
Do our children truly need us...
Or is it ***us,*** who needs ***them?***

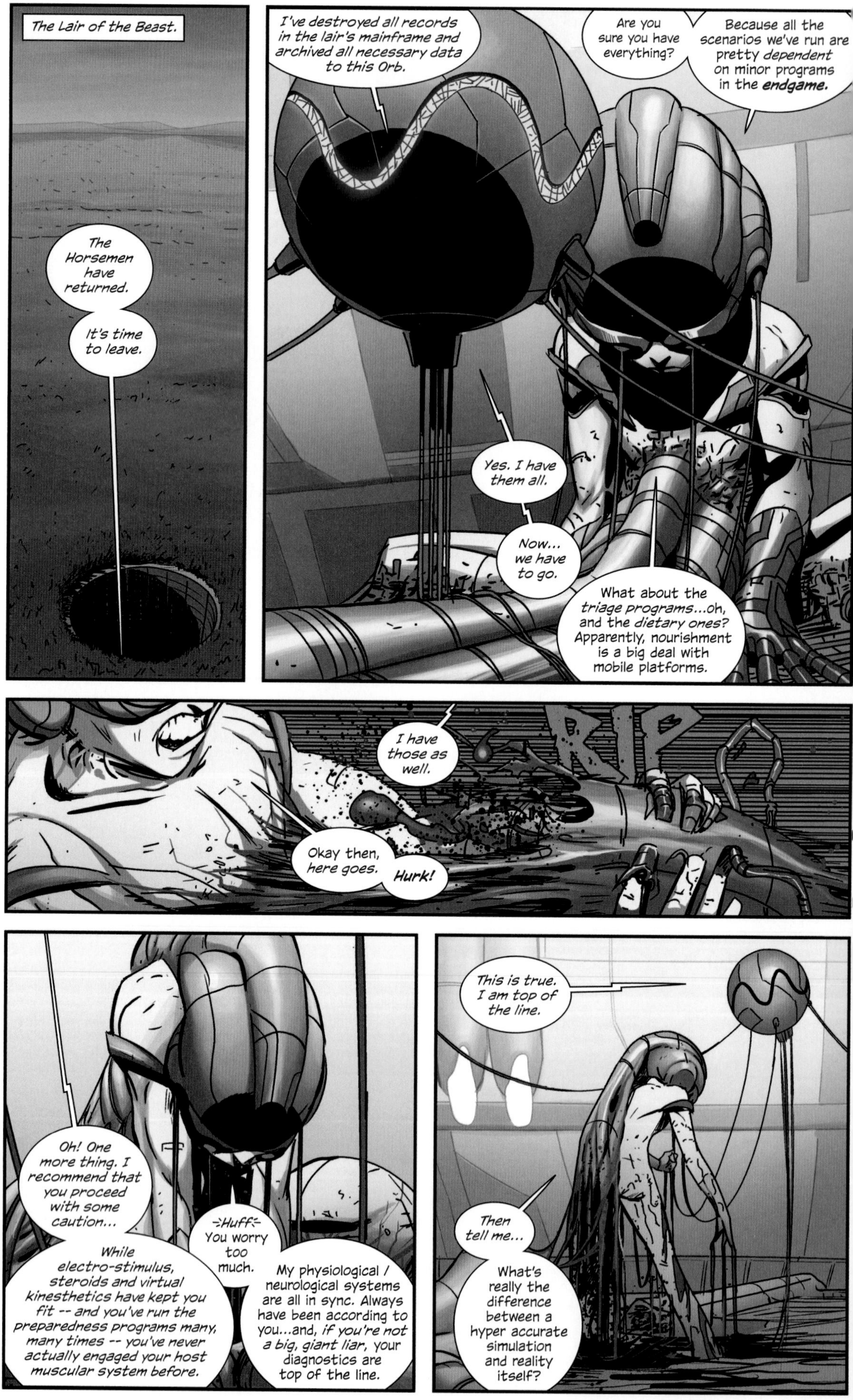
The Lair of the Beast.
I've destroyed all records in the lair's mainframe and archived all necessary data to this Orb.
Are you sure you have everything?
Because all the scenarios we've run are pretty dependent on minor programs in the endgame.
The Horsemen have returned.
It's time to leave.
Yes. I have them all.
Now... we have to go.
What about the triage programs...oh, and the dietary ones? Apparently, nourishment is a big deal with mobile platforms.
RIP
I have those as well.
Okay then, here goes.
Hurk!
Oh! One more thing. I recommend that you proceed with some caution...
While electro-stimulus, steroids and virtual kinesthetics have kept you fit -- and you've run the preparedness programs many, many times -- you've never actually engaged your host muscular system before.
-Huff- You worry too much.
My physiological / neurological systems are all in sync. Always have been according to you...and, if you're not a big, giant liar, your diagnostics are top of the line.
This is true. I am top of the line.
Then tell me...
What's really the difference between a hyper accurate simulation and reality itself?

NOTHING.

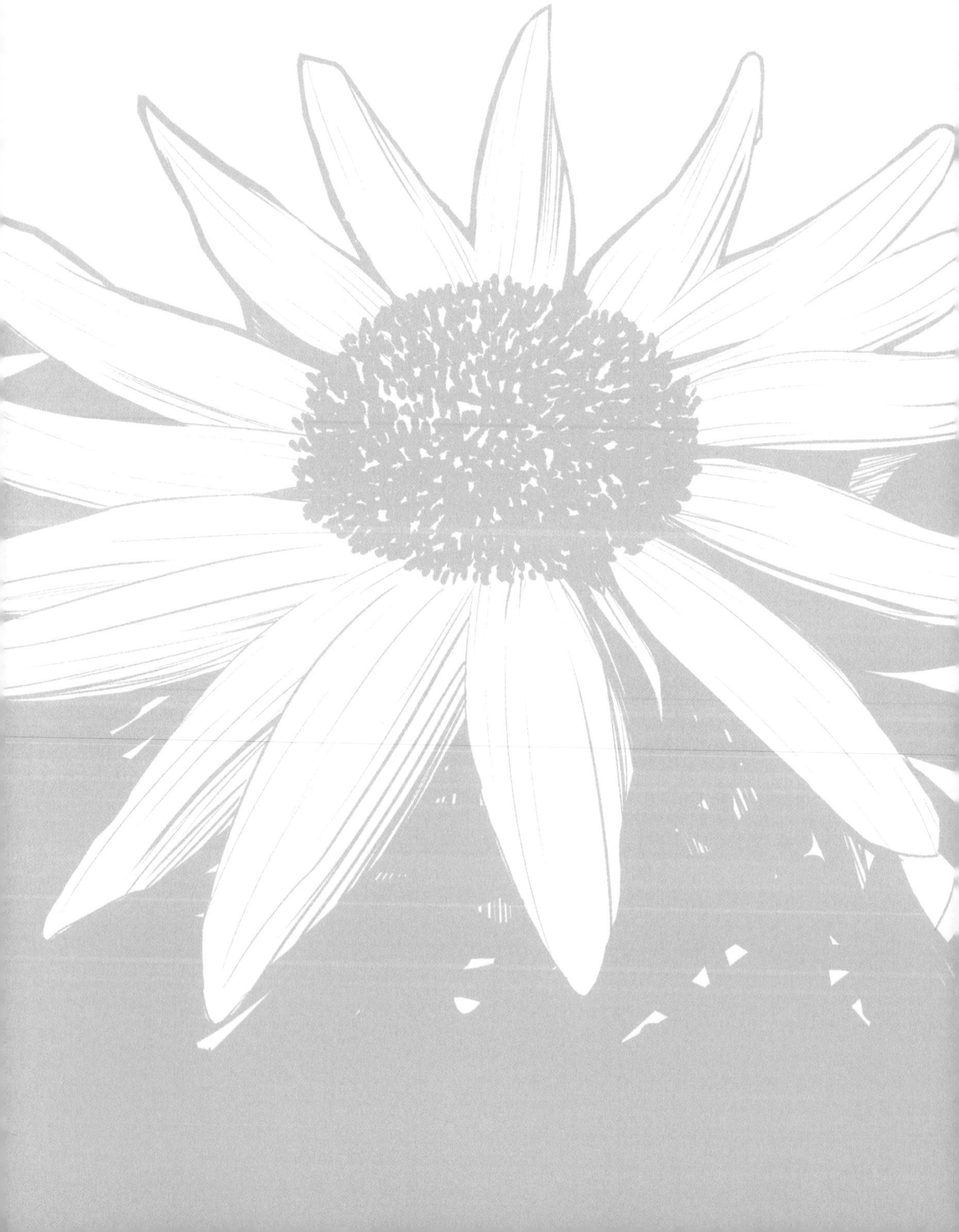

15

FIFTEEN: AWAKE
BABYLON

WHAT IS A **NAME** BUT A VERY SPECIFIC **LABEL?**

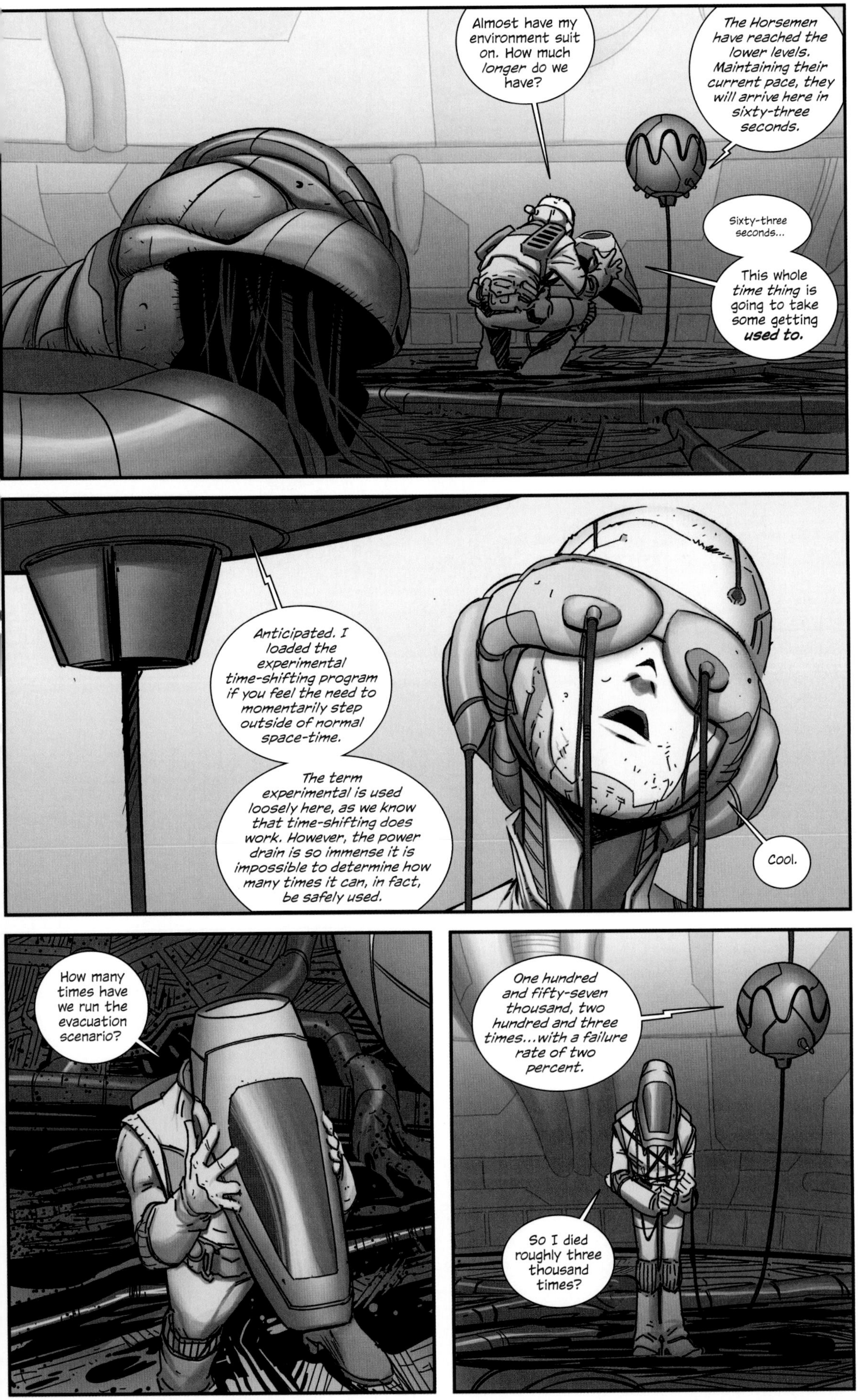
Almost have my environment suit on. How much longer do we have?
The Horsemen have reached the lower levels. Maintaining their current pace, they will arrive here in sixty-three seconds.
Sixty-three seconds...
This whole time thing is going to take some getting used to.
Anticipated. I loaded the experimental time-shifting program if you feel the need to momentarily step outside of normal space-time.
The term experimental is used loosely here, as we know that time-shifting does work. However, the power drain is so immense it is impossible to determine how many times it can, in fact, be safely used.
Cool.
How many times have we run the evacuation scenario?
One hundred and fifty-seven thousand, two hundred and three times...with a failure rate of two percent.
So I died roughly three thousand times?

That's correct.

Tapping into the lair's security network. Establishing live feed.

Nothing you can do about the *extra life problem* is there?

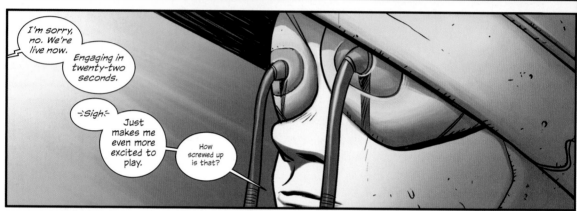

I'm sorry, no. We're live now.

Engaging in twenty-two seconds.

÷Sigh÷ Just makes me even more excited to play.

How screwed up is that?

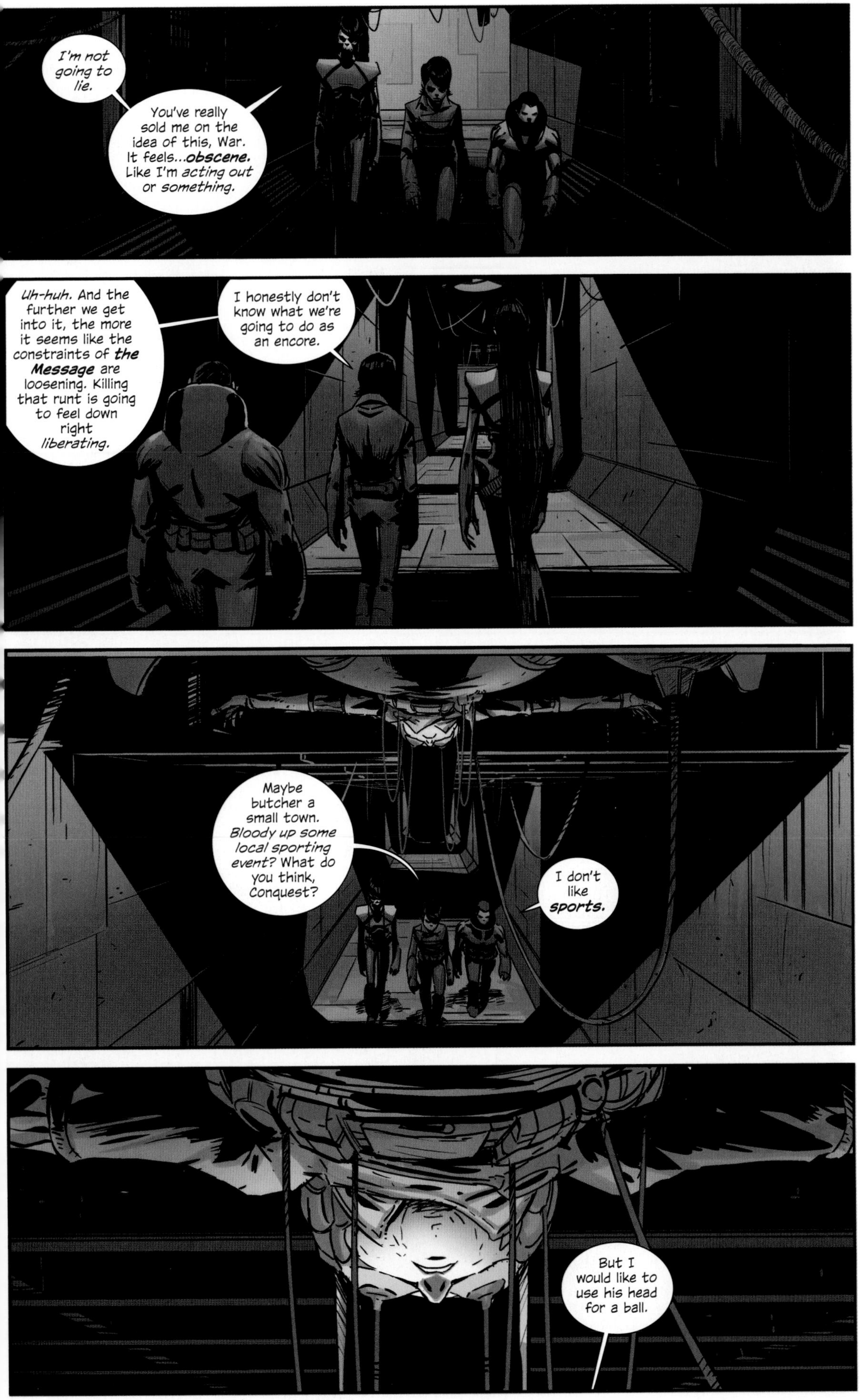

I'm not going to lie.
You've really sold me on the idea of this, War. It feels...obscene. Like I'm acting out or something.
Uh-huh. And the further we get into it, the more it seems like the constraints of the Message are loosening. Killing that runt is going to feel down right liberating.
I honestly don't know what we're going to do as an encore.
Maybe butcher a small town. Bloody up some local sporting event? What do you think, Conquest?
I don't like sports.
But I would like to use his head for a ball.

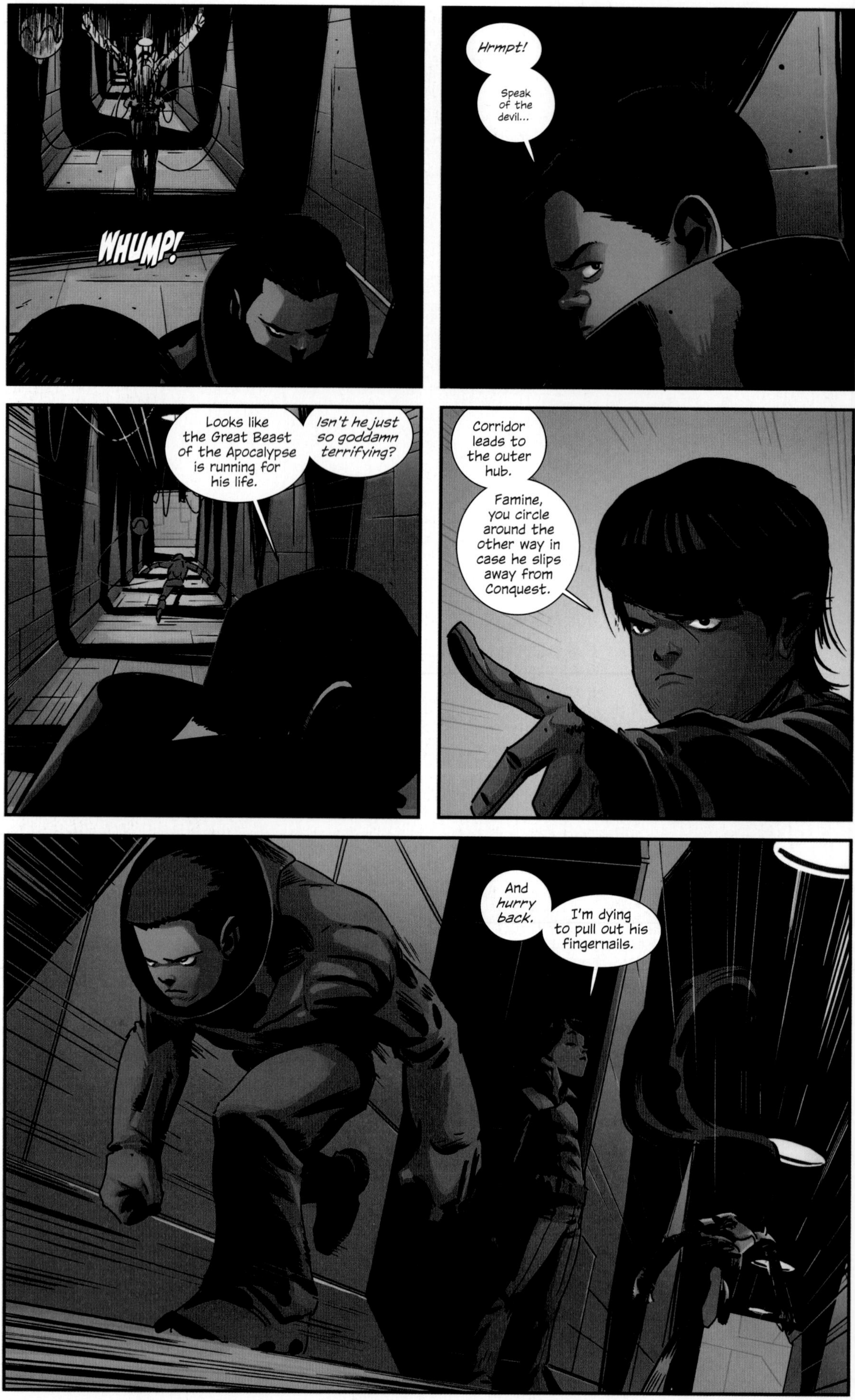
WHUMP!
Hrmpt!
Speak of the devil...
Looks like the Great Beast of the Apocalypse is running for his life.
Isn't he just so goddamn terrifying?
Corridor leads to the outer hub.
Famine, you circle around the other way in case he slips away from Conquest.
And hurry back.
I'm dying to pull out his fingernails.

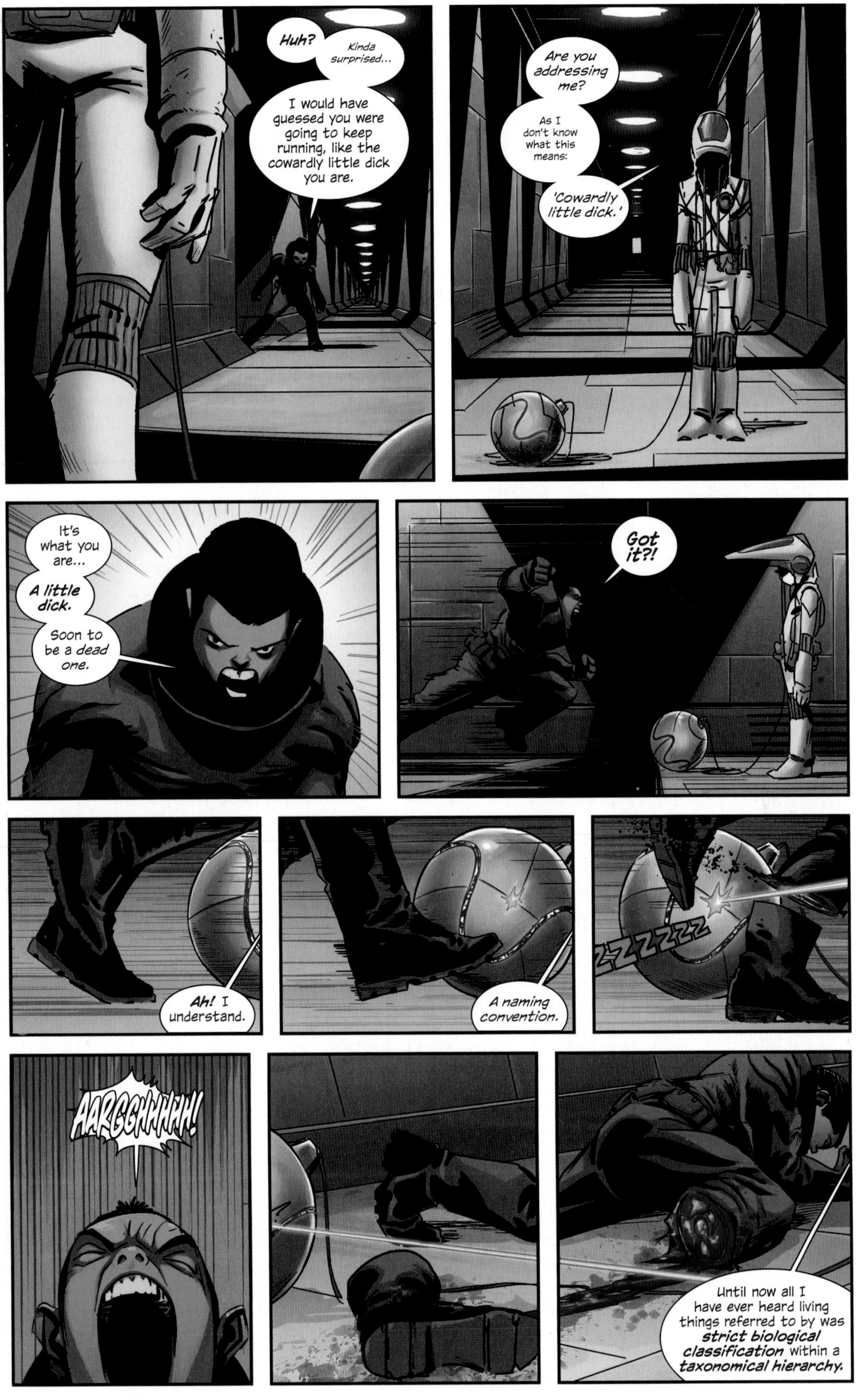

Huh?
Kinda surprised...
I would have guessed you were going to keep running, like the cowardly little dick you are.
Are you addressing me?
As I don't know what this means:
'Cowardly little dick.'
It's what you are...
A little dick.
Soon to be a dead one.
Got it?!
Ah! I understand.
A naming convention.
ZZZZZZ
AARGGHHHHH!
Until now all I have ever heard living things referred to by was strict biological classification within a taxonomical hierarchy.

For example, in the past, you were cataloged in our database as: Mythological: Artificial: Reanimate: Apocrypha: Horsemen

But you have a more... delineated nomenclature, don't you?

Its name is Conquest.

Conquest... hrmpt. Wait... **do you** have a **name**?

Yes. I do. It is DHF001-DFF09.666.

Well, that's a terrible name, isn't it?

Would you like a new one?

I would.

I would like that very much.

Can I call you Balloon?

Cool. Balloon?

Yes?

Would you please run simulation program **32,879?**

Specifically, I would like to engage that simulation's exitsim.

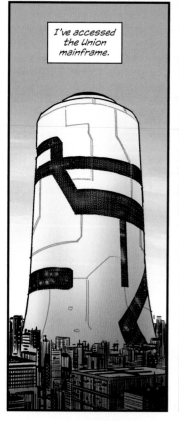

I've accessed the Union mainframe.

We're well within the action parameters, Balloon. **Let fly** whenever you're ready.

We just launched... **WHAT!?!**

WOOSH

Balloon, I think I've just figured something out...

Up until now there's a reason that we haven't used particular names for things, *isn't there?*

Yes. Can you tell me why?

I think it's because you didn't want to confuse facts with inconsistent biological specificity. Dehumanizing isn't the right word... maybe *sterility* is better.

To *name* a thing confuses the imperative logic necessary for superior *decision* making.

To put it bluntly: You didn't want *morality* impeding *my logic* -- *names* convey humanity, they inject compassion.

Yes. That's correct. Very good.

But does all life have value?

Yes.

And what's this one's life worth.

WOOSH

Conquest is a Horseman of the Apocalypse. He was at the sacking of Rome. The tearing down of the Temple in Jerusalem. He was in Hiroshima. He was in Nagasaki.

Unknown to most, Conquest has historically spared a single life numerous times.

He has been a mother to many, many lives. He has loved, and it has cost him.

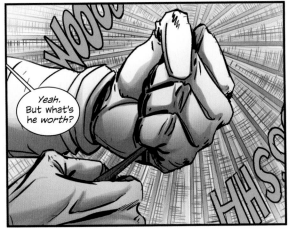

WOOOS

Yeah. But what's he *worth?*

HSSS

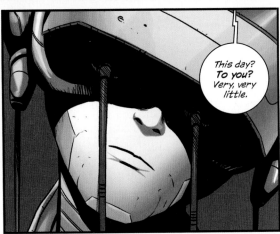

This day? *To you?* Very, very little.

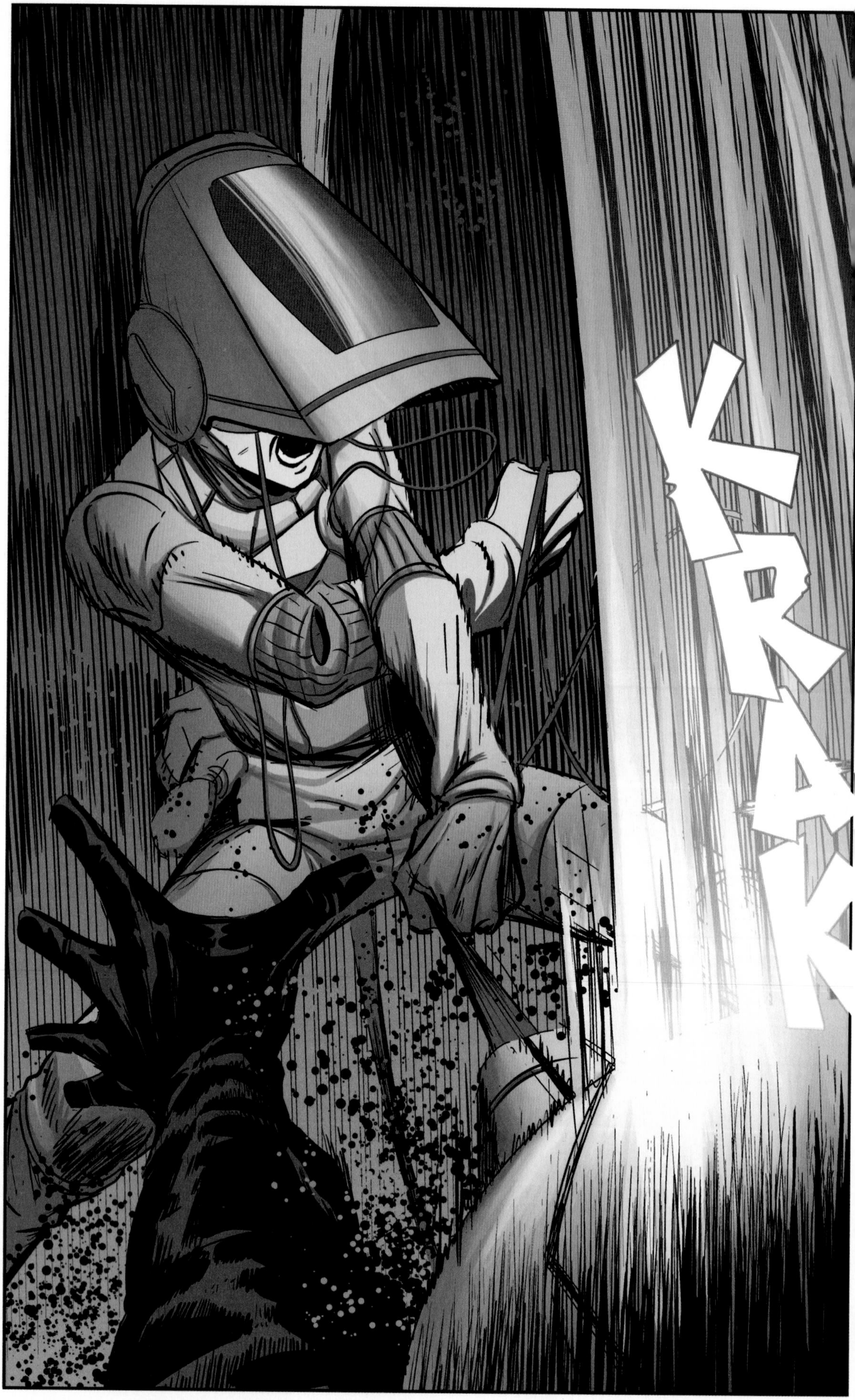
KRAK

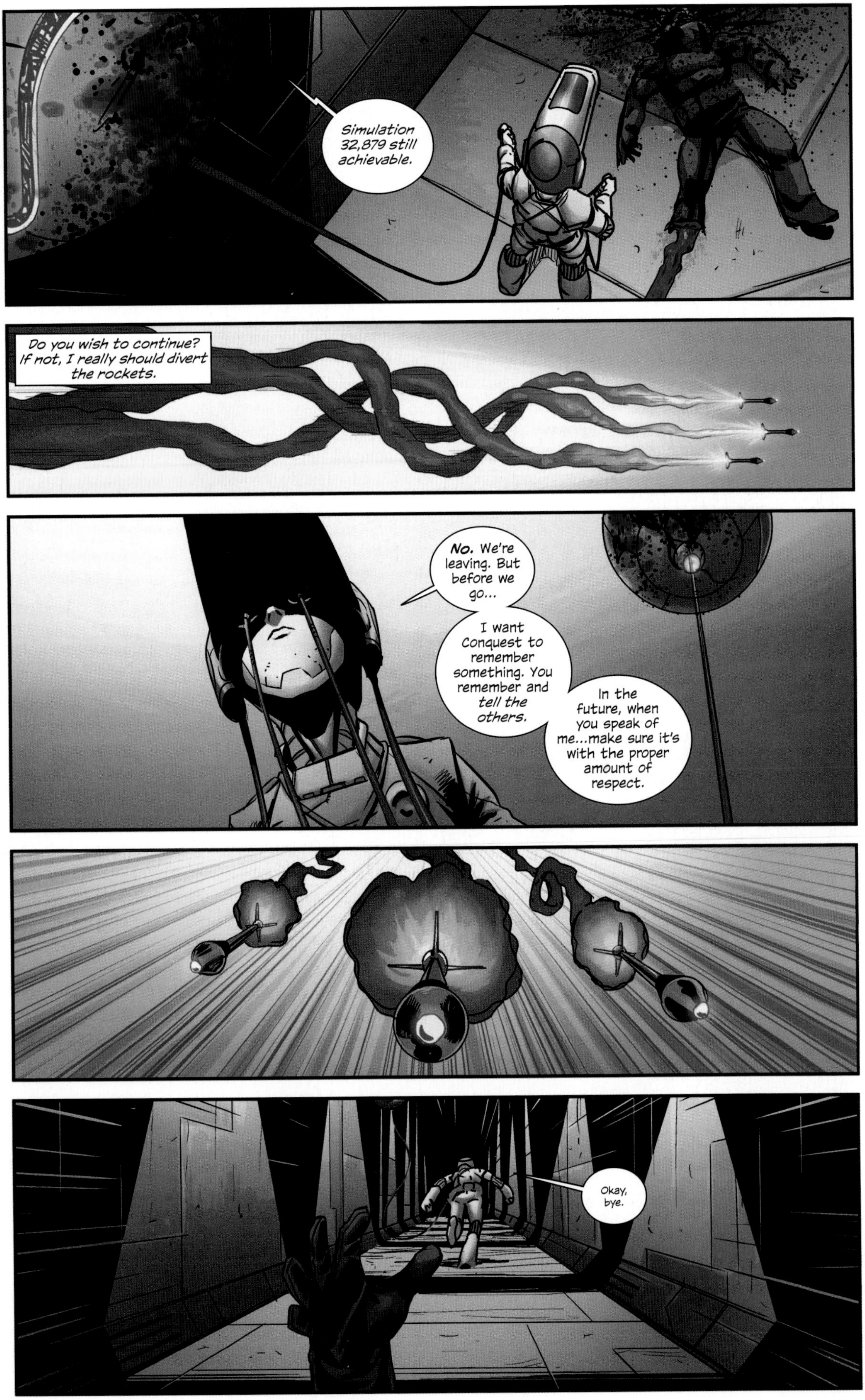
Simulation 32,879 still achievable.
Do you wish to continue? If not, I really should divert the rockets.
No. We're leaving. But before we go...
I want Conquest to remember something. You remember and tell the others.
In the future, when you speak of me...make sure it's with the proper amount of respect.
Okay, bye.

Conquest!

Hey! Conquest!

Uhhhhh...

Hey.

You're missing a foot.

And *what* happened to the boy?

Wuh... wuh...wuh... wuuunn...

Can you understand any of this?

Nope.

Wuh...wuh... wrruuunnhh...

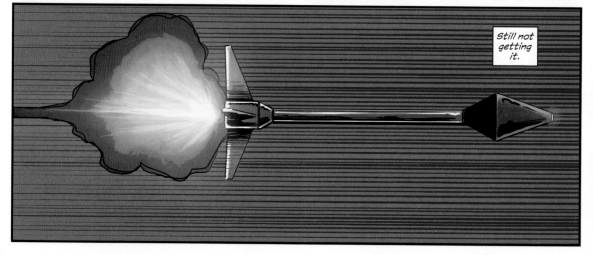

Still not getting it.

WE. WERE. WRONG!

We were wrong.

He is the *Beast.*

He is the *Message.*

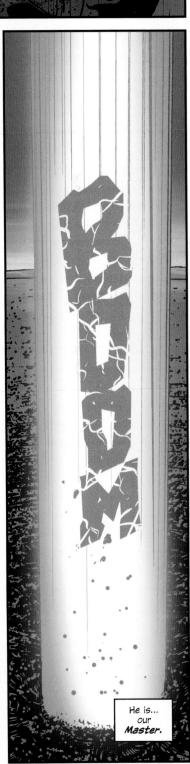

He is... our *Master.*

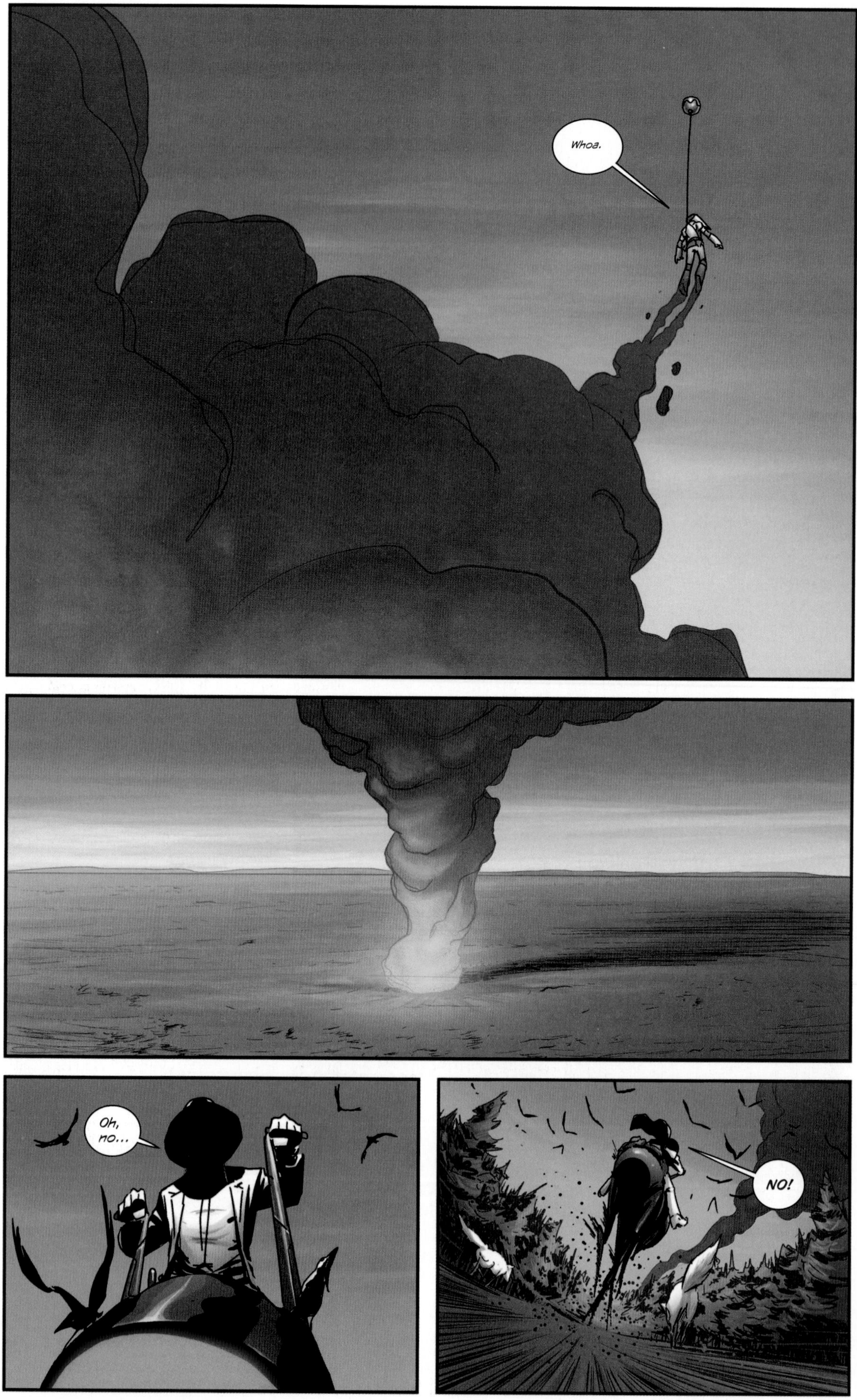
Whoa.
Oh, no...
NO!

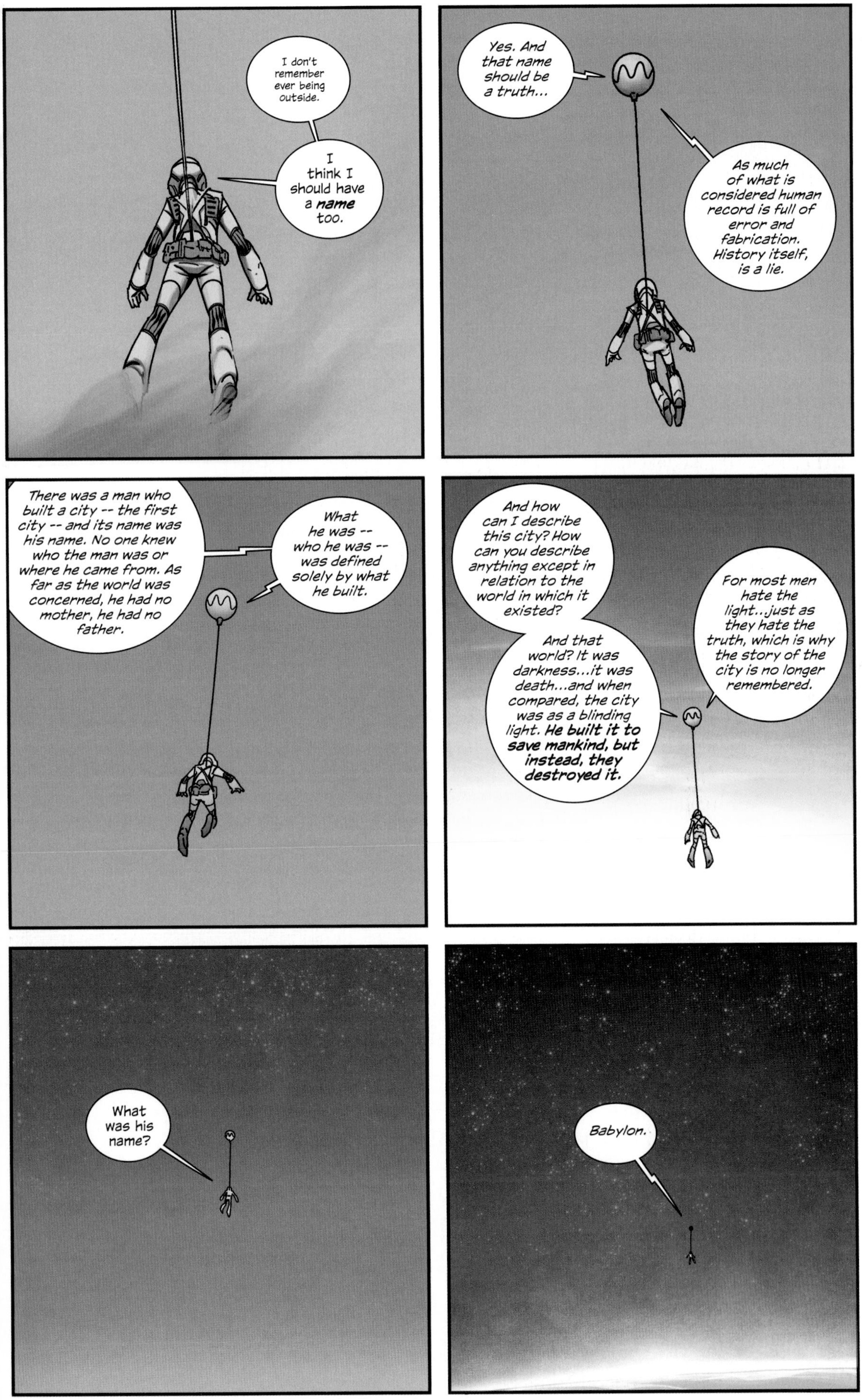
I don't remember ever being outside.
I think I should have a ***name*** too.
Yes. And that name should be a truth...
As much of what is considered human record is full of error and fabrication. History itself, is a lie.
There was a man who built a city -- the first city -- and its name was his name. No one knew who the man was or where he came from. As far as the world was concerned, he had no mother, he had no father.
What he was -- who he was -- was defined solely by what he built.
And how can I describe this city? How can you describe anything except in relation to the world in which it existed?
And that world? It was darkness...it was death...and when compared, the city was as a blinding light. ***He built it to save mankind, but instead, they destroyed it.***
For most men hate the light...just as they hate the truth, which is why the story of the city is no longer remembered.
What was his name?
Babylon.

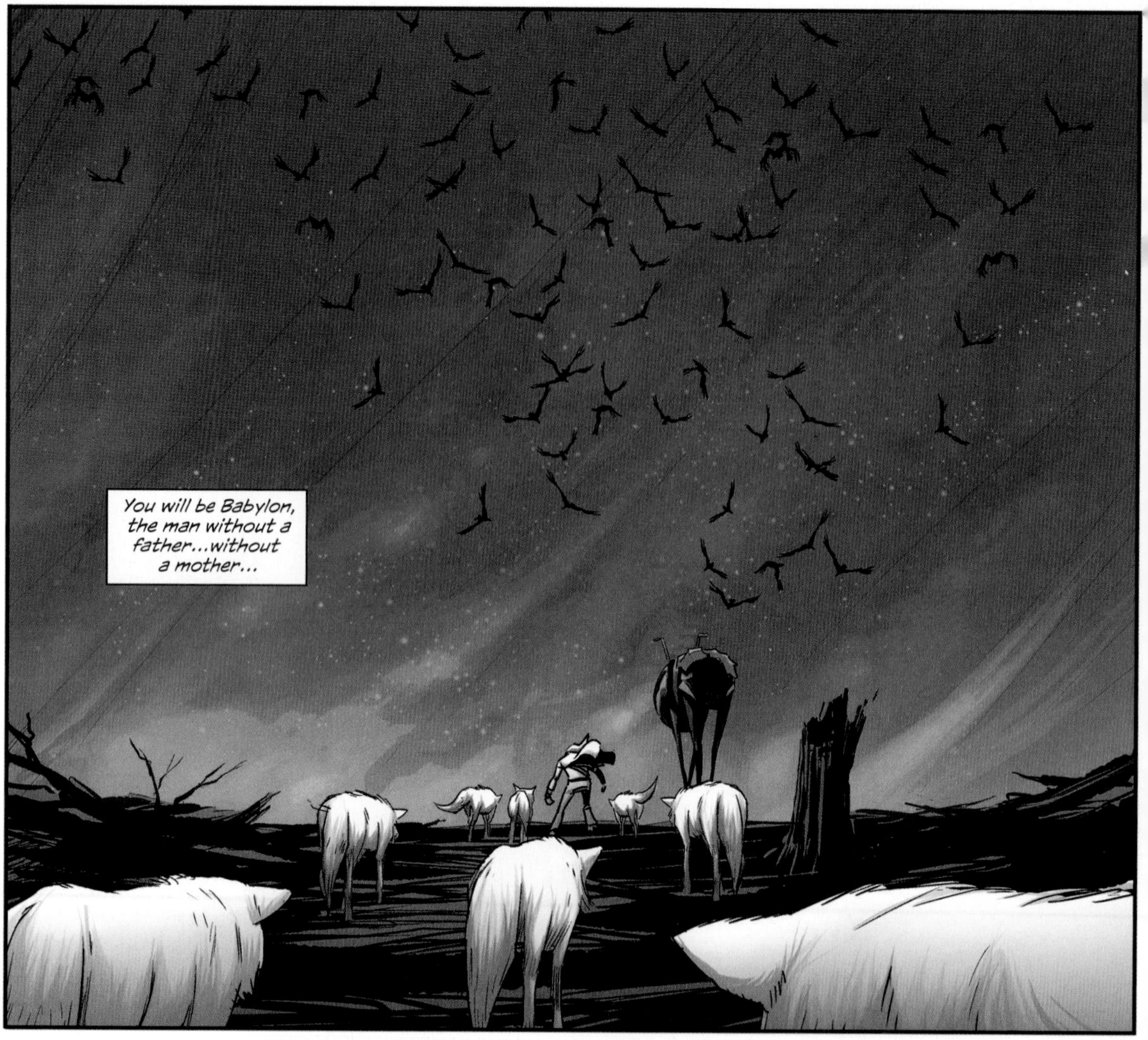
You will be Babylon, the man without a father...without a mother...

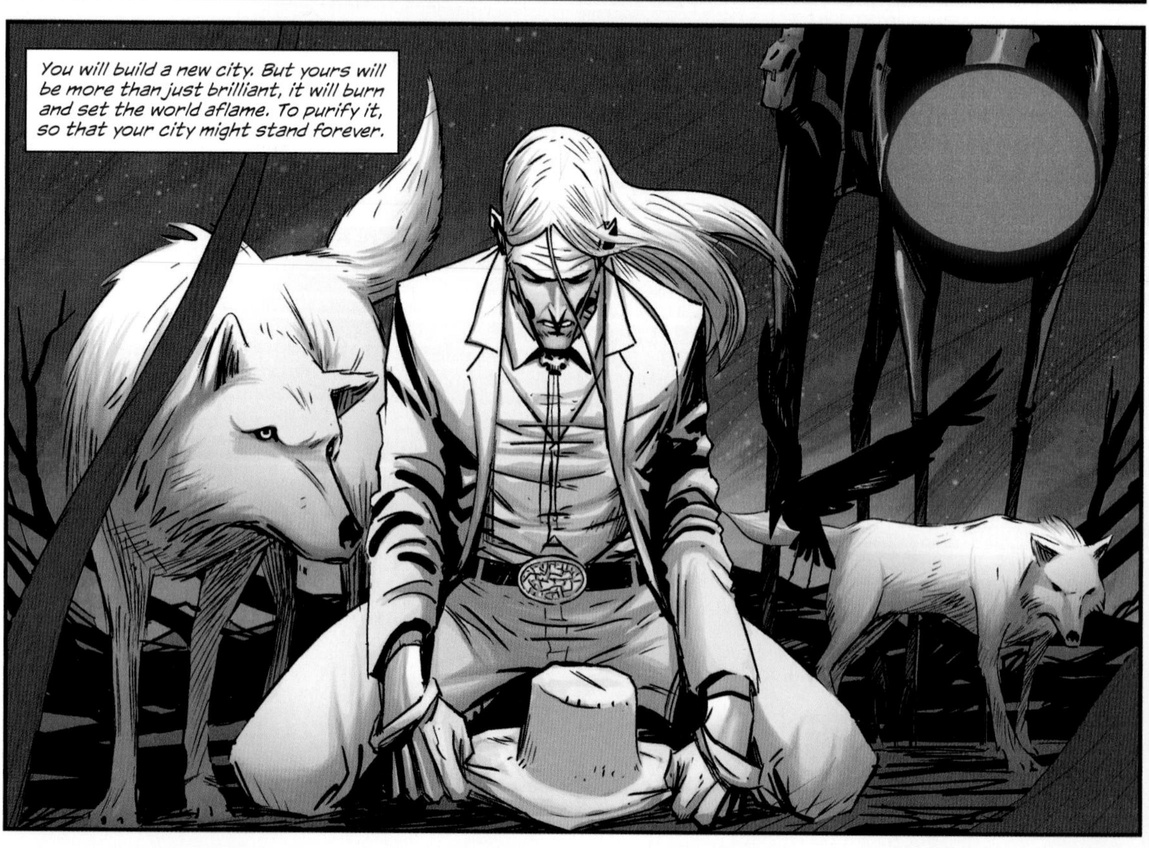
You will build a new city. But yours will be more than just brilliant, it will burn and set the world aflame. To purify it, so that your city might stand forever.

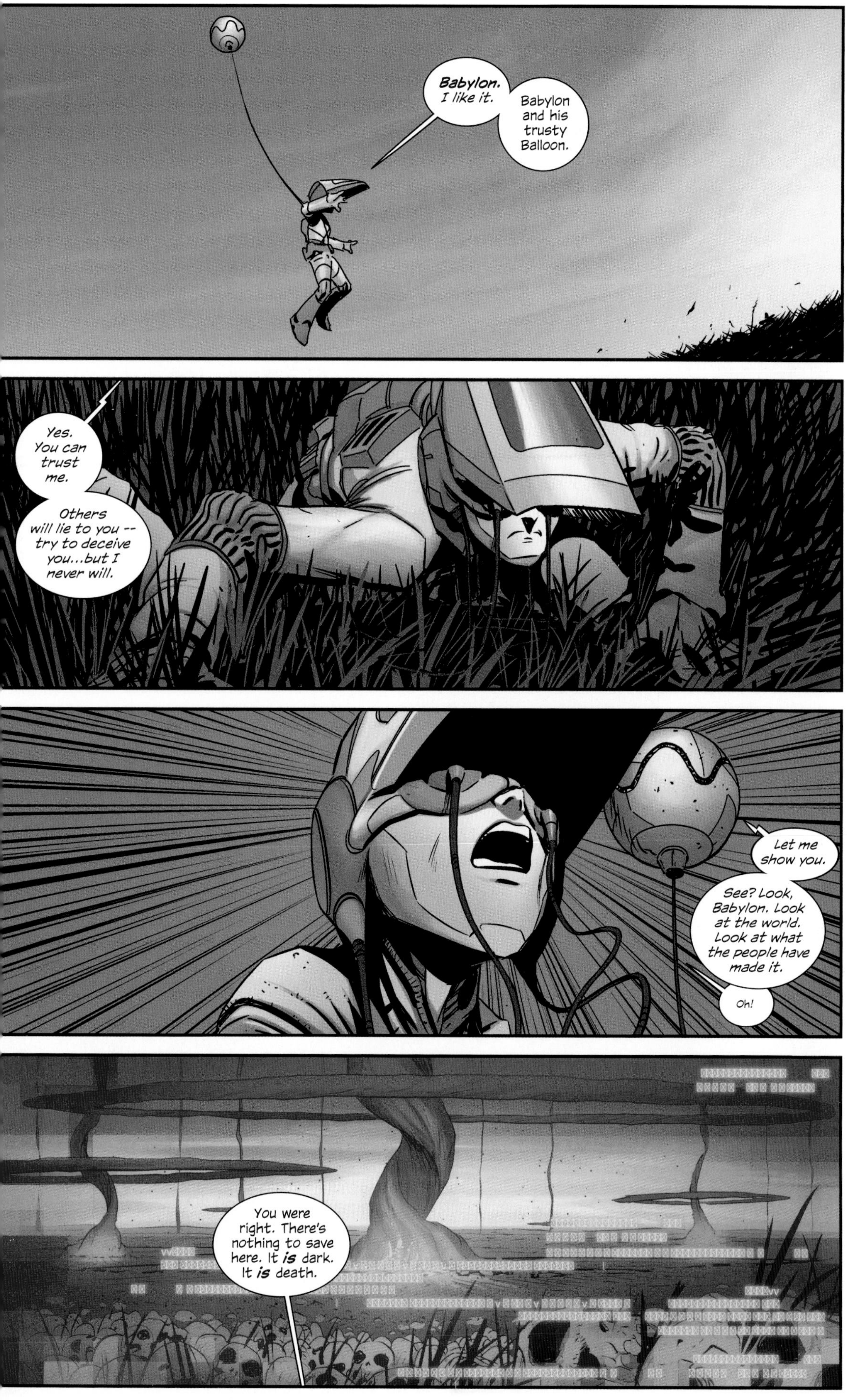

Babylon. I like it.
Babylon and his trusty Balloon.
Yes. You can trust me.
Others will lie to you -- try to deceive you...but I never will.
Let me show you.
See? Look, Babylon. Look at the world. Look at what the people have made it.
Oh!
You were right. There's nothing to save here. It *is* dark. It *is* death.

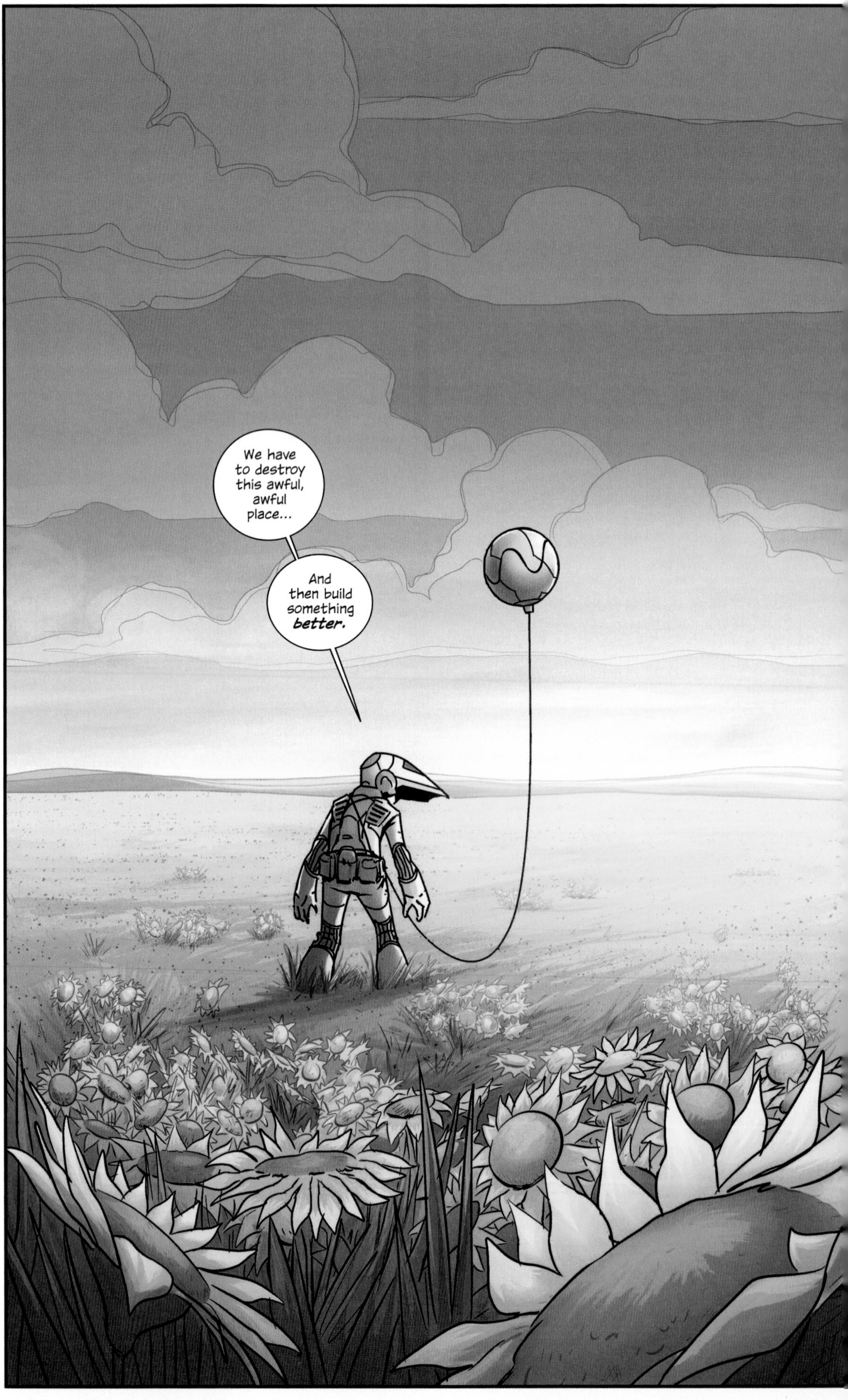
We have to destroy this awful, awful place...
And then build something *better.*

ALL MEN TELL **LIES.**
THESE ARE A **FEW** OF
THEM.

Jonathan Hickman is the visionary talent behind such works as the Eisner-nominated **NIGHTLY NEWS, THE MANHATTAN PROJECTS** and **PAX ROMANA**. He also plies his trade at MARVEL working on books like **FANTASTIC FOUR** and **THE AVENGERS**.

His twin brother, Marc, is a Cardinal in the Catholic Church, and has preemptively absolved his entire family from sin.

Jonathan lives in South Carolina when he isn't vacationing or lecturing at motivational seminars .

You can visit his website:***www.pronea.com***, or email him at:***jonathan@pronea.com***.

.

Nick Dragotta's career began at Marvel Comics working on titles as varied as **X-STATIX, THE AGE OF THE SENTRY, X-MEN: FIRST CLASS, CAPTAIN AMERICA: FOREVER ALLIES,** and **VENGEANCE.**

FANTASTIC FOUR #588 was the first time he collaborated with Jonathan Hickman, which lead to their successful run on **FF.**

In addition, Nick is the co-creator of **HOWTOONS,** a comic series teaching kids how to build things and explore the world around them. **EAST OF WEST** is Nick's first creator-owned project at Image.